CHARLOTTE HAWKINS BROWN
AND PALMER MEMORIAL INSTITUTE

CHARLOTTE HAWKINS
BROWN

& PALMER MEMORIAL INSTITUTE

What One Young
African American Woman
Could Do

Charles W. Wadelington

Richard F. Knapp

The University of North Carolina Press

Chapel Hill & London

Designed by April Leidig-Higgins
Set in Monotype Garamond by G&S Typesetters, Inc.

Publication of this work was supported by a generous gift from
the Charlotte Hawkins Brown Historical Foundation, Inc.

The paper in this book meets the guidelines for permanence and
durability of the Committee on Production Guidelines for Book
Longevity of the Council on Library Resources.

Library of Congress Cataloging-in-Publication Data
Wadelington, Charles Weldon.
Charlotte Hawkins Brown and Palmer Memorial Institute:
What one young African American woman could do /
Charles W. Wadelington and Richard F. Knapp.
p. cm. Includes bibliographical references (p.) and index.
ISBN 0-8078-2514-X (cloth: alk. paper).
ISBN 0-8078-4794-1 (pbk.: alk. paper) .
1. Brown, Charlotte Hawkins, 1883–1961. 2. Afro-American
women teachers–North Carolina–Biography. 3. Women school
administrators–North Carolina–Biography. 4. Palmer Memorial
Institute (Sedalia, N.C.) I. Knapp, Richard F., 1945–. II. Title.
LA2317.B598W33 1999 371.1′0092–dc21 [B] 99-19929 CIP

03 02 01 00 99 5 4 3 2 1

For our children

CHARLES, CHARLZINA,

DEBORAH, AND MARY ELIZABETH

and for

ELIZA SEARCY RUSSOM DICK

CONTENTS

ILLUSTRATIONS

PREFACE

DESPITE AT LEAST a century of various sorts of reform in American primary and secondary education, the issue remains one of constant discussion. Studies focus on this strength or that deficiency, SAT renaming and rejiggering, political correctness, political incorrectness, teacher burnout, overfunding, underfunding, and a myriad of other conditions calling for more reform. As taxpayers supporting the public schools, nearly all Americans, even if they are not parents of schoolchildren, have a stake in education.

This debate extends to the state and local levels. Because of our personal experience with our own four children in parochial, independent, and public schools, we are deeply interested in the discussion of alternatives for the most effective education of children such as public schools of differing sizes, charter schools, parochial schools, independent schools, and even home schools.

The debate is hardly new, and the essence of the question was a critical issue a century ago. In North Carolina, Palmer Memorial Institute, its predecessor Bethany Institute, and its partial successor the Sedalia Public School were examples over a period of decades of the alternatives that still face the state and the nation. In particular, Palmer showed what one capable and determined young African American woman could do to educate children and how her methods developed over half a century of success and national attention. Today her odyssey, which was intertwined with the African American experience during much of the twentieth century, offers valuable insight into educational alternatives for America. Clearly new ideas and the willingness to try them are needed in the contemporary educational arena. Charlotte Hawkins Brown offered one cohesive set of educational concepts. Although it no longer exists (and its principles are out of fashion in most circles), Palmer flourished for over sixty years and was in various ways a pacesetter for African American public and private education. Her school deserves to be remembered both because it is part of America's African American heritage and because it has addressed some of the vexing matters that still arise in educational controversies.

For these reasons, among others, we have written this book. It is the product of a journey that began in 1983 when Wadelington joined the Historic Sites Section of the North Carolina Department of Cultural Resources as a researcher for the then unborn Charlotte Hawkins Brown Memorial State Historic Site at the former Palmer Memorial Institute. The memorial became the first North Carolina state historic site to honor both African American education and women. Wadelington studied various aspects of Brown and her work over the years and then collaborated with Knapp on the manuscript that evolved into the current study. The research for this work draws on the incomplete papers of Brown and her school; numerous interviews with former students, teachers, family members, and associates; other manuscript collections up and down the eastern seaboard; and state and local records in North Carolina.

We have incurred numerous debts to colleagues, informants, and other supporters in the course of producing this book. Any listing of authors' debts is bound to be incomplete, and we are grateful to all who have aided our work. Marie Hart and Gayle Wulk shared information they learned while making a pathbreaking video on Brown. Three Palmer graduates, Maria Hawkins Cole, Marie Gibbs, and Representative H. M. Michaux; Senator William Martin; and Larry Misenheimer, among others, were instrumental in convincing the North Carolina Department of Cultural Resources to begin the Charlotte Hawkins Brown project. Historic Sites administrators James R. McPherson and Rob Boyette have been patient and supportive in allowing the authors time to complete the project. Rick Jackson willingly fulfilled our numerous requests for photographic services in a timely manner. Onetime Brown project director L. Annette Gibbs tirelessly encouraged as well as participated in early research efforts. Over the years, Historic Sites secretaries Bridget Jordan, Josephine George, Denise Walker, Coutanya Coombs, and others graciously typed many drafts of the manuscript.

The Charlotte Hawkins Brown Historical Foundation, guided by Harold Webb and others, offered moral support and contacts with dozens of people who remembered Brown and Palmer. Among them were two of Brown's first students, Vina Wadlington Webb and Ada Hooker, who at 104 recalled Brown as a young woman. The foundation also generously supplied a subvention supporting the publication of the book.

Charlotte Hawkins Brown with bust of her mentor,
Alice Freeman Palmer, 1952. Courtesy of Alex Rivera; NCDAH.

John Hope Franklin initially encouraged Wadelington to write a book
on Brown by commenting after Wadelington asked why more was not
published on her, "It's up to you, young man." He also later agreed to
read the manuscript. Paul Bitting, Percy Murray, and William S. Powell
also read various drafts. Robert M. Topkins was a diligent early reader;
his insight, keen eyes, and red pencil vastly improved the final product,
and his input proved crucial to its completion.

Former Palmer teacher Ruth M. Totton gave several interviews and read the entire manuscript. Founding historic site manager Jeanne Rudd extended office space and ongoing support; her assistant, Palmer graduate Barbara Wiley, supplied information on Palmer's later years. Enthusiastic young historians Lydia Hoffman and Valinda Littlefield continuously shared new perspectives and discoveries about Brown. Richard L. Wharton provided a rarely viewed glimpse of Brown and the inner workings of Palmer's directors. Ambassador Galen L. Stone, grandson of Brown's chief benefactor, shared details of his family's close association and friendship with Brown. Many other individuals contributed valuable interviews and other leads, including former Palmer presidents Wilhelmina Crosson, Harold Bragg, and Charles W. Bundrige; numerous former teachers and students at Palmer; and Hawkins family members such as Charlotte Hawkins Sullivan, Ruth Hawkins, Ruth Hughes, and André Vann.

Staff at the Arthur and Elizabeth Schlesinger Library on the History of Women in America at Radcliffe College demonstrated extraordinary professionalism and answered many queries before they were even asked. At the Amistad Research Center at Tulane University, the help of Clifton Johnson, Rebecca Hankins, Elise Cain, and others greatly enhanced a lengthy research trip to New Orleans. Staff at other repositories, including the Bennett College Archives, University of North Carolina at Chapel Hill libraries, North Carolina State Archives (especially Ed Morris and Steve Massengill), Rockefeller Archive Center, Duke University libraries, Harvard University libraries, Cambridge Historical Society, North Carolina Agricultural and Technical State University library, University of North Carolina at Greensboro libraries, Greensboro Public Library, Guilford County offices, Franklin D. Roosevelt Library, and other agencies, proved efficient, helpful, and willing. At the University of North Carolina Press, Editor-in-chief David Perry offered friendship, thoughtful criticism, and encouragement as we revised the manuscript for publication. Project editor Paula Wald carefully guided the book through copyediting and production. While all of these people and others helped in various ways, we, of course, bear sole responsibility for any errors in fact or interpretation that may appear.

We offer this book to readers in hopes that they will strive, as Charlotte Hawkins Brown did, to remember a diverse heritage and make a difference in American education for coming generations.

INTRODUCTION

IN THE FALL of 1901, Charlotte Hawkins (1883–1961) jumped off a Southern Railway train in the unfamiliar backwoods of Guilford County, North Carolina. She was black, small of stature (just under five feet tall), single, and barely eighteen years old and had come alone from Cambridge, Massachusetts, to begin her first real job teaching African Americans at the American Missionary Association's (AMA) Bethany Institute. Boston at the time was one of the oldest and finest cities in America—a city of colleges, good public and private schools, and modern conveniences. Poverty and racism also existed in Boston, but moderate numbers of African Americans lived there in a generally benign society with a long-standing reputation for tolerance and fairness to their race. Charlotte, who later claimed she had experienced little racism while growing up in Boston, was a graduate of a fine public high school, where she received a solid education. She also had studied a year at college.

The place in the woods where Charlotte jumped from the train did not have a platform. The place she walked to, several miles distant, had none of the advantages of Boston. Sedalia, as her future home ten miles east of Greensboro would later be named, was a small, primarily African American community lacking any cultural amenities. There was no electricity, no telephone, and no library. In the early Jim Crow days, African Americans (even those in the tiny middle class) in North Carolina recognized their second-class status and challenged the system only at their peril. At the time, a hundred or so lynchings a year occurred in the South. Public schools in the state—segregated, of course—were in general woefully inadequate and poorly attended. Numerous black schools still occupied rural one-room log structures. Illiteracy and intolerance were common. Both blacks and whites were suspicious of the short, aggressive young stranger with the clipped Yankee accent. It was not at all an auspicious setting for the beginning of a career. Many, if not most, would-be teachers would have returned to Boston on the next train.

Artist's depiction of eighteen-year-old Brown arriving in Guilford County,
North Carolina, from Cambridge, Massachusetts, in 1901. NCDAH.

But Charlotte Hawkins was persistent and determined, and she stayed for over half a century. When the AMA closed the failing school at the end of her first year of teaching, she boldly remained to begin her own school despite the lack of any material resources. Fifty years later, she would retire as the head of Palmer Memorial Institute, by then nationally known and the school of choice for upper-class African Americans along the eastern seaboard and beyond. With perseverance, intellect, faith in God, powers of persuasion, and some good luck, Brown accomplished far more than most people might have even with considerably more initial resources. She blended racial accommodation and activism into her own formula for success based on education, hard work, propriety, and social graces. This formula, reinforced by her personal example of achievement in a segregated society, continued to work its magic for well over fifty years. Of the hundreds of African American schools in the state around 1900, only Palmer gained national renown for academic excellence, outlasting virtually every other African American school existing at the time of its creation.[1]

Although the historical impact of Charlotte Hawkins Brown as an individual is substantial in itself, her career at Palmer exemplifies a number of central themes in African American history. As a speaker, teacher, and writer, she stood out as an example of the yearning for education as a means to achieve racial and individual success of generations of freed blacks. She was part of the rising group of middle-class black women leaders, often clubwomen, who as elite African Americans hoped their race would gain respectability through education and then acquire full economic, social, and civil rights and freedoms. As such, she espoused the ideology of racial uplift, which some African Americans believed would bring dignity and respectability as well as economic and cultural security. Brown was a practitioner and preacher of propriety, the traditional defense of African American women in a male-dominated racist society. In these and other ways, she represented the yearnings for middle-class respectability and education of the self-styled African American elite in the early 1900s, who often distanced themselves from the poorer, cruder masses. Brown's own life seemed to prove that her formula had substantial practical merit, and she spread her philosophy tirelessly to her students and other audiences. Many contemporary historians judge Brown by current standards and see her as old-fashioned and unprogressive rather than recognizing her achievements under Jim Crow. This book attempts to view Brown objectively in the context of her own times—the era of Jim Crow, accommodation, and overt racism wherein even many educated whites believed without question in African American inferiority.[2]

Palmer Memorial Institute began in 1902 as a rural African American school founded by Brown. It continued as a unique private school for nearly seventy years, a half century of which it was under her resourceful leadership. The academy evolved from a poor, one-room school to a preparatory school attracting elite African American students from many states, the Caribbean, and Africa. Brown's extraordinary achievements demonstrated what one African American woman could accomplish in the racist South during the height of Jim Crowism.[3]

The purpose of this study is to bring to full light the educational career of Charlotte Hawkins Brown. In doing so, it is virtually impossible to separate her adult life from the development of the institution she founded. Brown was Palmer Memorial Institute, and Palmer totally exemplified the beliefs and values of its founder. Unlike most African American schools, Palmer was the direct result of the efforts of one able and ambitious black woman rather than of white paternalism. Educated in the North and initially espousing a Washingtonian racial philosophy, Brown later promoted a doctrine of social graces that embodied W. E. B. Du Bois's "talented tenth" theory that the ablest one-tenth of African Americans be educated to their highest potential and that they in turn teach the masses as a solution to America's "Negro question." When she died, her school did not survive the challenges of integration and inept management, yet the small institute had proudly produced over a thousand graduates, many of whom went on to professional careers and positions of leadership. This book explores how and why Brown accomplished those achievements.

African Americans had been part of North Carolina's history almost since the earliest days of European penetration. In 1790, the first U.S. census included 100,000 slaves and 5,000 free blacks. Nevertheless, after centuries of enslavement, most of the state's African Americans existed as a poor, uneducated underclass.[4]

Prior to the Civil War, little was done to educate African Americans in North Carolina. Quakers instructed some African Americans, despite colonial restrictions. After independence, North Carolina tolerated the illegal education of some slaves until the 1830s. Following the Nat Turner slave revolt of 1831, however, new slave codes and laws suppressed African American uplift and learning throughout the South.[5] Nevertheless, John Chavis, a free black born in North Carolina around 1763 and educated at Princeton College, returned to North Carolina to preach, but when state law forced him to stop preaching in 1831, he began teaching. Soon new legislation forbade educating blacks, but Chavis continued to teach in semisecrecy.[6]

After 1863, as the Civil War raged, educational opportunities improved slowly for African Americans thanks to the U.S. government, religious agencies, and charitable groups. That year, the federal Freedmen's Bureau opened schools in North Carolina at New Bern, and teachers came from New England agencies to teach freedpeople. Many southern whites resented their work, but one group—the Peabody Fund, established by philanthropist George Foster Peabody in 1867—gained some local cooperation because it also helped white schools. In 1869, a state law called for the creation of public schools for all children, but the term "all" was not equally applied. Thus northern philanthropic agencies operated schools for African Americans well into the 1900s.[7]

Central among those groups was the American Missionary Association, which employed Charlotte Hawkins Brown in October 1901. Established in 1846, the AMA soon dominated evangelical abolitionism, drawing most of its funding from New England Congregationalists and providing a few schools for African Americans in the antebellum South. Unlike many manual or vocational training programs established after 1865, AMA schools supported classical liberal education.[8] In the 1850s, missionaries founded a dozen or so churches in Randolph, Guilford, and nearby counties in North Carolina. The association's stated mission in the South was to bring the Gospel, freedom, and education to all, but particularly to blacks. Before the Civil War, only eight AMA domestic missionaries were teachers.[9]

The AMA, realizing by 1866 that normal schools and colleges were needed to produce black teachers, was a pioneer in African American education throughout Reconstruction. By 1875, graduates of AMA normal schools and colleges were instructing 150,000 students in numerous common schools. Although providing a liberal Christian education was the schools' major objective, the association recognized African Americans' need for economic freedom. To that end, most AMA schools had manual labor departments—not unlike the department Brown established—in which students worked off part of the cost of their education.[10]

The AMA established hundreds of schools and churches in North Carolina, opening more schools than in any other state. By 1900, it operated seven main "graded" (grades 1–6) and normal schools for African Americans from the seacoast to the piedmont: Washburn Seminary (founded in 1863) in Beaufort; Gregory Normal Institute (1865) in Wilmington; Hillsborough Academy (ca. 1884); Peabody Academy in Troy; Douglass Academy (ca. 1900) in Cleveland County; Brick Agricultural, Industrial, and Normal School (ca. 1896) in Halifax County; and Lincoln Academy (ca. 1896) near King's Mountain. Three principals were black, but most teachers were single white northern women. Campuses typically contained several buildings. Student bodies ranged from 135 to over 300 pupils.[11] In contrast, Bethany Institute (1870) in Guilford County, where young Brown began work, was merely a nominal normal school. Below those larger schools were scores of smaller schools, most with grades 1–6. Many of these common schools were connected to small Congregational churches and taught by the pastors. These mostly rural schools were often the only schools available. Bethany was such a school before the AMA, in its eagerness to set up rural normal schools, elevated it to normal school status even though it did not meet the standards for existing normal schools. Undoubtedly, the AMA felt that in time Bethany would meet those requirements.[12]

By 1900, non-AMA religious normal schools and colleges for African Americans also existed in North Carolina. Six of them became the core of the state's enduring group of historically African American colleges and universities. The largest, with 400 students, was the Raleigh Institute for Theological Training of Freedmen (now Shaw University), started in 1865. Brown's mother attended Shaw's elementary school for a time. The other five were Biddle University (1867; now Johnson C. Smith University) in Charlotte; Saint Augustine's Normal School and Collegiate Institute (1867; now Saint Augustine's College) in Raleigh; Scotia Seminary (1870; now Barber-Scotia College) in Concord; Bennett Seminary (1873; now Bennett College) in Greensboro; and Zion Wesley Institute (1879; now Livingstone College, unique with solely black management) in Salisbury. Another group of schools, vibrant around 1900 but destined not to survive, included Franklinton Institute and Albion Academy in Franklinton; Kittrell Normal and Industrial School in Kittrell; Methodist Episcopal Academy in Asheville; Congregational High School in Wilmington; Whitin Normal School in Lumberton; Winton Academy in Winton; and Yadkin Academy in Mebane.[13]

Black education also benefited from emerging national philanthropic organizations. Several arose in the early 1900s as new multimillionaires, such as steel baron Andrew Carnegie and oil tycoon John D. Rockefeller, distributed their benevolence. Such men promoted educational reform and other causes by establishing various charitable foundations.

The Slater, Jeanes, Rockefeller, Phelps-Stokes, and Rosenwald Funds cooperated in their struggle for African American uplift through learning. Those funds were inspired by Peabody's gifts a generation earlier. John F. Slater of Connecticut provided $1 million to educate African Americans. Anna T. Jeanes, a Philadelphia Quaker, sent Rockefeller's General Education Board (GEB) $200,000 for schools in the rural South. Then she created a $1 million endowment with an integrated board to aid rural southern black education. For several decades after the GEB's founding in 1902, it supported African American education, including public training, normal, and industrial schools. The GEB assisted the Jeanes Fund's training of rural women and children in cooking, canning, sewing, and sanitation. The Phelps-Stokes Fund used $1 million from the will of Caroline Phelps Stokes of New York to support the education of blacks in Africa and the United States. The Rosenwald Fund was established by Julius Rosenwald of Sears and Roebuck, a trustee of Booker T. Washington's Tuskegee Institute. Rosenwald duplicated Tuskegee's well-kept, small rural schools in locations where people of both races contributed funds; the schools were required to have industrial education, a garden or small farm, extended terms, and increased teachers' salaries. Later the Rosenwald Fund helped build over 5,300 schools in two decades across the South.[14]

The Rockefeller-funded Southern Education Board (SEB) seemed crucial to the other funds' success. The SEB, which did not oppose southern whites' racial views, was formed in 1901 primarily to convince whites to support public schools with tax dollars, but many SEB programs were incorporated into black schools such as Palmer, which would offer teacher training for kindergarten through normal school education.[15] Just six months before Brown's arrival, SEB representatives met in Greensboro to discuss the educational needs of African Americans. Two attendees at this conference became links between the SEB and Palmer: Greensboro educator Charles D. McIver, whose wife was an early supporter of Palmer, and New York philanthropist William J. Schieffelin.

Although the charitable funds provided crucial aid, blacks' educational fate ultimately depended on state government and politics. In 1900, North Carolina's public education for both races was among the poorest in the nation. Democrat Charles B. Aycock, a racist educational reformer, was elected governor that year. He believed that the primary reason for improving education was to train white voters. Uncharacteristically, from 1895 through 1898 Fusionists—agrarian Populists (many former Democrats) and Republicans (many of them African Americans)—had controlled state government. In 1900, Democrats used the Fusion period to justify white supremacy and African American disfranchisement as safeguards against "Negro domination." [16] It is no wonder, then, that Aycock, whose view on education for African Americans was limited, was chosen to rescue the state. He and other educational liberals cleverly used the race question despite opposition to their centralizing educational tendencies from white rural fundamentalists and blacks who recognized the inequities of public education. A related issue was the state's need to educate a cheap, docile, but effective African American labor force. Yet the political threat of African American voters was the center of the white supremacy campaign behind the school reform movement around 1900.[17]

Although Aycock ran highly racist campaigns in 1898 and 1900, he supported limited African American education and improved public schools. He believed that segregation and disfranchisement would end the race problem in politics, while education for all (albeit unequal) would advance the state and prepare African Americans for full future citizenship.[18] Aycock increased state funds for public schools, raised teacher standards, and lengthened the school year to eighty-five days. He and others campaigned across the state for local tax funds to support education, which funded the construction of hundreds of schoolhouses, but African American schools still lagged substantially behind. By the time Brown arrived in Guilford County, the state had begun an unequal program of educational uplift for both races based on white leaders' views of African Americans as docile laborers and "happy Negroes."[19]

In North Carolina, the aim of public "colored schools" was to provide basic instruction and industrial training. From 1876 to 1900, the state also had developed normal schools. Seven normal schools for African Americans were consolidated into four at Winston, Elizabeth City, Franklinton, and Fayetteville. State funds barely paid current expenses. Aycock's men proposed improvements and asked for $20,000 for buildings, equipment, and development of domestic science and industrial training. Decent lower education was a challenge given the low pay of African American teachers and the poor attendance of students. Teachers received $89.13 for just over four months of work; most needed other employment for the rest of the year. In 1900, African American illiteracy in North Carolina was 47.6 percent. Only 69.3 percent of African American children were enrolled in public schools, and barely 42.3 percent were in daily attendance.[20]

Charles B. Aycock, elected governor of North Carolina in 1900 after a
Jim Crow campaign that also promoted better public education. NCDAH.

Aycock's reforming state school superintendent, James Y. Joyner
(1862–1954), believed in the innate inferiority of African Americans but
felt they had a right to rudimentary education and sought increased
funds for black normal schools. In 1904, African American students,
about one-third of the school-age population, received about one-fifth
of the school money. Joyner argued that they should be educated to be
obedient, self-restraining, and industrious. Thus the reformers allowed
African American public schools to offer basic courses, but even normal schools taught no Latin, a task left to private institutions.[21]

Aycock's state school superintendent James Y. Joyner, who believed
in the innate inferiority of African Americans but urged greater
public funding to provide them with rudimentary education. NCDAH.

In such times, the idealistic young Brown returned to the state of her
birth to teach. Her strong mother and grandmother had greatly influenced her persuasive, dominant personality. Brown was a diligent worker
and developed a lifelong tendency to work to the point of sacrificing
health, marriage, and economic security. Missionary zeal led her to accept an offer by the AMA to teach at Bethany Institute. She began to re-
organize the declining school, but the AMA closed it. Brown stayed, however, and virtually single-handedly founded her own school, Palmer

Memorial Institute. She raised funds in the North and South from supportive whites, often women, but her first trustees were all African Americans.

Brown continued to develop Palmer, acquiring new land and buildings and receiving increasing biracial support. Palmer gained respectability by securing the backing of national figures such as Booker T. Washington, Harvard president Charles W. Eliot, and Boston philanthropist Galen L. Stone. Initially Brown found the emphasis on industrial training an effective fund-raising tool but maintained a parallel liberal arts curriculum and slowly moved away from Washington's accommodationist philosophy. Financial support from Stone, biracial backing, and northern fund-raising greatly strengthened Palmer in the 1920s.

Seeking long-term institutional stability, Brown negotiated the takeover of Palmer by the AMA in the 1920s while remaining as president. Meanwhile she became a nationally known speaker stressing cultural education as a means to racial uplift and gained a reputation as the "first lady of social graces" after an appearance on national radio and the publication of an etiquette book. At the state level, she was a leader in women's organizations. Back at Palmer, Brown set up a junior college. After her uncompromising rule led the AMA to disown Palmer in 1934, Brown rejuvenated the school as an independent academic finishing school that increasingly drew middle- and upper-class students from across the United States. In the 1940s, she paid off most of the school's debts and raised a $100,000 endowment. Palmer became the school of choice among the African American elite.

After fifty years of service, Brown retired, turning the school over to a handpicked loyal successor. Palmer continued to flourish for fifteen years. Then inexperienced new leadership, excessive spending, and competition from newly integrated public schools proved fatal to Palmer. Eventually the state of North Carolina acquired the run-down campus as the first state historic site to honor African Americans and women. In particular, however, the site recalls the outstanding life and work of Brown and her nationally exemplary school, for Brown's story centers around Palmer and begins and ends in North Carolina.

Chapter One

FROM NORTH CAROLINA
TO NEW ENGLAND AND BACK

LOTTIE HAWKINS was born on June 11, 1883, in the small town of Henderson, North Carolina. She later recalled that her early childhood home played an important role in her life. Brown's birthplace was a "little cottage by the side of the road that sat almost on the spot" where her grandparents were once slaves. Her mother, Caroline (Carrie) Frances Hawkins (1865–1938), was the youngest of twelve children born to Rebecca (ca. 1826–1901) and Mingo Hawkins. The identity of Brown's father is a mystery. She believed that he once belonged to a family on an adjacent plantation. At various times, she and others referred to her elusive father as Edmund Hawkins, Willis Hawkins, John Hawkins, Edmund Hight, and Edward Hight.[1]

Brown's maternal grandparents were slaves on large plantations in what is now Vance County. Brown's authorized biographer, Cecie Jenkins, claimed that Rebecca, a slave on the Hawkins estate, was a descendant of the English navigator John Hawkins. Rebecca was said to be very light in complexion with blue eyes, yellow hair, an aristocratic demeanor, and a strong and resonant voice. She was characterized as unlettered but very businesslike and a lover of beauty and fine things.[2]

In the two generations before and after emancipation, the close links between the white and black Hawkinses influenced Brown greatly. She believed that Rebecca's well-bred young master was in fact her grandmother's half brother. Although the white Hawkinses did not openly acknowledge Rebecca's kinship with them, she was clearly a favorite slave. Brown claimed that it was through Rebecca that she and her mother inherited intelligence, good character, pride, and an appreciation of beauty.[3]

In contrast, the origins of Brown's grandfather, Mingo, are contestable. It is uncertain whether he was once a farmhand on an adjacent

Brown, circa 1905. This may be the earliest surviving image of Brown. NCDAH.

plantation or whether he preceded Rebecca on the Hawkins estate. Jenkins declared that none of the descendants took much interest in his origins and that he died fairly young prior to Lottie's birth. Historian Tera Hunter's more recent study followed Jenkins's lead and argued that Mingo was a common field hand when he married the privileged Rebecca. Yet he reputedly was a skilled carpenter, and by 1870, he owned a forty-acre farm in Vance County where he resided with Rebecca and their children. That a man just five years out of slavery owned a farm was notable considering the growing number of black and white North

Carolinians who were forced into tenant farming, sharecropping, and peonage.[4]

Oral histories indicate that Rebecca had been a breeder slave on the Brodie plantation before going to the Hawkins farm and that her last name before marrying Mingo was Brodie. It appears that Rebecca had twenty-one children in all. The type of slavery Rebecca endured was not the harsh slavery that Brown romanticized. According to Hunter, Brown's grandparents' experience was typical of elite slaves whose covertly positive relations with their masters caused them to internalize the values of well-to-do whites. Faithful slaves were given rewards such as better food, shelter, and clothing. Rebecca also received land and a chance for economic independence after emancipation.[5]

A privileged class of slaves helped masters regulate a social order within the slave community that clearly defined the roles of the superior master and inferior slave. The elite slaves' kinship and contact with other slaves gave masters an advantage in controlling common field hands. Ironically that cultural unity created resentment between the two classes of chattel. The presence of elite slaves fostered the idea that adherence to their masters' regulations was a means by which blacks could elevate their status. Privileged slaves also reinforced the concept of perpetual slavery; those who broke the rules were punished by removal from upper-class status. While light-skinned Rebecca may have considered her elite status positive, in actuality her status reinforced the slave mentality. Whether or not Rebecca realized her "place" is immaterial; even if her owners favored her over other slaves, they did not recognize her as an equal.[6]

Brown's pride in her ancestry was based on the belief that her forebears descended from the well-known English sea dog Sir John Hawkins of Elizabethan days, as claimed by the white Hawkinses. Members of the Hawkins family of Granville and Franklin Counties played important roles in local and state history. Historian Samuel Peace began their genealogy with Philemon Hawkins, who settled in Virginia in 1717.[7]

John Davis Hawkins (1781–1858), alleged father of Rebecca, nephew of a U.S. senator, and brother of Tar Heel governor William Hawkins, was the son of planter Philemon Hawkins III and Lucy Davis. Three Hawkins generations, including John and his father, were born at the Pleasant Hill plantation near Middleburg, now in Vance County. John graduated from the University of North Carolina in 1801. A planter and lawyer, he ran Pleasant Hill, which covered almost 10,000 acres. Like his

John D. Hawkins, North Carolina plantation owner and alleged
great-grandfather of Brown. Courtesy of Margaret Story Haywood; NCDAH.

brother William, John was a Democrat. John and his wife, Jane A. Boyd (d. 1827), had thirteen children. He apparently also sired offspring by slave mistresses, such as Rebecca's mother.[8] His son Alexander Boyd Hawkins (1825–1921), also born at Pleasant Hill and a graduate of the university, was a planter in Florida and later a businessman in Raleigh. Rebecca's other famous half brother, William J. Hawkins (1819–1894), shared the same birthplace and schooling and received a medical degree at the University of Pennsylvania. By 1850, he owned twenty-five slaves and real estate valued at $13,000. He was a Raleigh banker and president of the Raleigh and Gaston Railroad for many years. From that professed patrimony, certain Hawkinses of African American descent, in slavery and freedom, acquired knowledge of the finer cultural aspects of life and some economic advantages uncommon for former slaves.[9]

Charlotte's mother, born free in November 1865 as Rebecca and Mingo's twelfth child, was influenced even more by persistent southern white upper-class cultural values. Because of a fondness for light-skinned Carrie, Jane A. Hawkins (1827–1898), Rebecca's white half sister who was a spinster, reared her in the "aurora of the 'big house.'" Brown later recalled that Carrie's high level of culture was "absorbed from her association in early childhood with one of the finest white families in the south."[10] Carrie's most outstanding recollection of "Miss Jane" was her challenge to Carrie to strive as an African American woman for certain high values. "If there be anything like a colored lady," Jane announced, "I want you to be one." Perhaps Carrie never viewed herself or her race as inferior until such statements were made. Perhaps Jane was attempting to prepare Carrie for black womanhood. African American women faced the constant fear of coercion and rape by "blameless" white men. To avoid such attacks, Carrie and other upright black women of her day used sobriety, propriety, and the mammy stereotype as a defense.[11]

With cultural values from Rebecca and Jane firmly instilled, Carrie aspired to material and cultural achievements. Jane reportedly sent her for a time to the primary school at Shaw University in Raleigh. She was well on her way to becoming a "colored lady" under Jane's tutelage when, just shy of her seventeenth birthday, she became pregnant.[12] No one documented the response of her benefactress, but no doubt Jane was not pleased. Carrie moved from Jane's commodious home on fashionable North Blount Street in Raleigh to Rebecca's house in Henderson when she gave birth to Brown. Disappointed in her lapse, Carrie maintained a strong lifelong faith in a forgiving God and prayed that He would fulfill in her first child what she had "wanted to do and be and could not."

Jane A. Hawkins, who raised Brown's mother, Carrie Hawkins, circa 1887.
Courtesy of Margaret Story Haywood; NCDAH.

Brown in a later autobiographical account recalled as a child sometimes hearing from Carrie's bedroom "heartbreaking sobs of 'Oh, God, you know,—you understand.'" For years, Carrie worked industriously to overcome the circumstances of Brown's birth by molding the girl into a capable and proper young lady.[13]

Brown's family is said to have lived in the finest residence owned by

African Americans in Henderson. The home reportedly was built by Carrie's brother, Grant Hawkins. It was a white five-room frame cottage with four wooden columns in front. The house was fixed romantically in Brown's memory; it was painstakingly clean, and its interior walls bore copies of masterpieces. The columns, which towered high above little Lottie, created a mental impression that influenced her entire life not merely figuratively but tangibly as well, as seen later in Palmer's architecture. A pedal organ positioned deliberately in the hallway so as to be visible from the front door further emphasized the family's desire for culture. Brown could not recall if anyone ever played the organ, but it served as a symbol of middle-class respectability. At that time in America, the piano represented not only the virtues of music but also the virtues of home, family life, respectability, and the highest values of womanhood. Music allowed women expression otherwise frowned on by men. With such a background, the Hawkinses bravely sought opportunities normally not offered to southern blacks of that day.[14]

At the time of Brown's birth, African Americans in North Carolina lived in the ardent grip of post-Reconstruction politics. Democrats replaced Reconstruction Republicans, and blacks faced growing discrimination by white employers and legislative bodies that reinforced the stereotype of social, economic, and political inferiority. Wealthy farmers used sharecropping to exploit black tenants by burdening them with continual debt, which prevented them from escaping economic enslavement.[15]

Henderson in the 1880s was no exception, nor did its white citizens reject Jim Crow. Incorporated in 1841, the village experienced an increase in population from only 186 as late as 1860 to 1,751 in the 1870s. Local leaders convinced the state legislature to create Vance County in 1881. Although the growth of the town and the creation of the county presented a promising future for whites, African Americans confronted racial violence and received few advantages. The state rapidly forced blacks into second-class citizenship by enacting black codes and black laws. This repression, commonly called Jim Crow, placed African Americans in a subordinate position in a segregated and unequal society.[16]

The term "Jim Crow," derived from the name of a character in a song, became synonymous with the system of racial segregation codified in the turn-of-the-century South. Jim Crow laws forcibly segregated blacks in communities, schools, hospitals, prisons, restaurants, and cemeteries. Restrictions also applied to water fountains, rest rooms, employment, and public transportation. African Americans by law could not use white facilities. Even the U.S. Supreme Court in *Plessy v. Ferguson* (1896) sanctioned the "separate but equal" doctrine. Jim Crow was a primary reason that African Americans migrated to the North, where they hoped to find better opportunities. Many blacks in the upper coastal South, chiefly from Virginia and northeastern North Carolina, moved to Massachusetts. Former slaves such as Rebecca wanted a better life for their descendants, and her daughter Carrie was no exception. Although the Hawkinses had some advantages, Jim Crow nevertheless segregated them in society, giving them reason to migrate as well.[17]

How did Vance County African Americans learn of the advantages of the North? In 1870, Bostonian Washington H. Davis bought the Collins Hotel in Kittrell, a town near the Hawkins plantation. After completely glassing in the building's front and south sides, he reopened it as the Davis Hotel in 1871. From October to May, the Glass House was filled with New Englanders, mainly wealthy sportsmen and people suffering from illnesses such as tuberculosis. The famous resort employed many former slaves as domestic and grounds workers. These workers probably heard stories of opportunities in Boston from guests of the Glass House. Indeed, the Hawkinses' decision to move to Boston was influenced as much by knowledge of a potentially better life in New England as by local racial restrictions.

The Davis Hotel burned in 1893, ending an era of cultural exchange between northern whites and southern blacks. The 1890s, a decade leading up to the full flowering of Jim Crow, also ended an era of political achievement by blacks such as Henry Plumber Cheatham. Cheatham, born a slave in 1857 near Henderson, was register of deeds for Vance County from 1884 to 1888. He was a congressman from 1889 to 1893, one of the last southern black congressmen until the 1960s.[18]

African Americans increasingly were lured to Boston by social, racial, and economic conditions. From 1865 to 1910, the African American population of greater Boston increased 561 percent, compared to an overall rise of 225 percent. The African American population in Cambridge, where Brown's family settled, grew twice as fast as that of Boston; the university town by 1900 had a third as many African Americans as did all of Boston proper. Yet by 1910 only 4 percent of Cambridge citizens were African Americans; Boston was only 2 percent black. This increase in population was almost entirely the result of immigration. By the time Brown's family moved to Boston in 1888, over half of black Bostonians were southern born. The majority of those immigrants came from the coastal upper South.[19] John Daniels's pioneering study,

In Freedom's Birthplace: A Study of the Boston Negroes (1914), argued that African Americans were making substantial economic progress in Boston by 1900, which attracted those still in the South. Blacks who moved to Boston from the South during the 1890s often greatly increased their skills in contrast to others with similar abilities in the 1865–80 period. For instance, an African American might have begun work as a day laborer and advanced to become a teamster or carpenter. While some gained higher status and pay, others in lower occupations managed by thrift to advance their economic security. Blacks increasingly held more jobs above the lower occupations, and apparently men's earnings rose enough to permit the percentage of women who were employed to decline. Recent studies, however, argue that nearly all African Americans in Boston remained locked in lower-status, menial jobs because of racial discrimination.[20]

African Americans of northeastern North Carolina nonetheless chose Massachusetts over other northern states. Especially after the Civil War, Boston had a reputation for liberalism. Families such as the Hawkinses thought they had a greater chance to gain economic, political, social, and educational opportunities in Boston.[21]

The Hawkinses' reasons for emigration surely included fear of lynchings. From 1880 to 1899, an average of 188 lynchings occurred annually in the South. Ida B. Wells, an African American pioneer in the antilynching cause, wrote: "There is nothing we can do about lynching now, as we are out numbered and without arms. . . . We must leave a town which will neither protect our lives and property nor give us a fair trial in the courts." This fact, along with growing disfranchisement, was a strong motivation for flight, and from 1880 to 1890, some 65,000 African Americans left. That exodus greatly expanded after World War I, totaling an estimated 1 million people by 1930.[22]

Whatever finally led to their decision to leave, Brown's family left North Carolina in 1888 for Boston, which Brown later wrote "had become the Mecca for many of the progressive negroes." She continued, "My earliest recollection is that of traveling towards the railroad station with my mother, and hearing stories of the big sea animals who would swallow us up if we were not careful on that boat trip from Norfolk to Boston." Brown further recalled the "great commotion of the large packing, the childish joy of adventure, as we were carried to the station in so many wagons and buggies to take a train for Norfolk, Va. where we youngsters—my brother, my younger aunts and I—were told that a boat bigger than the house in which we lived would take us to Boston."[23]

Artist's depiction of African Americans at a railroad
station waiting to leave North Carolina for the North.
From *Frank Leslie's Illustrated Newspaper,* February 15, 1890.

The move to Massachusetts was a major turning point in Brown's life. The trip took her from the land of her nativity to a place of far greater freedom and opportunity. Brown's mother sought the best for her children. Denied so much in their home state, they followed others who envisioned greater opportunities in the North.[24]

One of Brown's few memories of her life before moving to Boston was of a childhood speech that she felt had a lasting impact on her life: "My mother dressed me in white with blue ribbons on my hair and stood me beside her on the settee in the Church when I was about three years old to say my first speech, 'Suffer little children to come unto me, and forbid them not, for of such is the Kingdom of Heaven.'" This memory symbolized Brown's continuing devotion to religion and public speaking. Brown recalled fondly that at the conclusion of such performances she would "catch the pennies and nickels" thrown by the audience. Except for those appearances, Brown considered her childhood average, full of the excitement of a child who accepted things as they were without question.[25]

Because Brown moved to Boston at such an early age, she endured very little overt racial prejudice in the South. In later years, she remarked that not once in her Cambridge childhood did anyone make her feel different from her white classmates. In fact, at school she associated mostly with whites. The one setting in which she associated mainly with blacks was at church. Brown and her mother were faithful members of the Union Baptist Church in Cambridge, a large black institution. There Brown further developed her singular skills as a public speaker.[26]

The year after Brown arrived in Boston, her mother married Nelson Willis, a North Carolinian born in 1867. The union lasted over thirty-five years. Willis returned to North Carolina from Boston to accompany the Hawkins contingent on their move north. He was said to be a quiet, kind man. The marriage endured the tragic ending of five pregnancies in miscarriage or early childhood death. In part to fill this void, Carrie regularly cared for two or more foster children. Willis worked as a day laborer for a number of years and later was employed by the Cambridge waterworks. Although closer to her mother, Brown fondly recalled Willis as "a wonderful stepfather."[27]

The Willises' first known address in Cambridge was 70 Hastings Street. Brown's immediate family lived there until 1895 and then moved two blocks west to 37 Clark Street, not far from Harvard University, where they lived until 1901. From 1888 to 1901, nuclear groupings of the extended family rented various apartments and row houses within a four-block area in Cambridge's African American neighborhood. During the 1890s, Rebecca lived at 15 Clark Street, on the same block as her daughter.[28]

The Willises rented their home and sublet rooms to other African Americans from North Carolina. About 150 blacks from North Carolina and Virginia and some 500 or 600 white immigrants lived in the neighborhood. Carrie and Nelson also earned money by running a laundry, a common occupation of minority women who sought to become independent wage earners. Carrie eventually employed several neighborhood women but always did the intricate work, such as pleating and ruffling, herself. Lottie, too, spent countless hours ironing handkerchiefs in the basement and delivering laundry to patrons. Over the years, the entrepreneurial Willises worked hard to be self-supporting while saving a significant amount of money.[29]

Decorations in the Willises' home were similar to those in Carrie's North Carolina house. Cleanliness and orderliness always were the rules, and the walls were adorned with pictures complementing the decor of the house. Carrie's desire to obtain the better things in life for her family can be seen in Brown's experiences as a New England youngster. For example, Carrie arranged for Lottie to begin piano lessons at age seven to encourage her to develop a deeper appreciation for music. Lottie demonstrated uncommon musical ability and was persuaded by her mother to take training in voice.[30]

During this period, Lottie's determination and nascent ability as a leader began to grow. Noticing a group of younger children at her Sunday school who received no special attention, she successfully organized a kindergarten class. The church also provided a means for her to refine her oratorical skills. Brown recalled one such event: "Before I was fourteen years of age, I had been chosen orator on a very distinguished occasion, when the minister of the church was celebrating his 15th anniversary as pastor." Selection as principal speaker was a lofty honor; Lottie delivered her address before luminaries such as the governor of Massachusetts and his council. In her autobiography, she wrote: "I can see myself bowing again and again as my ears made me the proud possessor of the comments heard on the platform: 'She's going to be a mighty speaker some day, I expect to hear from that girl in the future.'"[31]

These were not the only distinctions Lottie received, for she had a sharp mind and worked diligently to perform tasks well. She was only five years old when she arrived in Cambridge and barely seventeen when she graduated from high school after a program often requiring thirteen

Mother at 59 yrs.
1924 - 69 Dana St. Cambridge, Mass.

Caroline Hawkins Willis, age fifty-nine, in 1924.
Schlesinger Library, Radcliffe College.

years. Thus it appears that her mother either quickly enrolled her in primary school or that she completed her primary education in less than the usual three years, a feat then achieved by a mere six or seven out of a hundred students.[32]

Brown did outstanding work at the Allston Grammar School in Cambridge and probably skipped a grade there also, as did about 30 percent of her peers. Her efforts were rewarded when she was named graduation orator for her class. This event was a high point not only for Lottie but for her mother and grandmother as well. "What joy in the heart of that little girl! And what gratitude and thankfulness in the soul of a devoted mother who was beginning to see the realization of her dreams."[33]

Brown then entered the Cambridge English High School in 1896, an outstanding accomplishment for a child with her background. During high school, she continued to develop an insatiable thirst for art. While most of her peers spent their money on candies and clothes, Brown used her extra funds to buy pictures for her room, a choice reminiscent of Carrie's and Jane's appreciation of art. She later explained the source of her interest in art and beauty in the home: "My first lessons in interior decoration were learned from my mother, for whatever fortune may bring me now no greater beauty can stir my soul than did the little bedroom off my mother's room, the furniture made out of wood boxes, which were covered with blue cambric and dotted Swiss muslin. My bed looked too pretty at night to disturb, and I suspect I slept many times on top of the bed rather than under the cover. I can see the mirror now, set back beyond parted blue and white ruffles, stiffly starched and immaculate."[34]

The English High School, founded in 1847, played a critical role in Brown's career as an educator. The school was part of the Cambridge Latin and English High School until 1886. The Latin High School was a preparatory school, and the English High School emphasized general and commercial education, domestic science, and preparation for scientific training. The curricula of the Latin and English schools were largely similar; the Latin school, emphasizing the classics, was among the finest preparatory schools in the nation.[35]

While enrolled at the English High School, Brown made many friends among administrators and teachers. Ray Greene Huling, an honors graduate of Brown University who had become principal of the school in early September 1892, was one such friend. His fifteen years of leadership were the most successful in the history of the school. Besides Huling, only three of twenty-three faculty members were men. In addition,

Ray Greene Huling, principal of the Cambridge English
High School, circa 1893. Courtesy Cambridge Historical
Commission; from *Latin and High School Review* 8 (1893).

393 of 546 students in late 1899 were girls; Brown's class had almost
twice as many girls as boys. This massive female presence must have
reinforced her strong feminist legacy. Among the teachers with whom
Brown developed lasting friendships was Caroline Close, for years head
of the English department. Following Brown's graduation in 1900, the
two remained in regular contact until Close's death in 1920.[36]

Such longtime friends and supporters influenced Brown's career in
various ways. Huling was so impressed by one of her crayon portraits
that he displayed it prominently in the school's hall. Of this Brown wrote:
"I remember ... students hurrying to the chapel, and I went along ...

and how abashed I was when I saw that a crayon portrait . . . was being exhibited to the whole student body." This encouragement led to Brown's drawing portraits of fellow students to earn extra money. Some of her early work would remain on the school's walls as late as 1926.[37]

Money was always a concern in Brown's family. Although her parents provided adequately for the children, frugal Carrie discouraged unnecessary extras. One oft-told example stood out in Brown's memory: "In the month of April [1900] I hurried home one day to tell mother that the girls had decided they would wear silk slips under organdy dresses for graduation and that we were all going to buy silk hats and trim them with lilies of the valley to wear with our graduation dresses on Sunday." Her mother looked up sternly from her ironing board and said: "You can have the organdy but mother will not buy silk for you, you can only have silk when you work and earn the money." Brown was determined to have the silk slip and hat, so she asked Grace Deering, a supportive teacher, about ideas for work. In a few days, Deering informed Brown: "I have a friend who would like to have some nice girl come and amuse her baby in the afternoon." Deering knew that Brown could sing and liked children and felt that it was "just the thing for her." And just the thing it was; Brown knew much about caring for babies because her parents' home was "seldom ever free of one." The job paid a generous $3.50 weekly for two hours per day.[38]

Brown readily accepted the job and hurried home to inform her mother. Because Brown had never "worked a day out for anybody before," Carrie feared her plan was just a whim. But Brown, with her goal in mind, stuck to her baby-sitting duties during those bright April days. Those experiences, retold many times by Brown, would have a far greater impact on her life than merely providing money to buy a silk slip. Through both happenstance and Brown's hard work, they helped set her on a course that would forever change her life; the lives of more than a thousand men, women, and children; and the educational history of an entire state. About that time, envisioning her name on an impressive high school diploma, Brown adopted what she considered a more proper name than Lottie Hawkins. She chose Charlotte Eugenia Hawkins, an appellation she believed as elegant as those of Boston's finest young men and women.[39]

Other early influences also steered Brown toward a career in education. Through the black church, Brown became familiar with such outstanding African American educators as Booker T. Washington, W. E. B.

Du Bois, Lucy Craft Laney, and Maria L. Baldwin and their great work among African Americans, particularly in the South. Those contacts shaped her destiny.

Brown first learned of the educational work being done in the South in 1897 when Booker T. Washington gave a lecture at Boston's Ebenezer Baptist Church entitled "The Negro in the South." Brown remembered Washington's appeal to northern blacks that Sunday: "You, who have had the opportunity for education in Massachusetts, should help your own people in the South. Massachusetts does not need you. Come over into Macedonia and help us." Exposure to Washington's philosophy made a lasting impression on Brown.[40]

Booker T. Washington (ca. 1856–1915) was born a slave in Virginia. Overcoming poverty through hard work and perseverance, he received an education at Hampton Institute in Virginia and went on to establish Tuskegee Institute, a manual training school in Alabama. By accommodating the dominant white society, his career and influence rose in the late nineteenth century. In the mid-1890s, African Americans faced a crisis that seemed to threaten their very existence. Reconstruction and postemancipation progress in the South lay in ruins, and African American citizens were confronted with rising racism, increased lynchings, disfranchisement, and riots. Then in 1895 Washington delivered a controversial address that was considered demeaning to blacks at the Cotton States International Exposition in Atlanta that became known as the Atlanta Compromise.[41]

The speech marked Washington's emergence among whites as the foremost spokesman for African Americans. His selection as speaker signified his acceptance by much of the white leadership of the South. Washington called on African Americans to settle temporarily for second-class citizenship. By submitting to white social and political rule and focusing on economic initiative and self-help, Washington claimed, blacks would eventually acquire property, wealth, and respect. Those resources, along with high moral character, he argued, would bring about first-class citizenship.[42]

To allay white fears, Washington publicly disapproved of black involvement in politics, condemned migration north, renounced agitation for first-class citizenship, and urged African Americans to adjust to existing southern conditions. He believed that blacks' humble submission to racism would lead whites to realize the wrongs committed against African Americans. This philosophy encouraged African Americans' obedience to whites, forbearance of the wrongs dealt them, and faith in whites' ultimate justice toward them. Washington hoped that blacks' high moral character would eliminate racial animosities.[43]

It is not known how much the ideas of W. E. B. Du Bois influenced Brown during her early years. Du Bois, Massachusetts's native son, was also a well-known African American spokesman by the late 1890s. In fact, as a student, Brown personified his famous "talented tenth." Later, as a teacher, she employed his theories to uplift rural African American students. Born in western Massachusetts, William Edward Burghardt Du Bois (1868–1963) received a B.A. from Fisk University in 1888 and a second B.A. from Harvard in 1890. He earned an M.A. (1891) and a Ph.D. (1895) from Harvard and later studied in Germany. Whether as editor, professor, or public lecturer, Du Bois advocated elimination of racial inequalities. His attempts to reveal and correct such social ills in America inevitably brought him into conflict with Washington. In a remarkable career spanning over seventy years, Du Bois remained a firm critic of the suppression of African Americans.

Du Bois's ideological response to problems arising from the African American presence in the United States contained two conflicting concepts. The first was total integration of African Americans into American society; the second promoted black nationalism and separatism. Since total integration was rejected by most Americans, he adopted the second. Du Bois was aware of his "twoness," as he called it; he suggested that time and circumstance determined which option was appropriate. Toward the end of the 1890s, he placed great value on education as the solution to the problems of African Americans. He believed that to raise the masses, a black elite, or "talented tenth," would have to be created. That group in turn would uplift all African Americans.[44]

Surely knowledge of Washington and Du Bois inspired would-be educator Brown. Yet awareness of such *men* left room for doubt about the role of an African American woman in the uplift of her people. Brown, however, was encouraged by the accomplishments of African American women educators such as Maria Baldwin and Lucy Laney.

Maria L. Baldwin (1856–1922), an important model for Brown, was an outstanding educator in Cambridge. Her achievements not only gave Brown confidence but also stamped on whites an enduring impression of the intellectual abilities of African Americans. This recognition inspired Brown, who knew Baldwin personally and relied on her for advice. Born and educated in Cambridge, Baldwin was principal of the well-known Agassiz Grammar School for twenty-three years. The elite school had no other African American teachers and only a few black students. Baldwin's considerable ability and high degree of tact made her a competent and much-respected educator. Brown was fully aware that Baldwin was the only African American in greater Boston to hold such an important position.[45] In Brown's assessment, "My mother's plans for me were my greatest inspiration, but the position as a Master in one of the select schools of the city of Cambridge held by a beautiful brown-skin woman, Maria Baldwin by name, gave great courage to my desire to forge ahead and become. But the face of the black woman, Lucy Laney, thrown upon the canvas one night in a Cambridge church and a white man's description of her achievement in spite of her color determined my career as an educator and builder."[46]

Lucy Craft Laney (1854–1933) was proof of what one young black woman could do in the Jim Crow South. Laney believed that educated Christian women would uplift the race's youth and masses through schools dedicated both to academic subjects and community service. She was convinced that women were natural teachers of young children and that effective kindergarten and primary education could eventually be a major part of elevating African Americans. Laney, a member of American Missionary Association (AMA)–sponsored Atlanta University's first graduating class, was a pioneer among black female educators in the South. To meet what she considered the special needs of black children, Laney established the Haines Normal and Industrial School in Augusta, Georgia. For Brown, a role model such as Laney was vital because Laney proved that a dark-skinned African American woman could make a difference.[47]

Other racial concerns also shaped Brown's views of proper training for African American youth. She said that Jane Hawkins's challenge to her mother to be a "colored lady" "burnt its way into my very soul, and I now suspect my first real knowledge of difference in races was born when I heard it." But that was a memory of the Old South and had little to do with life in liberal Boston. Brown was aware of race and color differences between herself and her classmates in Boston but maintained that she "knew nothing of segregation; there were for me no barriers of which I was conscious. I went where I wanted to go, sat where I wanted to sit, and had scores of intimate friends, young and old, in both races."[48]

Brown did recall one racial incident during high school. The small group of African Americans at school participated in school affairs with other ethnic groups. But Brown suggested that if the few "Negro students got together" and held a dance, they could unite a "large group of friends." These African American students organized the Cambridge

High School Associates.[49] The dance was an elegant event, publicized by the *Boston Herald.* Brown was proud of the media attention and thought the occasion was welcomed by all who read the article. This was not the case, however, and Brown later claimed that her awareness of racial segregation and perceptions of African American inequality developed from this incident. Years later, Brown recalled one northern white person's response to the function:

> I received a letter from the president of the Cantabrigia Club of which the members represented the best Cambridge families. The writer was also wife of the editor [of the *Herald*]. Mrs. M——asked me to come to see her immediately. I naturally felt very important. . . . Imagine my surprise when this woman told me, in a strong forceful way, that I had committed a terrible error. She told me of the fight they were making to include Negroes in all things and that never again must we be guilty of having anything separate and apart in our school. "It will defeat our purpose," she said. Here I was in the lead of a segregated movement and didn't know it—doing then what I have been forced to do for forty years since.[50]

To be sure, Brown at an early age was aware of her blackness and, regardless of the covert nature of racism in Cambridge, needed encouragement and guidance to achieve her goals.

Influenced by her teachers and other educators, Brown developed a great interest in education beyond high school. Cambridge itself, with the Willis home near Harvard and Radcliffe, was surely an incentive for attending college. Perhaps Brown's classmates, a number of whom were children of well-known writers, poets, and educators, instilled in her a determination to obtain higher education. Whatever the reason, Brown, upon graduating from high school in June 1900, had a compelling desire to become a teacher.

While Brown was working as a baby-sitter, an incident occurred that became the most repeated anecdote of her life. Watching the children was easy work, and Brown often studied as she tended them. "One day, while rolling the baby carriage with one hand and reading my *Virgil* held in the other, there passed me briskly a woman dressed in black. She turned and smiled, and then turned again. Finally she came back. After tickling the baby under its plump little chin, she asked, judging I suppose from the fact that *Virgil* was a text used in the senior classes—'Are you a senior?' I answered, 'Yes, I am.' 'In which one of the schools?,' she asked. 'The English High School,' was my reply."[51] This pleasant talk held no special interest for Brown at the time. The woman did not identify herself, and Brown returned to her walking and reading.

The incident, however, did not end there. A few days later, Huling called Brown to his office: "Mrs. Alice Freeman Palmer inquired about you, Lottie, and wanted to know who was the little brown skin colored girl wheeling a baby carriage in the vicinity of the school. I told her that it must be you." To Brown, Palmer's name had no significance. Later she remembered Palmer as "a person who went out of her way to be kind." [52]

Alice Freeman Palmer (1855–1902) was born in rural New York. Her mother nurtured Palmer's intellectual curiosity, administrative abilities, and unselfish nature. Palmer entered Windsor Academy and at fourteen became engaged to a teacher. The engagement ended after Palmer realized that college meant more to her than marriage. Like Brown, Palmer had to convince her parents that a college education was worthwhile. She received a B.A. at the University of Michigan in 1876. Three years later, she became head of the Department of History at Wellesley College in Massachusetts. During her first year there, the college president reportedly stated to a trustee: "You see that little dark-eyed girl? She will be the next president of Wellesley." [53]

Palmer indeed became the second female president of Wellesley in 1881 and built the institution into a solid college. That same year, she was a founder of the American Association of University Women (AAUW), serving two terms as its president. More important to Brown's future, Palmer was chairperson until her death of the AAUW committee on fellowships. Of significance to Brown as well, the governor of Massachusetts appointed Palmer to the state board of education. This was the position she held when Brown reencountered Palmer's name while considering which normal school to attend. [54]

Like Palmer, Brown dreamed of a college education, but her mother had other thoughts. Although Brown wanted to attend Radcliffe, Carrie saw no need for college since very few women or men of any race were college graduates in 1900. Even Massachusetts did not require a normal school certificate to teach in public graded schools. Carrie felt her daughter had ample training to become a teacher and advised: "Some little political pull, good reputation, and fine high school scholarship were the requisites for appointment." No argument could justify her daughter's desire to attend a four-year college. Brown therefore approached her mother with the compromise that she attend one of several excellent two-year normal schools around Cambridge. This led to her rediscovery of Palmer: "I began to flood the mail with requests for normal school

Alice Freeman Palmer, second female president of Wellesley
College and mentor of young Brown. NCDAH.

catalogs, and imagine my surprise when I opened one from the state
normal school at Salem, to see the name 'Alice Freeman Palmer' on the
front page as a member of the board of education of the state of Massachusetts."[55]

Remembering Huling's reference to Palmer, Brown resolved to ask
her for help. As Brown saw it, "God had chosen to work a miracle." She
wrote: "I immediately decided that I would write and tell her that I was
the little brown skin colored girl whom she had seen wheeling the baby
carriage and reading Virgil." Brown had no doubt that Palmer would "at

least give her audience and listen to her proposition." Only a few days after she mailed her letter, Brown received a reply. Palmer had remembered her! Not only that, but she offered to aid Brown financially. Without making any inquiries into Brown's economic situation, Palmer even volunteered to take care of incidental expenses at any normal school in Massachusetts. Brown was overwhelmed by Palmer's generosity. She wrote: "I naturally chose Salem, as it was possible to commute back and forth from Boston." Palmer's aid must have eased any remaining concerns on the part of Brown's mother.[56]

Palmer had not assumed responsibility for the expenses of Brown's education carelessly. Before investing her time and money, she had consulted Maria Baldwin, who she knew was Brown's mentor. Baldwin told her that she had advised Brown to study current events and read noteworthy books to enable Brown to compete with upper-middle-class white children, who were exposed to intellectual discussions at their dinner tables. Baldwin also assured Palmer of Brown's high moral character. In addition, Palmer discovered that Brown had been an excellent student at the Cambridge English High School. Another possible reason Palmer acted without further consultation with Brown was that this black girl wheeling a carriage and reading Latin reminded Palmer of her own determination as a youth to attain higher education. Thus advised, Palmer agreed to assist a career in education that became far more brilliant than any she might have imagined.[57]

Thus in the fall of 1900, at the age of seventeen, Brown began studies at the state normal school at Salem. Placing great confidence in her benefactor's guidance, she applied herself fully to her work and did remarkably well. She advanced to the class of 1902 but could not complete the final year of study because she received a compelling proposal that would lead her back to the state of her birth, North Carolina.

The prelude to the invitation occurred one spring day in 1901 as Brown commuted from school to her home in Cambridge. As she boarded a train with several white schoolmates, she noticed that a friendly looking woman continued to glance at her. Brown thought the woman was looking at her because she was the only African American in the group. Eventually the woman moved to the seat beside Brown and began a conversation. She was a field secretary for the AMA, the chief Christian philanthropic agency operating schools for African Americans in the South. She explained to Brown that the AMA was seeking qualified black teachers for its schools, and Brown said that she was immensely interested in teaching African American youth. The woman promised to send materials to Brown about teaching opportunities. Brown later stated: "God directed a woman, filled with the missionary spirit, to me to encourage my already burning desire to return to the state of my birth and help my people. I cannot tell in detail, but step by step I was led directly to do what I had dreamed of since childhood. I could not get away from the idea that God wanted me for this kind of work."[58]

Initially, Brown had no idea that the AMA position would be in North Carolina, but the package she received offered a choice between a job in that state or a job in Florida. Because the North Carolina job paid very poorly, Brown in September prepared to take the position in the Florida school. She could not resist the lure of her native state, however. Explaining her final decision, Brown wrote: "I was about to go to Florida to . . . a well-organized school, [when] there came a second letter from the [AMA] board. . . . This letter told me of the little mission school they were supporting in McLeansville, N.C., as the post office was then known."[59]

This is how Brown came to accept the AMA's appointment as a missionary teacher at Bethany Institute in rural Guilford County. In 1901, she still lacked one year of study before she could graduate from the Salem normal school. Because the AMA could not hold the position open until after she graduated, Brown had to choose between graduating with her class and going to North Carolina. She chose the latter and arranged to finish her studies in absentia and remain in the class of 1902. Thus this brave, determined young African American woman left her family in Boston for a challenging, lonely AMA assignment in a backwoods corner of piedmont North Carolina. Little did she know that her relationship with the AMA would not endure and that the rural school ultimately would evolve during a half century of her strong leadership into the nation's preeminent African American preparatory school.[60]

The AMA school to which Brown would report, Bethany Institute, had begun in eastern Guilford County in 1870 with the arrival of a white missionary from Iowa, Esther Douglass. Douglass began holding services in an old foundry where Confederate munitions had been made and soon asked the AMA for funds to build a church. Local African Americans aided in clearing land at the church site.[61] In 1873, John Scott, the mission's first pastor, again asked the AMA for funds ($500) to construct a church. African American residents were eager to have a new place of learning and worship.[62]

Douglass continued as both teacher and lay preacher until the Bethany school was dedicated in January 1874; after that time, her work was mainly educational. Black walnut gun stocks once used to make rifles were transformed into seats for the new mission.[63] The church was an instant success, and Scott expected that the number of congregants would soon reach the maximum seating capacity. Moreover, the place that would become Sedalia gained a reputation for racial goodwill, in part because of Douglass's efforts; despite nearby Ku Klux Klan activity, the locality enjoyed racial tolerance.[64]

Douglass provided continuity for nearly a decade, running the mission by herself for a time after Scott's departure. The school was soon too large for one teacher, yet most pupils made progress. Adults studied in night school. Due to Douglass's dedication, the mission addressed the basic educational needs of rural Guilford's African Americans. Douglass continued to serve as both educator and evangelist alongside a string of part-time ministers.[65]

In 1878, Reverend Alfred Connet of Indiana became the mission's first full-time pastor. With increased enrollment, he informed the AMA that dormitories were needed at once, for "white people do not wish to take in boards, unless at high fees." In 1879, Douglass was removed, leaving Connet as minister and teacher.[66] He served until 1891 and made Bethany more than a common school by obtaining textbooks for primary through normal school instruction. Trying to convince the AMA to reclassify Bethany as a normal school, he noted that it had "improved in numbers and in regularity of attendance. The number enrolled is 84."[67]

By 1880, Bethany was drawing students from four counties. Thirteen were paying boarders, of whom ten were "professors of religion," two were preparing for the ministry, and one was a minister. Seven of the students in normal school classes the previous year had become teachers. Several African American neighbors provided buildings for student housing, and other black families agreed to take in boarders. The school added a second room and expected twelve to fifteen pupils to obtain teacher's licenses that year.[68] Although Connet's wife was concerned about Ku Klux Klan activity and local whites who shunned her, a surprising number of whites attended revival services with blacks at Bethany Congregational Church, some every night.[69]

In 1881, Connet successfully directed a two-month summer normal institute to train African American teachers, the first such effort—public or private—in the area. Bethany was in its heyday, and church and school had good attendance.[70] Bethany had about eight acres, including a spring, a cemetery with some fifty graves, and an orchard with about a thousand trees and vines that produced a dozen kinds of fruits. Classes included algebra and Latin to prepare students for teaching or AMA colleges. Connet and his wife taught most classes, and his daughters tutored individual students. The school enrolled about eighty students. Fifteen of them had taught at one time, and three went on to attend Hampton Institute, Fisk University, and Talladega College.[71] In the 1880s, the number of AMA schools and churches in North Carolina increased greatly. Connet continued at Bethany for a time, but his dream of establishing a full-fledged normal school fell short.

In 1893, Elizabeth Smith, an African American, began teaching at Bethany. The next year, her husband, Reverend George S. Smith, became Bethany's first African American minister.[72] The Smiths were AMA missionaries at Bethany and a nearby church. That same year, George Smith died. Mr. and Mrs. S. S. Sevier, also African Americans, replaced the Smiths at the second church school, while Elizabeth Smith continued as teacher at Bethany along with S. S. Sevier as preacher.[73]

In 1897, Reverend Manuel Liston Baldwin became minister and principal. A graduate of the AMA's Talladega College in Alabama, Baldwin was ordained in 1896 as an AMA missionary. At Bethany, he found teacher Minnie A. Green and 145 students, an enrollment that was a sizable increase over that of previous years and was comparable to the enrollment at other AMA normal schools. Like Connet, Baldwin hoped that the school would attain normal school status. By this time, many AMA schools were run by African Americans educated at AMA schools and colleges. Baldwin supervised both church schools, and his wife Edith joined him as a teacher. Soon two other African American teachers arrived: Eliza and Dulcina Torrence.[74] They remained through the 1900–1901 school year and were replaced the next term by Malsie D. Green of Pekin, North Carolina (probably Minnie Green's sister), and the exceptional Charlotte Eugenia Hawkins, newly arrived from Massachusetts. The AMA recognized Bethany as a normal school in 1901 and must have expected the bright northern-trained Brown to strengthen it substantially.[75]

As Brown prepared for a career as an AMA teacher, she carefully reviewed her instructions from the association. She could not have foreseen, however, the magnitude of the difference between metropolitan Boston and rural North Carolina. Even Brown's mother had not heard of McLeansville but thought it must be near the small town of Greensboro.

On Brown's journey to North Carolina in early October, after the train passed through the places she knew, such as Henderson and Raleigh, she began to ask the porter where McLeansville was. He replied that it was only a stop in the woods and that if they were not careful the train would pass it. Fearing this warning, Brown continued to question him. After hearing her reminders once too often, the porter angrily told her that he would be sure to let her off the train.[76]

After she left the train, the only indication that Brown could find that she was in McLeansville was a faded wooden sign; there were no buildings or other manifestations of a real town. She began to doubt the wisdom of rejecting the job at the well-established school in Florida. After recovering from the shock of finding herself in such a remote area, Brown realized that no one was there to meet her. She was also the only passenger to get off at that stop.

Finally Brown saw an elderly white couple coming out of an old wooden store in the distance. Thinking that this might be her only chance to obtain directions, she approached them. Remembering her mother's warning about how southern whites treated African Americans, she summoned her courage and cautiously asked directions to the Bethany school. Her appearance was pleasant, and her clothes were like those worn by teachers in Massachusetts. Astonished by her New England accent and dress, the white couple said they knew nothing of Bethany but offered to let Brown follow them down the narrow dirt road in hopes that she would meet someone who could give her directions. After following them for some time, Brown spotted a black woman working alone in a field.[77]

Approaching the woman without hesitation, Brown asked for directions to Bethany Institute. The woman, also amazed by Brown's speech and appearance, answered: "Law, child, I knows that school, but it be a right far piece from here. Wait a bit and I'll have Ely hitch up the mules and drive you down there." Relieved, Brown waited until the woman finished her work, then climbed into the wagon with the woman and her husband behind two sleepy-looking mules. The ride was rough because the dirt road had many holes, but it was better than walking. During the trip, some four miles including her walk from the whistle-stop, the woman engaged Brown in conversation and unknowingly provided an example of some of the prejudices that Brown would face. The woman stated: "Child, that be one mean place. You got to watch everybody, white folks and niggers alike. They's all mean. You got to watch 'em all, even me."[78]

At last, Brown reached the school and was shocked to find a run-down structure. With a sickened heart, she heard the words, "Here be the school." She recalled: "It was unpainted and much weather-beaten.

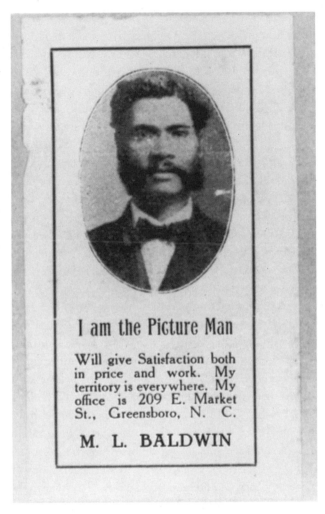

I am the Picture Man

Will give Satisfaction both
in price and work. My
territory is everywhere. My
office is 209 E. Market
St., Greensboro, N. C.

M. L. BALDWIN

Manuel L. Baldwin, principal of Bethany Institute
when Brown arrived there. NCDAH.

Large, gaping holes showed forth where window panes had once been.
The yard was unkempt and grown up with stubble." As the couple drove
off, she felt abandoned and helpless in her chosen field of labor.

Next to the school was the home of Manuel Baldwin. He was thirty-
eight when Brown arrived and had been married for eighteen years to
thirty-seven-year-old Edith; they had five children aged three to fifteen.
Brown went to the house and was welcomed somewhat doubtfully by
Baldwin. She remembered: "No one seemed to be expecting me. . . . I
felt as though I wanted to go back home. I did not then know, as I now

do, that God knew what was best for me. I wanted to enter His service, but had not thought of entering such a barren field. However, after thinking over my desire, I said, 'This is God's way; I must be satisfied.'" After talking with Brown, Baldwin remembered that the AMA had written him about a Miss Hawkins, but he had no idea when she would arrive or that she would be an African American. Because she was coming from Cambridge, Baldwin had assumed that the AMA was sending a white woman.[79]

That night after dinner, Brown prayed for some understanding of why God had directed her to such an unpromising field of labor. As she searched for answers, she came to the conclusion that God had chosen this backwoods place as part of her destiny. Therefore, with characteristic determination, Brown accepted the challenge. The next morning, the church school and Baldwin's home seemed even more miserable. A narrow red clay road separated them from a large field of briar and stubble containing a dilapidated blacksmith shop. Brown described the vista: "A short distance up the road in one direction stood another little building designated as the white school house. In the other direction—not too far—stood a general store bearing the name R. B. Andrew." Brown could not help but reflect on the life she had left in Cambridge. Nevertheless, she firmly believed that Bethany was where she belonged. With such conviction and faith in God, she overcame much of her depression.[80]

Brown's faith that God had led her to Bethany was comforting but did little to change the harsh realities of impoverished rural life. About fifty children arrived for school on the morning of October 10, 1901, her first day as a teacher. Boys and girls, dressed in all types of clothes, came prepared to learn and greeted her warmly. Classes were held in the church, and the pupils sat in the pews. Each pew had a long board attached to the back with hinges that could be lowered and used as a writing surface. Baldwin and his wife did some teaching, Malsie Green provided elementary instruction, and Brown taught the advanced students, mostly tenth and eleventh graders expecting to teach the following year.[81]

Brown came to Bethany with a well-planned curriculum based on her own experience in progressive Boston and naively anticipated teaching her poor rural students some of the same academic material she had learned in an elite urban public high school. The young instructor was sure she knew what to expect from students who would be teachers the following year but, after questioning several pupils on academic subjects, noticed that they were slow to respond. At first, she thought they were sluggish due to the shock of having a teacher their own age. But she discovered a more serious problem: the students' education level was far below Boston standards. Brown first had assumed that her pupils had followed the same course of study she had taken in Massachusetts. Obviously this was not the case; Bethany's tenth and eleventh graders were actually on fifth- and sixth-grade levels. Brown finally placed even her most advanced pupils in lower grades to bring them up to speed. Although they were understandably not pleased, most of the pupils endured this and were eager to learn; after a difficult period of adjustment, they settled into the stiffer curriculum.[82]

Several students had problems other than adjustment to new academic requirements. Some were ill clad. Many had to walk long distances, in some cases ten to fifteen miles, to attend classes. When the weather was bad, those students remained at home. Missing even one day made it very hard to keep up because the school term lasted only four to five months. The term was short because most children worked on their parents' sharecropping farms during the spring, summer, and fall. This left only the harsh winter months for formal education. Brown was determined to find a solution to winter transportation problems. Observing that Green and several female students were boarders in Baldwin's home, she reasoned, as Connet had earlier, that if additional boarding arrangements could be made, many more students could attend the school.

To solve this problem, Brown asked Baldwin for use of the run-down blacksmith shed across the road from the school as student housing. He agreed, and the old shop was made into female dormitory space. Students and parents assisted in repairing the structure, which when finished contained classroom space downstairs and living areas upstairs for Brown and fifteen girls. These improvements were made while the school was still under AMA control with Baldwin as principal. For the first time, school and church were held in separate buildings.

To help feed the new boarders, all girls at first, many parents paid tuition in food instead of money. Female students prepared their own meals but had inadequate training in food preparation because of their rural upbringing and simple diet. Many girls had not learned to eat a healthy variety of foods because their regular fare consisted of corn bread, beans, potatoes, and molasses—the typical unbalanced diet (minus the meat) of most poor southerners of the era. Meat was rarely served, although small bits of pork were often used as seasoning.[83]

Expenses for board and tuition were $5 per month. Boarding girls

Old blacksmith shed that served as Palmer's first classroom
and dormitory building, circa 1917. NCDAH.

shared laundry and housekeeping duties. Brown assigned a certain task
to each girl for a prearranged period of time, then another housekeeping duty was assigned. From its early days, the Bethany school had a
steady supply of fresh drinking water, but it had to be drawn by hand
from a well. Chores included cooking, washing, making mattresses by
hand, and filling oil lamps each day. The average daily attendance at the
improved school was around fifty-five students of all ages.[84]

Once Brown solved the problem of the lack of boarding facilities for
girls, she was determined to find space for boys to live near the school.
She again approached Baldwin for assistance. He agreed to give the
school an old house about a quarter of a mile from the blacksmith shop.
The house was in good condition, and again with the assistance of students, parents, and others in the community, it was transformed into a
dormitory.

Brown made these improvements during her first year at Bethany. In
addition to teaching, she did much other work with little assistance from
Baldwin. Except for contributing two run-down buildings, he more or
less had given up on the school and devoted his energies to church affairs.
Even the AMA, which had contracted to pay Brown $25 a month during
the school term, was reducing its commitment to Bethany Institute.

Nevertheless Brown, confident in God's plan, continued her efforts.

Having met the basic needs for housing, she set about making greater improvements. Because the boys' dormitory was in much better condition than the girls', she decided to move the girls into the same structure. The new boys' and girls' dormitory housed forty persons, including Brown. It was perhaps the first coeducational dormitory in North Carolina. The new living arrangement was not without restrictions, for Brown was a strict disciplinarian of high moral character. Students were separated by floors, with girls upstairs and boys downstairs; Brown personally supervised all of their activities to ensure proper conduct.[85]

With limited support from Baldwin and the AMA, Brown struggled along under great hardship and pressure. Not only was she forced to endure a shortage of funds and moral support, but also she faced racial prejudice from blacks as well as whites. Local whites were biased against her for several reasons: she was an African American, she was a woman, she was a Yankee, she had been well educated (far better than most whites), and she had come "to teach their niggers." Many local African Americans also were suspicious of her motives. They did not like the fact that Brown was attempting to change their way of life. They viewed the ideas and actions of the nicely dressed, well-spoken young black woman from the North as absurd. Faced with such suspicions, Brown had to convince blacks and whites alike to place their confidence in her. This was not easy because North Carolina's tradition of inadequate education, for African Americans in particular, was deeply entrenched by 1901.[86]

Five years earlier, the U.S. Supreme Court in *Plessy v. Ferguson* had ruled that separation of the races was constitutional. The Court believed that equality could be achieved as long as equal facilities were provided for both races. A year before the famous *Plessy* case, Booker T. Washington had become the nationally recognized leader of African Americans by voicing his approval (and supposedly that of the black race) in the Atlanta Compromise of political and social racial separation. Clearly under such conditions anyone, but particularly a young black woman from Boston, would need to take great care to avoid transgressing societal norms or offending members of either race in the pursuit of excellence in African American education.[87] Yet Brown knew she would need to take risks (as she had in merely coming to Bethany) and reach out to whites—who had political and economic power—to secure financial support and recognition for her school.

Chapter Two

BETHANY INSTITUTE BECOMES
PALMER MEMORIAL INSTITUTE

WHILE BROWN prepared parents and students for her school's new role in the community, she began meeting with southern white educational leaders such as Jesse R. Wharton, Guilford County's superintendent of public schools. Brown had obtained her certificate to teach in the segregated schools of North Carolina in November 1901. As she began efforts to transform Bethany Institute into an authentic normal school, lack of funds caused many of the students' personal needs to be unfulfilled. The American Missionary Association (AMA) furnished little support, and most students were poor, making do with monotonous unbalanced diets, worn clothes, and old shoes. To overcome this, Brown taught boarding students to live economically. Furthermore, she knew she had to find some way to secure permanent support.[1]

Although she assumed that the AMA's limited aid would continue, Brown sought ways to obtain additional funds. She was confident that she could get help from people like Alice Freeman Palmer and other New England friends who had encouraged her to work in the South. After conceiving a plan to solicit financial support and compiling a list of prospective donors, Brown composed a standard letter of appeal describing Bethany's needs and had pupils copy it. The tedious letter-writing sessions often lasted into the early morning, producing hundreds of letters each time. After mailing the letters to possible benefactors, Brown and the students prayed for their success. Each time a contribution was received, the bond between Brown and her students grew stronger. When a large gift arrived, "shouts gave way to tears."[2]

Poor living conditions and limited capital were not as difficult for Brown to endure as lack of mental stimulation. She was accustomed to association with educated people, but the residents of rural Sedalia were generally ignorant of the world around them. They were hardworking people who lacked formal education and cultural training. Less than fifty families, nearly all of whom were African Americans, lived within three miles of Brown's little school. Handicapped by poverty and lack of education, they were often unresourceful and unprogressive. In contrast, the young teacher characterized life in a nearby area that lacked a school as "almost savagery." Brown found her neighbors uninterested in books, newspapers, and music, and her female students offered only limited companionship. Intellectually starved, she turned to the dictionary and a worn set of encyclopedias. By reading them daily, she gathered much information and developed a love of words that became almost an obsession. Greensboro was the nearest town with educated African Americans, including teachers at schools such as Bennett College and the North Carolina Agricultural and Mechanical College for Negroes. It was ten miles away, however, by horse, wagon, or train. Brown concluded that the solution to her problem was to pursue a broad correspondence with friends and potential supporters, creating a substantial network of allies and advisers.[3]

Exacerbating the difficulties of gaining support, a major crisis arose at the end of Brown's first year at Bethany Institute. During and immediately after the Civil War, the AMA had taught newly freed slaves basic reading, writing, and math. By the end of Reconstruction, it had begun divestiture of primary and secondary schools as local authorities gradually accepted responsibility for some African American education over several decades. The AMA then devoted its resources to its two-year normal and industrial institutes and its colleges.[4]

In 1902, the overextended AMA announced that it would close Bethany and other small schools in order to focus its support on more-established normal schools. This disclosure came as a complete shock to Brown, who had the option of either accepting a new assignment with the AMA or continuing her school alone. Inspired by community members' pleas that she remain at the school, Brown bravely chose the latter. Fund-raising became an even greater concern. After many hours of prayer, Brown decided to approach it from more than one angle. In addition to continuing the successful letter-writing campaign during the school term, Brown resolved to devote her efforts during the summer to securing funds.

Brown decided to return to New England in the summer of 1902 to personally contact prospective donors, concentrating on churches and summer resorts. She hoped to raise enough money to continue to operate the abandoned AMA school. In Cambridge, she collected money, clothing, and furniture from a few African American churches and white friends. She then planned to visit resorts around Gloucester, Massachusetts, to present a program including one or two jubilee melodies, a recitation of poetry by the contemporary African American poet Paul Laurence Dunbar, a ten-minute talk on Palmer, and a collection.[5]

At the resorts, many hotel keepers turned her away, but Brown posted notices and prayed for audiences. Some nights, she gave presentations at up to four hotels, walking six miles between hotels. Her efforts brought her many friends and supporters. After two weeks, she had secured $75 of her $100 goal. After raising another $15 the next day, she decided to remain one more night to attempt to collect the final $10. Waiting for the dinner hour to pass before beginning her program, she sat under a tree, weak from lack of food and rest. All at once tears swept down her face. Brown prayed for a sign that she was doing God's will. Suddenly a woman approached, saying that a hotel guest had invited her to a meal. She saw this event as confirmation that God would provide even daily food. With that faith, Brown raised the rest of the money and funds to pay her expenses back to Sedalia. She optimistically planned to open her school.[6]

Thus in the fall of 1902, Brown returned to North Carolina, virtually alone and with shaky finances, to open the first normal school in the state established solely by an African American woman. She had not received any pay since early in the year. Brown took up the seemingly impossible challenge due to strong support in the local community and her personal missionary zeal. Added to this was the attraction that the newly restructured school would be completely under her own direction. In fact, Brown's great sense of individualism and achievement as well as her apparent need to be in control must have influenced her decision.[7]

Although Baldwin no longer played a direct role in operating the school, he remained pastor of Bethany Congregational Church through 1903. The following year, he was replaced by Reverend Obediah W. Hawkins (Brown's uncle) but continued to serve two small AMA churches in Greensboro and Burlington. With the school under her complete control, Brown immediately began making plans to increase fund-raising activities. By happenstance, she made the acquaintance of Daisy S. Bright, wife of affluent New York businessman O. W. Bright, who owned a hunting lodge near Bethany. Brown cultivated the friendship, which was to last half a century, and Bright became a key supporter and regular weekly visitor to Brown's school during the winter hunting season. Bright soon introduced Brown to other affluent northerners who hunted in Guilford, such as Charles and Frances Guthrie of New York and Charles Fry of Boston. For Palmer's first few years, the northern hunters who had seen Brown's work and their wives (particularly Bright) were the main source of funds for the school. Brown realized that she would need the aid of leading southern whites as well. She also understood that, as a young, educated northern black woman, she would have to be cautious in a white male-dominated, racist South.[8]

Among the first southerners Brown approached was Charles Duncan McIver (1860–1906), first president of the State Normal and Industrial School for Girls in Greensboro. He was also president of the Southern Education Association, a trustee of the University of North Carolina, and secretary and district director of the Southern Education Board (SEB). Brown knew that his backing was crucial. After obtaining a letter of introduction, she traveled to Greensboro to state her case. His wife, Lula Verlinda Martin McIver (1864–1944), received the unexpected visitor in her husband's absence. Lula McIver later recalled listening to Brown's plans for the school: "Her daring, her enthusiasm, her faith intrigued me and I kept her for more than an hour, offering advice as to the best way to win friends."[9]

Alice Freeman Palmer was largely responsible for attracting early northern supporters such as Helen Frances Kimball, a high school classmate of Brown's from a wealthy family. Regarding Brown's ambitious but unproven plans to build a school, Kimball wrote: "If I did not believe you intended to be truthful I should never have been interested in you. Truth is the corner-stone of character." Kimball showed interest in the scheme but did not fully endorse it. She advised Brown to wait for wider support. Accepting that advice, Brown increased fund-raising efforts in New England.[10]

To be sure, Brown devoted considerable energy to raising funds the first year after the closing of the Bethany school, but her efforts were complicated by the sudden death of Palmer. The loss was a dreadful blow to Brown; not only was Palmer her friend, but she had provided the foundation of what Lula McIver termed Brown's "air castle." Deeply grateful for Palmer's assistance and encouragement, Brown named her "air castle" the Alice Freeman Palmer Memorial Institute after George Herbert Palmer gave Brown permission to use his wife's name in 1903. Nearly two decades later, at the dedication of the Alice Freeman Palmer Building, he called Brown "another Mrs. Palmer; her whole attitude, full of enthusiasm, full of self-devotion, full of sympathy with everybody, full of resource for means to carry out her great ideas."[11]

Bethany Congregational Church, circa 1903.
Brown is in the front row, to the right of the small child.
Reverend Obediah W. Hawkins is standing,
ninth from left. NCDAH.

After the demise of Palmer, Brown knew that she must intensify her efforts to ensure the growth of Palmer Institute. Brown and her students continued writing letters and praying for contributions. Vina Wadlington Webb (1890–1986), a member of the 1907 second graduating class, recalled: "We were . . . like family. Any time Miss Hawkins left or returned from a trip there was occasion for serious rejoicing." [12]

Although she was only seven years younger than Brown, Webb shared a special mother-daughter relationship with her. The youngest daughter of George Washington Wadlington and Louise Wharton Wadlington, Webb had spent her childhood under Brown's care while she was being educated at Palmer: "My mother [died and] left us early when she was only 34. My father had the good wisdom to send me to live in this school summer and winter. [Brown] was a real mother; she could not have been more careful if I had been her own child." Webb was one of several young girls raised by Brown. These girls lived as if they were members of Brown's family. They ate their meals at her table, where she taught them to dine properly and speak softly. To remind her "children" of these lessons, Brown posted on the wall an inscription from Shake-

Charles D. McIver, first president of the State Normal
and Industrial School for Girls in Greensboro, circa 1900. NCDAH.

speare's *King Lear:* "Her voice was ever soft, gentle, and low; an excellent thing in a woman."[13]

Brown followed the example of more-established African American
schools by requiring students to work on campus. According to Webb:
"There were no hired maids or special dietitians. We took our turns in
the kitchen, gathered vegetables and fruit," and "prepared them for can-
ning, to help the kitchen for the following winter." By 1904, Brown had
raised $500 toward the cost of constructing the first new building on
Palmer's campus. Her hard work, however, led to mental and physical
exhaustion, a cycle that would occur a number of times throughout her
life. Brown nevertheless recovered after a period of rest.[14]

In April 1904, Baldwin and his wife donated fifteen acres to the trustees of Palmer, with the stipulation that the land had to be returned if the school ceased operation. The next year, Baldwin presented Brown with a challenge by offering to give the property without restriction if "subscriptions for said school were gotten." Baldwin's gift convinced Brown that her school was ready for its first new classroom building.[15]

The story of how Brown acquired funds to finance the completion of Memorial Hall is an excellent example of her unyielding determination and faith in God. Construction began in May 1905, and Brown hoped that the building would be ready by the fall term. She expected to have no trouble raising the $800 needed to finish the building because she had collected that amount each summer during her previous campaigns in New England. That summer, however, would be different. Having signed a contract to complete the structure without having the money in hand, Brown went north to raise the needed funds. She soon became ill from overwork, however, and was forced to spend almost nine weeks in a Massachusetts hospital. By the time she was released, it was nearly time to return to North Carolina. She had collected only $125 and had no idea where she would be able to quickly secure the remaining $675 to pay the builder.

Brown decided to call on Charles Guthrie in New York. She boldly went to the St. Regis Hotel and called Guthrie's room. His valet answered and said that Guthrie was not interested in the school and that his wife was the only member of the family who had any concern for it but was in Washington, D.C., at the time.[16]

Not knowing that the valet had refused her admittance without consulting Guthrie, Brown felt a deep despair. After she prayed for guidance, an idea came to her. Brown sent a telegram to Guthrie asking to see him, and to her amazement, he agreed. She returned to the hotel and was escorted to Guthrie's suite by the very valet who had rejected her. Brown spoke at length to Guthrie, but he talked of everything but money. After a while, Guthrie finally asked casually what the building would cost. Brown told him $800. As she departed, he presented her with the full amount. Shortly thereafter, Memorial Hall was completed in time for the fall term.[17]

Memorial Hall, a white three-story frame building with a wide porch that extended across the entire front, contained classrooms, faculty and staff offices, a library, a spacious kitchen, a laundry, and a dining area on the first floor. On the second floor were recitation rooms and a chapel.

The third floor, really an attic with dormer windows, was the girls' dormitory, and a school bell topped the structure. Memorial Hall engendered a feeling of community since it was the result of much mutual effort. "It was the center of campus activity, and it may be, that in this accomplishment, the true 'Sedalia Spirit' was born." In 1905, Palmer observed its first graduation exercises, an event long awaited by the three graduates. One graduate was Zula Clapp Totton, whose family had lived in the community since its founding and would provide Palmer with students and teachers for sixty years. Zula was perhaps the brightest student at Bethany on Brown's arrival. After graduation, she taught briefly at the AMA's Oak School in Mebane. Returning to Sedalia, Zula resumed a close relationship with Brown and continued to play a very active role at Bethany Church.[18]

To accomplish her academic goals and provide students with knowledge they could use in their later lives, Brown developed a curriculum based on her Massachusetts experience. In elementary grades, subjects such as spelling, drawing, and hygiene were combined with lessons in reading, writing, and arithmetic. In the upper grades, basic instruction continued along with classes in subjects demanding higher skills, such as literature, grammar, geography, history, and agriculture. Students expecting to attend normal school or college usually took advanced courses in education, civil government, North Carolina school laws, and a foreign language.[19]

Brown's choice of curriculum was influenced heavily by the subjects she had taken at the Allston Grammar and Cambridge English High Schools. In the Cambridge grammar school, for instance, students were exposed to classic American and British literature. In 1899, the school system had adopted a list of readings for grammar school students initially prepared for the National Education Association. Third- and fourth-grade students read such books as *Black Beauty, Robinson Crusoe,* and *Swiss Family Robinson* and memorized works by Whittier, Longfellow, Bryant, and Tennyson. Seventh and eighth graders read *Evangeline, A Man without a Country, Silas Marner,* and *Ivanhoe* and memorized writings by Longfellow, Bryant, Whittier, Emerson, and Lincoln.[20]

After grammar school, Cambridge students completed four additional years at either the Latin or English High School. The English High School had four prescribed courses of study: a general course, a preparatory course (for the scientific colleges), a commercial course, and a domestic science course. Each pupil had weekly music and drawing classes

Memorial Hall, Palmer's first new classroom
building (completed in 1905), in 1917. NCDAH.

as a first-year requirement and as an option in later years. No student
could begin two foreign languages in the same year, and two years of
study of one foreign language were required.[21]

In addition to Palmer's regular course of study, Brown emphasized—
particularly to potential contributors—industrial and manual training,
another curriculum taught in certain Cambridge public schools. Because
it adhered to Washington's philosophy of appropriate African American
education, Palmer was an attractive charity for whites. Early northern
supporters such as Mary R. Grinnell donated significant sums to domestic and industrial programs at Palmer. In fact, all of Palmer's early white
patrons, from both North and South, were firm believers in industrial,
domestic, and manual training. Brown's former high school teacher,
Caroline Close, compared Palmer to Tuskegee Institute: "I had the pleasure of hearing Mr. Washington at the Latin School Hall. . . . Several of
his illustrations were taken from his work at Tuskegee. Again and again,
your work came to mind. Is not Palmer a little Tuskegee?" Practical
training was not only crucial in acquiring white support but also instrumental in obtaining one of the largest in-kind contributions to Palmer,
a gift of about 70 of 200 acres purchased by Helen Kimball of Massachusetts "to teach advanced ideas of practical agriculture, and to help
support the school by the food-stuff raised."[22]

Another longtime friend and major donor, Frances Guthrie, sent

Brown a twenty-six-page document outlining her suggestions for a curriculum at Palmer. The document reflected what many whites felt should be taught to African Americans. Guthrie hoped that Brown would not try to teach her pupils more than "their natures are ready to receive" and noted that "though of your race, your pupils are not like you." Poor rural blacks would require years of training before being able to use an academic education productively without having it "*turn* their heads." Country bumpkins, black and white, were "nearly all *very* ignorant people" who considered education to be worthless nonsense. Warning against teaching a curriculum that could not be used by blacks without invoking white wrath and jealousy, Guthrie felt Brown's hardest battle would be against "prejudices of both colored and white neighbors" about "the possibilities of your work."[23]

Guthrie focused on the development of basic living skills, not industrial education or preparation for higher education, as the foundation on which Brown should build her curriculum. She felt rural blacks should be taught "simple and easily understood truths from the Bible" and "personal cleanliness and *modesty*." She believed that poor African American children lacked examples of cleanliness and that girls especially needed instruction in modesty and propriety to guard against rape, a view shared by many educated African American women.

Foreshadowing Brown's 1941 book on manners, *The Correct Thing to Do, to Say, to Wear,* Guthrie stressed that how African Americans presented themselves greatly determined how whites regarded them. She believed that with proper cultural training, African American women eventually would obtain respect. Even if Brown failed to teach children to read, Guthrie said, she would have done a creditable job by teaching them basic refinement and manners: "This would be first, then book learning. Essential reading and writing skills could be achieved concurrently through topics such as 'How I Clean a Room.' . . . Endless simple subjects such as these" would provide crucial practical knowledge. Guthrie warned Brown against attempting to teach African American children more than they or their parents could understand, but she was not altogether opposed to more advanced education for blacks. She felt that the children of Palmer's early graduates would "be the ones ready for the higher things." Guthrie told Brown that she had "the molding" of her race in her hands; "those who follow after you will put on the finishing touches."[24]

In order to keep money coming in, Brown continued to seek endorsements and/or donations from the Guthries and other early supporters such as Helen Kimball, Mary Grinnell, O. W. and Daisy Bright, Grace Deering, David Kimball (Helen's brother), R. B. Andrew (postmaster at Sedalia), Caroline Close, Una S. Connfelt (of New York), Maria Baldwin, Charles Fry, Ray Huling, W. H. McLean (chairman of the local school committee), Thomas Foust (Guilford school superintendent), and Charles and Lula McIver.[25]

Once Brown gained the backing of Lula McIver, she soon began wooing Charles McIver. McIver had substantial power to recommend support for Palmer by the Southern Education Association, the SEB, and the National Education Association. In her first known letter to McIver, Brown wrote of her efforts to "establish a good rural school" and to teach her students "morally as well as mentally." She reported that Palmer had property worth $800 as well as furniture and musical instruments of equal value. Brown also revealed that the school had been receiving county funds since 1902 to pay the faculty but that she had accepted no salary herself. School superintendent Foust probably had arranged this support as a way to maintain Guilford's Jim Crow school system. Although the county aid was no doubt a great help, Brown's school survived largely because of donations and its agricultural resources.[26]

Most important, by April 1904, Brown had formed a local board of African American trustees, "three fairly able colored gentlemen": Cain Foust Sr. (ca. 1828–1910), John H. Smith (1836–1911), and Reverend Obediah Hawkins. Establishment of a local board as well as a board of northern friends that same year was an important step in Palmer's development. Three men—Huling, Fry, and Bright—comprised the northern board. Prompted by northern advisers, Brown recognized the wisdom of consulting such bodies while continuing to retain absolute control of her school. During this early period, Brown had no success in securing McIver's blessing. Even positive letters to and from Booker T. Washington had little influence on McIver. To encourage him to visit Palmer, supporter Charles Fry sent McIver a report he had mailed to Washington. Fry had visited Palmer and was "much struck by the conduct and application of the students." He found that Brown provided an "ordinary English education" with a bit of Latin. She lacked, however, facilities for Washingtonian manual training but was "desirous of extending their lines. Neatness of dress, and of the girls' boarding house was a markedly pleasant characteristic." McIver, nonetheless, did not respond.[27]

Brown became more direct in her appeals to McIver; perhaps it was her persistence that finally won his support. She explained that "people to whom I had made appeals gave me your name as the principal gentleman I should see." In the next letter, Brown closed with the touching petition: "If you can say a good word for us anywhere, please say it." After a year passed and there was still no word from McIver, Brown could not conceal her anger: "Dear Sir, we do not by any means wish to impose upon your time, but we are still waiting for your visit." She asked, "Will you spare a few hours" to look over "our work since so much depends upon your estimation?" With the help of white southerners such as Thomas Foust, Brown's perseverance finally paid off and McIver eventually gave his approval without visiting the campus. On SEB letterhead, McIver endorsed Palmer as an effective school that was worthy of support. If Brown's determination in acquiring McIver's support was an example of her approach to others, there is little wonder that she raised so much money. Her ability to recruit friends for Palmer was one of her most outstanding qualities.[28]

Her tenacity was not always successful, however. Brown's attempts—which persisted for decades—to woo the new General Education Board (GEB) were in vain. The Rockefellers were pumping money into the GEB, adding $10 million in 1905 and $32 million in 1907, which elevated its resources far above those of other foundations aiding black schools. Perhaps a Boston supporter or Daisy Bright, who later interceded personally with John D. Rockefeller Jr. on behalf of Palmer, first made Brown aware of the GEB's largess. In August 1903, Brown began a vigorous letter-writing campaign to the GEB's heads that lasted for decades. "I'm willing to devote my life to the development of my less fortunate brothers and sisters," she proclaimed earnestly in her first letter. The young teacher asked the GEB to fund the construction of Memorial Hall and sent progress reports and annual letters seeking money for general support, salaries for agricultural instructors, capital improvements, and other needs. She asked prominent supporters to send testimonials and visit GEB headquarters in New York and entertained GEB inspectors at Palmer. But the GEB's response, while complimentary, was always negative. Claiming that many southern schools were similar to Palmer, the GEB explained that it preferred to fund public tax-supported schools that were not dependent on northern philanthropy. When it aided non-public schools, it chose institutions with more prospective long-term support, such as those affiliated with major religious denominations. Brown nevertheless made substantial progress without GEB support.[29]

The formative years between 1903 and 1907 were very important in the history of Palmer Memorial Institute. By the end of 1907, Brown had brought the school a long way to a certain stability. The staff included Brown; Lelia Ireland, an academic and domestic science instructor and graduate of Scotia Seminary in Concord, North Carolina; Charles G. Davis, a teacher of carpentry; and recent Palmer graduates Vina Wadlington and Claudia Jones, both of whom were assistants with primary school children. The campus consisted of several wooden buildings with Memorial Hall at the center and a school farm. Boys still were crowded into a small structure, but a new dormitory was under construction. Other buildings included a small, separate kitchen, a meagerly equipped laundry, and a crude barn. A fund-raising campaign for a domestic science cottage had been completed, and major contributors such as Grinnell and Edward S. Harkness, a New York businessman and philanthropist, had been enlisted. Daisy Bright, Grace Deering, Maria Baldwin, and Frances Guthrie also served as influential endorsers of Brown's work.

About ninety students attended the school in 1907, of whom fifty (eighteen boys and thirty-two girls) were boarders. Nearly all of the students were rural folk from the neighborhood or adjacent counties. A third were young adults, but most were in elementary school. Brown sought to attract young adults by offering free tuition to the first twenty-five "young working men or women" to enroll. She emphasized the quality of the education, the focus on morality and Christianity, industrial training and music instruction, and the promise of better jobs in a brochure for prospective students. Since the school had produced six teachers who worked in public schools, Palmer graduates were in increasing demand. In 1907, Palmer graduated its second normal school class, composed of eight girls and three boys.[30]

Ada Hooker, an early graduate who became a teacher, recalled her days as a boarding student at Palmer. In 1905, her father had brought eleven-year-old Ada to the school in a buggy from their Alamance County home and paid tuition with flour, corn meal, and chickens. Ada and five other girls lived in Memorial Hall and shared three beds. The school year lasted from October until May, and Ada went home only at Christmas and Easter. Her classes included arithmetic, writing, and sewing. Food was rough but passable—corn bread, fatback, grits, gravy, and peas. There was little recreation beyond reading books from the school library. Evenings were spent studying, and weekends were devoted to cleaning, washing, and ironing on Saturday and church on Sunday. Brown—who even then traveled a lot although she taught a few

Brown (back row center) and her faculty in 1907. NCDAH.

classes—was fair but strict and had a powerful temper. Unruly students simply were sent home.[31]

New graduates and friends brought additional funds, and Palmer expanded its agricultural and manual training programs, a move sure to find favor with many of the school's white supporters. By early 1908, Brown brought two new teachers to the campus, one from the North Carolina Agricultural and Mechanical College for Negroes in Greensboro and the other from Tuskegee. These teachers taught classes in agriculture, industrial arts, and home economics. Students taking the new courses learned by raising crops and making needed repairs to buildings and furniture. Academics were not neglected, but industrial and practical training at Palmer was necessary to expand the support of donors.[32]

From the school's very beginning, the practical, moral, and cultural aspects of life were emphasized. To develop students morally, Brown stressed religion. She proclaimed: "We believe in God. . . . Christianity [is] the basis of our training, the Bible [is] our chief text-book." Although the school was no longer formally associated with the AMA, Brown and her students continued to participate in Sunday and midweek activities at Bethany Church.

Brown was fully aware that for her school to survive in a segregated society, whites with money and connections would have to endorse it. To that end, she effectively defused the initial suspicions of some local

The Palmer family, circa 1907. Brown is in the front row, fifth from right.
Ada Hooker is in the second row, second student from left.
Vina Wadlington Webb is in the third row at the far left. NCDAH.

whites with her policies of propriety and accommodation to segregation. She had worked to develop the right mixture of black/white and
southern/northern support since coming to North Carolina and would
continue for decades to build what she considered a suitable diversity of
key supporters and board members. Brown carefully had crafted an
early Palmer letterhead to illustrate a geographical cross section of white
and black support, prominently listing the names of Palmer, Huling,
Fry, Bright, local white neighbors Andrew and McLean, and Washington. The entire lefthand margin of the page contained praise from Huling ("self-sacrificing . . . worthy young woman"), Fry ("very commend-
able"), Washington ("interests me very much indeed"), and Bright
("faithful and energetic").[33]

Another institutional strength of Palmer was its incorporation,
largely made possible by Frank P. Hobgood Jr., a young Greensboro attorney and son of a Baptist girl's college administrator. In November
1907, six years after Brown's arrival, she and Hobgood arranged the
school's incorporation, with John Smith, Cain Foust, and herself as

founders. The charter proclaimed that the school would teach "improved methods of agriculture and industrial pursuits generally." Although no part of the document specifically mentioned high school or normal school training, it allowed room for broader scholastic goals. Palmer students studied to become successful housewives, laborers, and farmers, while a few looked toward higher education. Achieving those goals, Brown stated, would allow Palmer graduates to "contribute to the best citizenship of their communities." The document provided a firm legal basis for Palmer as an ongoing institution.[34]

Chapter Three

BROWN'S HOPES AND DREAMS

WITH PALMER'S corporate charter in hand, Brown, who had matured from a bright and eager but inexperienced young teacher into an energetic, savvy fund-raiser and school builder, quickly moved to centralize her authority. To do so, in 1908 she convinced the board to adopt a formal constitution and bylaws that clearly gave her full power over the direction of Palmer. To increase her control over the trustees, Brown included in the bylaws a provision enabling the secretary of the board (Brown) to call a meeting at any time with only twenty-four hours' notice. The bylaws also made it possible for Brown to influence the type of school Palmer would become, and that was exactly what she had in mind when as an agent she began to sell the remaining 132 acres of the 200-acre farm purchased by Helen Kimball.[1]

The primary reason Kimball had bought the farm had been to provide Palmer with another sixty-six acres in addition to its original fifteen acres. The school's supporters thought this was sufficient acreage for Palmer to develop its industrial and domestic training facilities. They felt that if more land was needed, the school could purchase additional property later. Kimball warned Brown to go slowly on future purchases, but Brown pushed ahead with various land schemes.[2]

Kimball expressed confidence in Brown's "ability and good intentions" but was upset over Brown's loose handling of land transactions. To avoid future problems, Kimball advised Brown to work closely with attorney Frank Hobgood on such issues. Fearing that Brown might sell key school farmland to poor landless neighbors, Kimball wrote angrily that she had given the land to "teach the boys good agriculture" and to raise food for the school and that Brown did not have the "right to sell it." Kimball reiterated that Brown should consult experts before making important real estate decisions. She wrote: "It does not show lack of confidence in you to have someone else give the advice which we are not in position to give. There are matters of business . . . in which I have always found that a woman needs a man's help, no matter how capable she may be." Brown adhered to Kimball's advice and continued to consult Hobgood for nearly fifty years.[3]

Brown planned to sell land to local farmers so that a community of African American landowners would spring up around Palmer. Although Kimball shared that goal, she objected to Brown's failure to obtain legal surveys and deeds before selling land. She suggested that Brown write to Charlotte R. Thorn, founder of a school in Calhoun, Alabama, for suggestions on selling Palmer's land.[4]

Thorn had built the Calhoun school under the direction of Samuel C. Armstrong, founder of Hampton Institute, aided by Booker T. Washington. To Kimball, the rural school illustrated what could be done in an area where blacks had been "exploited by the whites in a cruel fashion." Washington had selected the site because African Americans there lived in "conditions under which they could not advance economically or educationally," and he was largely responsible for incorporating the school in 1892.[5]

Brown had acquired more knowledge of the success of schools such as Calhoun during a week-long visit to Hampton in 1907. Whether she wrote to Thorn for advice is unknown, but surely Brown learned the advantages of having a community of black property owners around the school. She believed that "community cohesiveness and economic stability would enable educational advancement to occur at a faster rate." Since most African Americans lacked money to purchase land, cooperative buying was a welcome option. Brown eventually established the Sedalia Home Ownership Association to make it possible for residents of Sedalia to escape the sharecropping system under which they lived.[6]

As Kimball's agent, Brown continued to sell farmland to local African Americans. She encountered more problems with Kimball, however. Although the original plan specified that only lots of ten acres or less were to be sold, for unknown reasons, she sold sixty acres to Thomas Foust, the white school superintendent. This irked Kimball, who wrote: "Are your arrangements of sale the same as at Calhoun? I understood that they would be. I thought that you proposed ten-acre lots, so as to help as many as possible to a start. I'm sorry that you should sell so large a portion as *60* acres to one person. Why was it?" But such rebukes did not dampen Brown's passion for acquiring and selling property, although Kimball continued to caution her to go slowly.[7]

Fiercely independent and unyielding, however, in 1908, Brown contracted on her own to purchase seventy-six acres adjoining Palmer. The deed listed Brown as trustee for unnamed parties. A later document revealed that she was trustee for herself, John Smith, and Jacob Smith, members of Bethany Congregational Church and Palmer supporters. Each of the three paid $100 toward the $300 down payment. Some two years later, the Smiths received about two-thirds of the property after paying off the note. Brown then received personal title to twenty-four acres of the tract and transferred it to Palmer.[8]

Brown's actions seemed impetuous and foolhardy to several northern supporters who, like Kimball, encouraged her to proceed more cautiously. For instance, Frances Guthrie advised Brown not to buy any more property. She wrote: "You already have some 200 acres. You've not begun to sell all that off yet . . . [and] until it is sold . . . [and] Miss Kimball repaid the $2,000—you are in debt. Even though not a pressing debt—*it is still a debt* . . . [and] must be seriously considered." Guthrie suggested that completion of the boys' dormitory (Grew Hall), repair of existing structures, and cultivation of the farm were of far greater importance than acquiring additional land. She believed that a small, well-run school would gain more support than a large, poorly managed campus with extensive landholdings.[9]

Besides expanding Palmer's real estate holdings, Brown considered other options for her school's future, in particular the possibility of Palmer becoming a segregated, tax-supported public high school. Palmer had been receiving modest but increasing public funds to educate blacks from the school's township since its inception. Brown was on good terms with Guilford superintendent Foust, and Palmer director Charles Ireland sat on the county school board. Furthermore, in 1907 the state had authorized the creation of standard public high schools with three- or four-year curricula and had approved two such schools for whites in rural Guilford, with a third following in 1908.

In March 1909, Wallace Buttrick of the GEB visited Superintendent Foust and asked that Guilford make Palmer the state's first rural public high school for blacks. In a few months, Foust, on behalf of his board, proposed the creation of a model farm and agricultural public high school at Palmer. Unwilling or unable to back his words with money, Foust suggested that the GEB give $6,000 and friends of Palmer give $4,000 to establish the model school. The GEB, with its focus on purely public secondary schools, rejected the plan. Brown then appealed in person to the school board to create a black public high school at Sedalia, but the board took no action and filed her statement for future reference. She then returned to the GEB with a more modest plan involving county, state, Palmer, and GEB funds. Although the GEB again declined to participate, Brown's promotion of Palmer as a county high school persisted without success for years. It would be only one aspect of her long search for institutional stability for Palmer.[10]

Meanwhile, although she was careful not to offend her white supporters, Brown moved forward with her plans to increase landholdings and construct campus buildings. Because many contributors had become personal friends, an open communication developed that allowed much flexibility. Brown sometimes disregarded the advice of her rich white friends. She defended her actions by professing that God would lead her down the correct path. Although she received many suggestions, Brown nearly always had the final word. For example, Kimball at one point wrote that the physical plant "ought not to be enlarged until the *money is in hand*." After Kimball vented her anger, however, she returned to a friendlier tone. She was unwilling to finance the construction of a girls' domestic science building but continued to make regular gifts. To secure funds for building that structure, Brown turned to another longtime friend, Mary R. Grinnell.[11]

Grinnell, a loyal supporter, regularly made a minimum annual contribution of $200, several months' wages for many in that era. Grinnell shared with Brown her views on running the school, which were similar to those of other disciples of Washington. Her beliefs about African Americans' intellectual ability also reflected her times. Grinnell explored the issue in a series of intimate letters with Brown and noted that many whites thought that "if a colored person cares for books it is because they have white blood in their veins." An acquaintance had asked Grinnell if she knew of any "educated colored person who had no white blood." Thinking Brown was of pure African blood, Grinnell had replied in the affirmative but later had second thoughts and quizzed Brown about her lineage. Grinnell believed she and Brown were close enough to speak frankly on the sensitive subject. "I should like to know your opinion," wrote Grinnell, "as I should regard it as more authentic than anything my white friends might tell me."[12]

Brown then explained her white Hawkins ancestry. Satisfied with the response, Grinnell became the primary benefactor of the new domestic science building. She happily sent an additional $200 for the facility and offered to cover the entire cost if it was not raised by September 1909. True to her word, she sent the money in July, two months early. Grinnell became engrossed in the project. Requesting that all of her donations be used for the building, Grinnell revealed that her motivations were unselfish by asking that the structure not be named in her honor. She recognized that a few friends "would understand who gave it." Brown, however, convinced Grinnell to accept the honor by arguing that naming the cottage for Grinnell would benefit Palmer. Soon Grinnell Cottage was in constant use for domestic science instruction. Its six bedrooms, dining room, kitchen, and reception room afforded ample space for girls to master the care of a home and yard. Before graduation, every senior girl resided there for one semester. Each girl performed various monthly duties, such as planning, preparing, and serving meals and caring for three small children. Nearly forty years later, other Massachusetts donors would finance the construction of an up-to-date replacement for the cottage and continuation of its training.[13]

With northern help coming on a more regular basis, Brown proceeded with her usual persistence to attain additional southern white support. Such support was necessary because in the South around 1910 independent schools needed at least the partial backing of the local power structure. Northern donors made it clear that they would not aid such schools indefinitely without local support. In addition, Palmer's physical plant was growing steadily, despite the warnings of major donors, and the growth brought added financial responsibilities. To meet these responsibilities, Brown wisely recruited C. A. Bray, president of the Home Savings Bank in Greensboro, as treasurer of Palmer in 1910. The school's board by then included four other local whites: Frank Hobgood, president; Cyrus A. Wharton, a prosperous farmer; Edward P. Wharton, a businessman; and Charles Ireland, owner of the Odell Hardware Company of Gibsonville. All board members had worked with Brown before or were involved with education, and all represented the business and professional classes, groups with greater access to financial resources than educators.[14]

By 1909, Brown also had broadened her own personal and professional activities to encompass local, state, and national organizations, several of which developed primarily through her efforts. That year, she became a founder of the North Carolina Federation of Negro Women's Clubs. She became president in 1912, a post she would hold for two decades. Affiliated with the National Association of Colored Women's Clubs, whose motto was "Lifting As We Climb," the group sought membership among various civic, religious, and social clubs rather than individuals. Groups promoting "programs of betterment of Negro womanhood" were welcome to join. Brown also became a member of the North Carolina Teachers Association (NCTA; now the North Carolina

Grinnell Cottage (completed in 1909), the
domestic science facility, circa 1917. NCDAH.

Association of Educators) and served as its president in 1935–37. Both
groups gave Brown access to a network of educated African American
women and their programs, and she would continue to play a leading
role in them at the state and regional level for decades. As a leader of the
NCTA, she sought to upgrade inferior African American educational facilities; to obtain better pay and treatment of African American teachers; and to instill in youth a sense of moral obligation, racial pride, and
the desire to become the best they could be. In attempting to fulfill
those goals, she boldly met with governors and other state leaders.[15]

Although Brown played an increasingly active role in state and national groups that fostered African American uplift, she did not abandon her interest in the local community. To improve conditions around
Palmer, Brown introduced the School Improvement League in Sedalia
in 1909. The primary purpose of the league was to transform schools
and homes into places of uplift and beauty. In pursuit of those goals,
Brown called on the professional skills of Virginia Randolph, who was
well known for her outstanding social work in the rural black schools of
Henrico County, Virginia. Randolph had transformed the poorest, unkempt schools and communities there into places of beauty. In the summer of 1909, Randolph visited Palmer, and her support for the ideas that
Brown advocated inspired the students and teachers.

Randolph's School Improvement League worked to make schools
and grounds attractive. She told Brown that students paid five cents a
month to help finance the league's activities, gave performances to raise

more money and to "elevate the community morally and educationally," and learned "to sew, make shuck mats, baskets, darn, and anything that will help them in their homes." They also learned some carpentry, spending half a day each week working to maintain the schools. Following the directions of Randolph, Brown began a program of beautification, cultural development, and moral uplift. Palmer students and teachers, as well as the Sedalia community, gave their full support. Students presented musical programs, fairs, and other entertainment. The league allowed residents to feel as if they were a part of Palmer and students to feel as if they were a part of the rural community.[16]

An important institution of that community was the church. Brown's teaching career started at Bethany Church, and her first interaction with local families occurred there. Bethany Church was a center of life at Palmer as well as in Sedalia. Over the years, Brown became a vital force in both church and community. She viewed the relationship between the church and the school as a tool to be used by Palmer's students and as a functional approach to education. Through Bethany Church, Brown became aware of and assisted the families in the Sedalia community.

In her self-appointed role as head of community uplift, Brown made Palmer the de facto social welfare department for Sedalia. For a generation or more, the rural, nearly all black community that was centered around Palmer and Bethany Church had been largely static. Modern conveniences were slow in coming, and poverty persisted. Besides selling land for small farms and homesteads, Palmer sponsored regular meetings at which local farmers could consult the school's farm expert and sometimes county extension agents. On occasion, faculty members took part in community cornhusking parties, which moved from farm to farm. Palmer's own successful farm demonstrated improved agricultural techniques, provided pure-bred livestock for crossbreeding to enhance local stock, and produced quality seeds for neighbors. In one year, five student farmers furnished 10,000 sweet potato plants to community farmers. At one point, Brown's agricultural teacher was coordinating thirty-one community projects.[17]

Palmer also helped improve public health and living standards in Sedalia. The school had a budget for community work in some years. Copying a program in Cambridge, Brown set up a nursery and kindergarten for the children of working mothers. Teenage female students, guided by Palmer's school nurse, cared for the children as part of their domestic science training. The school's parent-teacher association studied topics such as proper diet, home health care, and sanitation. The school nurse gave programs for the community on personal hygiene. A community clinic at the school, funded by government dollars, featured regular visits by a doctor, dentist, and nurse and monthly medical care for babies. Palmer's community committee organized a neighborhood civic club and distributed clothing in the vicinity. Girls in sewing classes made garments for Palmer elementary students who could not afford suitable clothing. Brown expected neighbors, black and white, to take advantage of not only Palmer's health services but also its plays, movies, musical programs, recitals, religious and other cultural programs, speaking engagements, and related activities as well as its library. Palmer's Christmas program of Handel's *Messiah* and carols was an annual treat for Sedalia. The school also had programs to support juvenile offenders and prison inmates. On occasion, tuition at Palmer was waived for needy community children. Finally, when possible Brown sent her condolences and sometimes food to neighboring families suffering from sickness or bereavement.[18]

As Brown continued her efforts to uplift African Americans through education, racial understanding, and better living conditions, several national organizations were forming to assist blacks in attaining social and political equality. Those groups called for immediate elevation of African Americans to first-class citizenship. Whereas Brown increasingly believed that racial problems could be solved through education and cultural training, those groups viewed justice and equality as purely a matter of law.

One such society, founded in 1909, was the multiracial National Association for the Advancement of Colored People (NAACP), an outgrowth of the earlier Niagara Movement. That movement began at a gathering led by W. E. B. Du Bois and others at Niagara Falls in 1905. It demanded full freedom of speech, voting rights, an end to racial discrimination, acknowledgment of human brotherhood, and respect for America's workers. The NAACP leadership was made up of a distinguished group of educators, publicists, bishops, judges, and social workers. The group vowed to strive for integration, educational and voting equity, and broad implementation of the Fourteenth and Fifteenth Amendments.[19]

Du Bois became the NAACP's director of publicity and research and was its only African American officer; his presence marked the group as radical. Since most white philanthropists regarded the NAACP as extremist, Brown could not support it openly. Fearing that involvement might jeopardize white support of Palmer, she wisely avoided association with the philosophy of Du Bois, who openly challenged Washington's Atlanta Compromise. Although the NAACP supported the expansion of economic opportunities for blacks, it initially did very little in that area. Another new organization, the National Urban League, however, devoted much effort to improving economic conditions for African Americans.[20]

The National Urban League developed about the same time as the Niagara Movement from several reform groups in New York. These groups accepted the Atlanta Compromise, and their memberships included such philanthropists as William J. Schieffelin and A. S. Frissell of Hampton. In 1911, three groups formed the National League on Urban Conditions among Negroes (later called the National Urban League). Unlike the NAACP, the Urban League attracted the support of Julius Rosenwald and Booker T. Washington. The society sought to improve opportunities for blacks in industry and to help rural African Americans who moved to cities by developing programs to train them in social work. Brown took an active interest in such efforts. She also participated in the Young Men's Christian Association (YMCA) and the Young Women's Christian Association (YWCA). Although the YMCA was segregated, she found herself in company with wealthy whites who could be of great help to Palmer.[21]

Brown's major work prior to 1910, however, was at her beloved Palmer. By that time, she had expanded both its physical plant and its reputation. In eight years, Brown had brought the school from a one-room dilapidated structure on fifteen acres of uncultivated land to an eighty-acre campus consisting of Memorial Hall, the main building; Grinnell Cottage, the girls' domestic science building; and Grew Hall, a two-story boys' dormitory probably funded by honorary board member Mrs. H. S. Grew. Brown had devoted much of her youth to the development of Palmer and had given little attention to the pursuit of personal happiness. Nevertheless, she still had dreams of having a husband, a family, and a home.

In June 1910, Brown began to consider seriously the subject of marriage. Before that time, the issue had affected her only indirectly. In 1908, Brown wondered about the consequences for Palmer of the impending marriages of two of her best teachers. Her confidant Caroline Close reassured Brown that "new workers will come to the front." Close asked: "What would Palmer do if you took a notion to be engaged too?" How would her marriage affect the operation and growth of the school? What role would her husband play? Long before Brown married, she and her closest friends discussed such questions.[22]

Mary Grinnell gave Brown advice on the subject in mid-1909, appar-

Palmer's wooden campus, circa 1915 (left to right): Grinnell Cottage (domestic science building), Memorial Hall (girls' dormitory and classrooms), Grew Hall (boys' dormitory), and Mechanical Hall (industrial training building). NCDAH.

ently in response to news from Brown. Grinnell counseled her that "the feeling you have about getting married is perfectly natural" and "if you have misgivings as to whether all the love and tenderness which you bestow upon the man are to be returned in equal measure you are only voicing the feelings of many a young woman whose misgivings have vanished as she has entered upon married life." The name of the man was not mentioned, but obviously Brown had met someone.[23]

Edward S. Brown (1873–1961) had been a teacher at Gilbert Academy in New Orleans. He was continuing his education at Harvard University when he met Charlotte around 1909. He had come to the home of Brown's parents in Cambridge to inquire about renting a room. Charlotte's mother politely received Edward and accepted him as a boarder. On the evening that Edward moved into the Willis home, he was greeted by Charlotte, who was home for a summer of fund-raising. She apparently fell in love at first sight. Charlotte took pleasure in introducing outgoing, fun-loving Edward to her friends.[24]

Charlotte was drawn to Edward because of his educational experience, demeanor, and good looks. She was curious about Edward's experiences teaching in the Deep South and his decision to attend Harvard. During their summer courtship, they enjoyed their time together. After Charlotte returned to North Carolina, they corresponded faithfully and courted each other on her trips home.[25]

The first written record of Charlotte's involvement with Edward is in a 1910 letter from Grace Deering, who said she was very happy for Charlotte but asked her to consider the matter of marriage carefully. She warned that it would be difficult for Charlotte to find time for her relationship with Edward because she devoted so much of her time to securing friends for Palmer. Her efforts to maintain both relationships must have proven too much for her because once again she became ill from overwork. The stress of realizing that her primary commitment would always be to Palmer no doubt contributed to her sickness. Deering wrote that "no one who works as you do could be well unless she was a giant to start with. You use up your strength, so that too little is left for the functioning of your body."[26]

Most of Charlotte's female supporters favored her marriage. Overall the women believed it would give Charlotte great joy and provide Palmer with another well-educated teacher. Grinnell, although happy for Charlotte, was concerned that their friendship might suffer. Kimball congratulated Charlotte, claiming to be "not so much of an old maid as not to believe in matrimony if it comes with deep and true love." Daisy Bright took the news calmly and merely asked the date of the event. Maria Baldwin compared marriage to service and viewed Charlotte's decision as a step to be taken with the same high purpose as her efforts for Palmer.[27]

Charlotte and Edward Brown were married in Cambridge on June 14, 1911, three days after the bride's twenty-eighth birthday, at the home of her mother. Edward had withdrawn from Harvard prior to the marriage. For the rest of the summer, the newlyweds remained in Cambridge while Charlotte raised funds for Palmer. When fall arrived, the Browns left for Palmer. At first, they worked enthusiastically together. Edward's professional contribution was similar to that of an assistant principal. In addition to teaching, he oversaw the boys' dormitory.[28]

All was not well for the newlyweds at Sedalia, however. One problem was that the couple lacked private living quarters. Charlotte lived with the girls and other female teachers, and Edward slept with the boys and male teachers. Searching for a solution, Grinnell wished that the couple had a "little place with three or four rooms" and hinted that supporters might pay for the house. Edward probably also had concerns about his role at the school. Since Charlotte maintained her tight control over Palmer, Edward no doubt felt he could only offer advice about "her school." Moreover, many of the students thought of Edward as "Mr. Hawkins" rather than "Mr. Brown." It is not known exactly what caused Edward and Charlotte to separate, but one historian has speculated that Palmer did not challenge him since it was Charlotte's school.[29]

Grinnell offered Charlotte her help in this predicament: "But how can we best help each other and what can I say that will make life more worth while to you?" Grinnell recognized the couple's serious problems and reassured Charlotte of the permanency of the bond between the two women. She observed: "I think that both you and Mr. Brown are . . . right but it is extremely difficult for either of you to see or really understand the other's way of thinking. . . . Your heart and soul are so wrapped up in the school that the most Mr. Brown could do for you would be to

Brown in her wedding gown, 1911. NCDAH.

Dairy barn on Palmer's farm, 1917. NCDAH.

aid the school, forgetting, hard as it may be to him, your personal needs and comforts for a time."[30] Grinnell told Charlotte that even if she and Edward agreed on their separation, some people would criticize her but that she should not worry about what others thought as long as she did what she believed was right. Grinnell said that she had asked God to give Charlotte courage to face life without Edward.[31]

Edward probably left Palmer for several reasons, including a desire to earn a real salary and a lack of commitment to a life spent fostering his wife's school. In addition, Charlotte's heritage of dominance possibly undermined the relationship. After separating, Charlotte and Edward corresponded, but he never returned to Sedalia to live. Charlotte continued her crusade alone despite thoughts of giving up her work at Palmer to join her husband. Grinnell cautioned: "Has Mr. Brown ever asked you to forsake your work in order to join him? If not why should you volunteer to go? If he felt hurt because he could not support you in Sedalia, does he now find the means to send you home a few pennies for yourself?" Brown must have experienced a great deal of pain from the separation, but her total commitment to Palmer and her sense of personal worth would not allow her to forsake her life's work. Grinnell reinforced Brown: "You may owe something to him as wife, but being a man he owes more than I fear he is now doing for you." Grinnell apparently thought each party had chosen career over love. She believed that Charlotte had selected love of her school over love of her husband. Grinnell was right; like several of her female forebears, Brown did not fit the stereotype of the submissive wife. The couple never reunited after their year at Sedalia, and in 1916, the marriage ended in divorce.[32]

Although Brown's separation was painful, she continued to nurture her first love, Palmer. She refused to allow anything, not even a husband, to stand in the way of her commitment to the school. Before Brown married, she shrewdly transferred to Palmer the title to all of the land she owned, as Bright had recommended, to safeguard the property from potential claims by Edward. Three months before her wedding, Brown sold one acre to Jacob Smith; two months later, she sold twenty-five acres to Palmer.[33]

To increase Palmer's holdings, Brown purchased 254 acres from white neighbors Walter H. and Eugenia M. McLean for $7,959 in 1911. With the purchase, Palmer owned an estimated 350 acres. Although most of Brown's supporters advised against further expansion until existing debts were paid off, Brown argued that the school needed the land to grow more food for its nonpaying students. Brown continued to refrain from placing property in her own name until her divorce was final. At that time, she purchased five acres from Robert Hughes for $150, which she borrowed from the Greensboro Loan and Trust Company.[34]

Once Brown increased Palmer's property holdings to more than 350 acres, she wanted to expand its physical plant. In developing a plan for expansion, she sought the counsel of several persons, including Monroe Work, a leader of Tuskegee Institute. Although most people advised Brown to go slowly, Work suggested that Palmer could be improved by increasing enrollment, concentrating on more practical literary and industrial instruction, and installing a new method of bookkeeping.[35]

To support her claims that Palmer's course offerings could be expanded without incurring extreme debt, Brown sent a copy of Work's analysis to all of the school's trustees in 1911. Even though his report was supportive of her ambitious plans in most areas, it did not endorse her goal to replace the existing wooden buildings with brick ones. Regardless of the abundant advice to maintain Palmer at its present level, Brown continued to push for further growth in all aspects of the school's organization and operation. By 1914, Palmer's physical plant included four main wooden buildings, all but one of which had been constructed in part using student labor: Memorial Hall, Grinnell Cottage, Grew Hall, and Mechanical Hall, the site of industrial work for boys and girls. Mechanical Hall was built and equipped at a cost of $1,000 as a gift from J. F. Twombly of Brookline, Massachusetts. A large barn also was built that year. Brown was determined, however, to secure funds to construct a more imposing campus.[36]

Chapter Four

A NEW RESPECTABILITY

ALONG WITH THE expansion of Palmer's physical plant, Brown made improvements in personnel, daily operations, and particularly fundraising. She reorganized the board in 1910 after appointing Greensboro banker C. A. Bray as treasurer. His first objective was to place Palmer on a more businesslike basis. In the same year, Helen Kimball donated $1,000 to begin an endowment fund. The following year, John F. Twombly, an honorary trustee, also gave $1,000 after hearing of Monroe Work's findings. Edward S. Harkness, an early contributor from New York, subscribed $5,000 to the endowment fund on the condition that Brown raise some $50,000 more. These gifts were substantial considering the fact that Palmer's annual budget was under $7,500. By 1913, Palmer's debt was less than $500, and it had paid nearly half of the cost of the farm purchased in 1911. As a result of such gains, by 1914 Palmer's property and equipment were valued at $35,000. Seven instructors taught 130 students, mainly local day pupils, academic subjects as well as "domestic science, domestic art, manual training, practical gardening, and agriculture." The academic calendar covered seven and a half months, and industrial work, mainly on the farm, continued year-round.[1]

From 1911 to 1914, Palmer's board had twelve members, with attorney Frank Hobgood as president and Daisy Bright as vice president. The expanded board included men and women, northerners and southerners, and blacks and whites and was far stronger than the initial board. Other members were Brown, Bray, Frances Guthrie, Mary Grinnell, Charles Ireland, W. H. McLean, Cyrus Wharton, Lula McIver, Lelia Ireland Yancey, and John Smith. Among the school's honorary trustees were Twombly; James B. Dudley, president of North Carolina Agricultural and Mechanical College for Negroes in Greensboro; and Kimball, Mrs. Robert Winsor, Mrs. Samuel Frothingham, and Mrs. J. S. Howe, all of Massachusetts. Palmer's leadership remained stable for the next several years.[2]

Brown and a colleague, circa 1911. NCDAH.

Of special note during that period was the developing interest of Boston financier and philanthropist Galen L. Stone (1862–1926), who would become Palmer's most important contributor. Born in Massachusetts, Stone graduated from Boston's English High School in 1878 and joined the *Boston Commercial Bulletin* as a clerk and accountant. Acquiring a knowledge of the stock market, he became financial editor of

Galen L. Stone, Palmer's major benefactor, circa 1920.
Courtesy of Ambassador Galen L. Stone.

the *Boston Advertiser* and earned a reputation as an astute analyst. In 1891, Stone decided to use his keen financial sense as a brokerage apprentice. Then he met Charles Hayden, and they formed the partnership of Hayden, Stone and Company. The business flourished, financing and managing steamship lines, manufacturing and industrial corporations, railroads, and mines. During his career, Stone served as chairman of the board and director of numerous major companies.[3]

To his credit, Stone used his wealth to support the arts and other charities. He was proud that his money and power had not been acquired by exploiting others. Among the recipients of his benevolence were Wellesley College, the Fogg Art Museum at Harvard University, the Boston Symphony, Massachusetts General Hospital, and the McLean Asylum in Massachusetts.[4]

Stone became interested in Palmer in 1913. Unlike earlier contributors, he did not restrict his donations to industrial and domestic education. Brown later wrote that Stone "put life and vigor" in her soul when he said, "I am not interested in educating and advancing Negroes, but in making American citizens." In contrast, Kimball, Palmer's greatest benefactor prior to Stone, believed that African Americans' ability to learn was limited. A disciple of Washington, she thought industrial education was the best training for blacks. Stone, however, felt African Americans should receive the best education available. Brown recalled that Stone remarked after listening to the school's quartet that African American melodies were beautiful but that Brown should "teach them to sing even the finest music."[5]

In 1914, Brown asked Stone to be local treasurer for the school in New York and pressed him to contribute a large gift. One longtime supporter applauded his involvement and wrote Brown: "It will be splendid if he does give $500. I will leave Mr. Stone to you." To Brown, Stone was a godsend because he was the first major supporter of considerable wealth who believed in higher education for African Americans. Stone's confidence was a tremendous boost for Brown because previously she had been able to enlist the support of only a few men. With his aid established, Brown continued to ask men of influence to sanction her work.[6]

One such long-sought endorsement finally came in 1915 from Booker T. Washington. After learning about Palmer from Monroe Work, Tuskegee board member Frank Trumbull, board president Seth Low, and his wife Margaret, Washington wrote to Brown: "I am sure that you have one of the best and most useful of the smaller schools in the South, and I bespeak for its most hearty and generous support." At last, Brown had received the written blessing of Washington that she had toiled for years to obtain because she believed it was crucial to Palmer's continued growth and favor with white donors. She visited Washington's home at Tuskegee on several occasions and often claimed to have been his disciple.[7]

Soon after endorsing Palmer, Washington died. Brown deliberately associated herself with his legacy and for many years honored a mandate to carry on his message. She claimed that she had "often intruded on the busy moments of his life to ask advice and help." Brown felt a close kinship to Washington because she had been reared and educated in New England, whose philanthropists had given liberally to causes such as Tuskegee. Later she acquired the support of some of Tuskegee's friends for her own school. Brown thought Washington's beliefs "transcended race, creed, condition and color." She said he believed that every African American could be made into a worthwhile citizen. Brown and Washington sought to remind whites that blacks bought a substantial amount of goods and deserved the attention of America's financial barons.[8]

Above all, according to Brown, Washington felt that his race was one of the "great divisions of the Human Family" and had "possibilities of achieving noble ends through the help of the dominant race." Both educators believed that the African American should "devote his every virtue to attaining the success he had set as his goal" and that lasting success was the "hard long pull of the rope that blisters the hand."[9]

Seth Low was one of the first wealthy northern whites from the Tuskegee group to contribute to Palmer and his support was a primary reason for Washington's endorsement. After Washington's death, Low intensified his efforts to gain friends for Palmer. Perhaps his major contribution was his strong recommendation of the school to Charles W. Eliot.[10]

Charles Eliot (1834–1926), president of Harvard from 1869 to 1909, was perhaps the most influential American educator of his day. His family was identified prominently with the rise of New England and Harvard. Born in Boston, he studied at the Latin High School and entered Harvard at the age of fifteen, graduating second in his class. His presidency marked a new era at Harvard. During his forty-year tenure, the university added graduate schools of arts and sciences, applied science, and business administration as well as Radcliffe College for women. Eliot supported universal education and social mobility regardless of race.[11]

Eliot's initial involvement with Palmer seems to have been largely the result of Low's support. Eliot contributed to and tentatively endorsed Palmer on the basis of his associates' recommendations. Brown acknowledged that his endorsement "opened some doors that otherwise would have been closed."[12] But because he had never visited the school, Eliot declined Brown's invitation to chair a fund-raising meeting. Undeterred by his refusal, Brown wrote back: "Your name will draw many persons who, perhaps, would not [otherwise] be interested; before that time I shall see to it that you receive . . . personal letters of commendation . . . so that you will not hesitate to speak in the highest terms." Brown again pressed Eliot to chair the meeting, proudly informing him that she had "succeeded in getting $6,000 pledged toward the $15,000" guaranty fund. Eliot nevertheless refused a second time, citing once again the fact that he had not yet visited the campus: "Under such circumstances I am not in the habit of giving such an endorsement as presiding at your meeting would signify."[13]

Finally realizing that Eliot would not fully support the school without seeing it first, Brown asked permission to mention his interest in the school on cards announcing the meeting. She also requested that he send a few invitations with his personal card.[14]

Other efforts to raise money during this period generally were successful. Brown impetuously began to solicit funds for different aspects of Palmer's growth before initial efforts were thoroughly organized. Campaigns for the building, endowment, and guaranty funds were led by various key supporters. Northern women such as Bright, Grinnell, Kimball, and Una Connfelt, directed by Brown, were primary fund-raisers for the school.

An excellent example of such efforts was Grinnell's work. She suggested that Brown write the treasurer of Grinnell Manufacturing Company, Otis Pierce, to request that, besides making an annual contribution, he include Palmer in his will. She targeted friends and family members, such as her brother, who was not in the habit of giving to charities. His surprisingly quick and positive response inspired her to write to Brown: "Too many burdens have to be assumed by women alone where the men ought to share them with us." Grinnell also felt that the school's trustees had an obligation to support Palmer personally and gave $1,000 or more in some years.[15]

Perhaps one of the greatest triumphs for Brown during this period was receiving an endorsement from George Herbert Palmer, the husband of Alice Palmer. Palmer wrote: "I gladly send the endorsement you request . . . [and] wish I might also send a more solid contribution. Long ago I chose the form of memorial for Mrs. Palmer to which I wished to devote my slender means. . . . Your work I watch with great interest . . . constantly surprised at what you manage to accomplish." Palmer's name, like that of Eliot, proved of substantial value to Palmer Institute.[16]

With growing support in the form of money and endorsements, Brown began 1914 on a high note. Palmer was receiving increased contributions from blacks and whites in the North as well as the South. Although most African Americans did not have the means to give large donations, many had enthusiasm and gave freely of their time. The largely black Sedalia community contributed $200 a year to pay the salary of one teacher, and southern white entrepreneurs recommended the school to northern businessmen.[17]

Brown's method of raising money changed little over the years. It involved writing letters and telling the story of the school at gatherings in homes, churches, and other places. One important tool was the Sedalia Quartette, originally composed of female teachers, including Brown, who gave performances along the eastern seaboard. Brown developed a standard program for the group, which typically began with the introduction of Brown by local sponsors. After Brown spoke about Palmer and the hardships she had endured, faculty, students, and singers presented African American spirituals and readings. Then a well-respected southern white person spoke in support of the school. Finally, Brown earnestly solicited donations. Unlike northern appeals, presentations to white southerners confirmed that the school was no threat to the social order. The Washingtonian message recalled the "good ole days" of presumed social stability.[18]

Between 1914 and 1917, contributions to Palmer increased enormously as Brown continued her personal appeals, letter-writing campaigns, solicitation of endorsements by key business and social leaders, and concert tours. In 1914–15, contributions from northern whites almost doubled to over $5,600. Brown also collected smaller amounts from African Americans and southern whites, receiving less than $100 from each group. An inheritance brought in $500, the Guilford County school board allocated $400, and the endowment fund yielded $55. Including tuition, farm profits, and miscellaneous income, the total funding of the school that year exceeded $10,000. It was as if Brown's "air castle," as Lula McIver called it, had finally landed on fertile soil. Moreover, Connfelt, Bright, and others had attracted the interest of Galen Stone and were working strenuously to secure his permanent support.

Another important person whom Connfelt interested in Palmer was Sara Roosevelt of New York, the mother of future president Franklin D. Roosevelt. Although her contributions were not large, she made yearly donations and allowed the school to use her influential name. In addition, Palmer caught the eye of several foundations supporting African American education, among them the Jeanes, Rosenwald, and Slater Funds. The attention of such agencies in turn impressed Stone; shortly after Brown told him of their support, he sent a $150 donation.

A notable exception to Brown's success in raising funds was the well-financed General Education Board (GEB). She continued to send a barrage of letters and endorsements and sought matching funds for land, new buildings, and salaries. Despite her persistence and a very favorable report by a GEB agent, however, the group declined to support Palmer.[19]

By 1916, Brown and her supporters were in the midst of a $30,000 building-fund campaign. Fund-raising events were held in the North and South among blacks and whites. The Slater Fund awarded Palmer a gift of $300 that enabled the school to divert other resources to the capital campaign. As Palmer steadily increased its ability to secure operating money, Brown gained the courage to amplify her search for capital funds. After raising $5,000, she asked Bright for help in securing $15,000 in the New York area. The final $10,000 was to be collected in New England, with the help of Charles Eliot and a group of upper-middle-class white women known as the Sedalia Club.[20]

The Sedalia Club was founded by Kimball in 1914 to advance Palmer's ability to provide industrial training to African American youth in rural North Carolina. Apparently two other southern black schools similar to Palmer already had clubs in the Boston area. Only nine women attended the club's initial meeting, at which the group elected Kimball its first president. One member cautioned, "You must not expect too much of us." The club grew to over 200 members, however, and its annual income in some years exceeded $10,000. Kimball remained president for about six years and then became honorary president. The Sedalia Club's contributions to Palmer were a welcome source of annual income.[21]

To stabilize the school's yearly operating budget, the Rosenwald Fund offered $2,500 over five years if Brown could secure an equal amount from other donors. Accepting the challenge, Brown met the requirement the first year and received $500. Although Julius Rosenwald congratulated the achievement, he had reservations about Brown's ability to complete the campaign. The following year, after sending the second installment, he enclosed a biography of Booker T. Washington written by Emmett J. Scott and Lyman Beecher Stowe and asked for Brown's impressions.[22]

Brown was aware of Rosenwald's Washingtonian views, which were revealed by his immense contributions to Tuskegee. In evaluating the laudatory biography, she chose her remarks carefully, as she was accustomed to doing to secure friends for Palmer. She attempted to increase

Rosenwald's interest in her work while maintaining her dignity. She wrote: "It is indeed a thrilling human story and I believe it should go hand in hand with the Pentateuch, for Dr. Washington was indeed our Moses. . . . I here resolve that tho the principles for which he labored so earnestly may be compromised or threatened, his faithfulness, his love for his race shall be the guiding star of my life in the humble but similar duty to which I feel God has called me."[23] By comparing the book to the first five books of the Old Testament, Brown placed it on a level with great sacred and historical works. Rosenwald regarded her fulsome remarks as inoffensive and continued to support her.

Brown also sought to place Palmer on a more secure foundation by turning it over to a state or church agency that would fund the school but allow Brown to maintain control. After Brown attended a meeting in Raleigh in 1914 on African American teacher-training schools, Palmer's board debated turning the school over to the state. Palmer continued to receive funding from Guilford County because of its reputation for providing the county with many of its best new teachers. Brown wrote Nathan C. Newbold, associate supervisor of rural schools, to propose that Palmer become a state-supported African American normal school, giving Thomas R. Foust as a reference. She made it clear, however, that she would agree to the takeover only if it did not change the way the school was run or diminish her own dominant role. For a time, Brown's proposal received serious attention by state officials, largely because of support from people such as Foust, W. T. Whitsett, and Charles Ireland, all Palmer supporters and members of the county's board of education. But in the end, the takeover was rejected; state leaders refused to assume responsibility without having administrative power.[24]

Although Brown refused to yield her authority to the state, she persisted, with some success, in seeking funding from various public and private agencies. In 1908, there were approximately 259 significant African American schools in the South, 37 of which were in North Carolina. All of them, except for Palmer and four state normal schools, were run by church groups. Apparently state officials were concerned that acceptance of Brown's restrictions would lead to controversy and a flood of similar requests. But Palmer continued to receive its yearly quota from the Guilford school board to supplement African American public school efforts. Although the county board of education rejected a request by Brown in 1915 that it run part of Palmer as a teacher-training school, Brown was able to get some additional public funding.[25]

Brown received assistance from Newbold in her ongoing but unsuccessful efforts to gain the support of the GEB. After the state rejected her
proposals that it fund Palmer, she asked the GEB for $1,500 each year for
five years to supplement the school's $6,000 operating budget. In ad-
dition, Guilford County and the Slater Fund promised $500 each. Thus
Palmer provided the only tax-supported education for African Americans in Sedalia for a generation. Other public funding was supplied by
the federal government through the Smith-Hughes Act of 1917. Under
the act, the federal government gave states money to support schools
such as the Agricultural and Mechanical College in Raleigh (now North
Carolina State University) and to subsidize agricultural, home economic, and industrial classes in public secondary schools. Palmer qualified for aid under the act and received three-fourths of an agricultural
teacher's salary. The increase in state, federal, and private funding led to
refinement of the curriculum to meet state requirements.[26]

Sex education, almost unheard of in schools during that time, was
one course that Palmer pioneered. Although sex education was not required by state or federal agencies, it was requested by the major contributor to Grinnell Cottage. Grinnell thought that the community and
the students, especially the girls, would benefit from studying a series of
textbooks titled *Self and Sex*. The books were purportedly helpful to parents and teachers in eliminating vulgarity. Sex education, however, was
only a small part of the blossoming of Palmer in its second decade.[27]

Along with sex education and the growth of Palmer's physical plant
came expansion of its more conventional course offerings. By 1917,
Palmer had increased its student body to 200 students. In reports to
supporters, Brown stressed the school's thrift and emphasis on industrial education. She noted that boys in the industrial department "earned
for the school over $1,200 by doing much of the mechanical work and
all work pertaining to the farm" and "applied their knowledge to making tables, mending chairs, building and repairing." Industrial work for
girls stressed practicality; each girl made underclothes and a dress for
herself. Many girls went north in the summer to earn money, often as
housekeepers, to complete their education. Although she emphasized
such vocational training, Brown did not omit the school's broader work.
She claimed that Palmer had revitalized Sedalia and made the people
"more intelligent, more thrifty and more law abiding." Brown stressed
that the institute provided grammar school training as well as classes in
domestic science, practical housekeeping, cooking, sewing, carpentry,

"The Finished Product, Class of 1916. Ready for service in the
school room, in the home, and on the farm. Faculty in the rear."
Brown is in the second row, fourth from left. NCDAH.

and agriculture. Among the instructors aiding Brown with this work
were Ghretta E. Scott and H. E. Wilson, both trained at Fisk University;
Esther L. Smith, Atlanta University; Gustava L. Alexander, Cheyney Institute; F. L. Brady and Bruce L. Bozeman, Hampton Institute; O. Williams, Wilberforce University; Mrs. Bozeman, Tuskegee Institute; and
M. M. Whittet, Palmer Institute.[28]

By 1916, Palmer had produced fifty-five graduates. Nearly a third
were teachers, and two were public school principals. One in seven was
a housekeeper. Others were engaged in industrial work, farming, and
skilled trades. Several went on to study theology and medicine. Palmer's
graduates reflected well on the growing institution. Brown announced
with pride that not a single graduate had ever been "arrested or accused
of misdemeanor" and that all were gainfully employed. Nearly a decade
later, by which time the roster of graduates would reach 100, most of
the women were elementary teachers or housekeepers, and farming
was the predominant male occupation. Girls always outnumbered boys
at Palmer, and as late as 1921, nearly all of the students were from rural
areas. Over half were from Guilford County, and three-fourths were
from Guilford and four adjacent counties. One-fourth were from fourteen other North Carolina counties. Seven students were from South
Carolina and Virginia. Forty-two of 259 students were in the high school
in 1921.

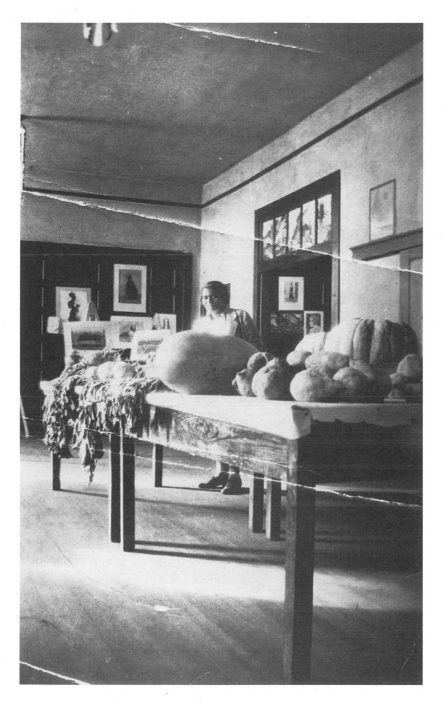

Brown examining produce from the school farm, circa 1916.
Schlesinger Library, Radcliffe College.

Students in dining hall, circa 1916.
Schlesinger Library, Radcliffe College.

Operation of the school farm was a major activity of the era. In 1915, Palmer's farm acquired "for the first time in its history a graduate in Agriculture, a wide awake Hampton man" (Bozeman), as director. The mixed-crop and demonstration farm yielded a variety of products and a profit for the school. Crops included wheat, oats, rye, corn, hay, millet, peas, peanuts, sweet potatoes, pumpkins, cotton, red and crimson clover, and alfalfa. Demonstration plots for classes featured cabbage, collards, turnips, onions, peppers, squash, okra, cucumbers, water-melons, cantaloupes, beets, spinach, rutabagas, white potatoes, lettuce, tomatoes, carrots, strawberries, celery, peaches, apples, plums, and pears. Palmer's dairy produced milk and butter for use at the school. Hogs, poultry, three mules, and a horse comprised the remainder of the livestock. The farm products in 1914–15 had a value of $890, mainly from corn ($250), wheat ($112), sweet potatoes ($104), and oats ($96). For at least three decades afterward, the farm, worked in large part by Palmer boys, would be a significant source of food and revenue for the school. Certain crops, such as sweet potatoes, sometimes produced twice the county's average yield per acre. As late as 1965, school leaders pulled boys from other chores to harvest sweet potatoes. Palmer's farm, managed for decades by Charlie Maye, regularly exceeded neighboring farms in productivity and profits.[29]

By the end of the 1910s, Palmer not only had developed a productive farm but also had reached a level of academic excellence equaled by few African American elementary or secondary schools in North Carolina. There were nearly a hundred private black schools in the state ranging from struggling parochial schools in small towns to colleges such as Biddle University in Charlotte and Bennett College in Greensboro. Many African American high schools, unlike Palmer, would close their doors with the spread of public high schools for rural African Americans in coming decades.[30]

In 1916, Palmer celebrated its fifteenth anniversary. The year held promise of good things to come. Brown invited supporters of African American education from across the country. She asked Mrs. Booker T. Washington to "bring Dr. Washington's message to these people in the rural districts." The anniversary festivities were a success and revealed Brown's love of ceremony and pageantry. She was disappointed, however, that many of her most faithful supporters, such as Maria Baldwin, Grace Deering, and Helen Kimball, were unable to attend.[31]

Various fund-raising campaigns were enjoying limited success, and the growing interest of Rosenwald and Stone held great promise. The $30,000 building fund, for instance, to finance a brick facility to replace Memorial Hall was well under way. The new structure would contain classrooms, administrative offices, a library, and an auditorium. Knowing that Alice Palmer had been greatly loved as president of Wellesley, Brown wisely named the campaign the Wellesley Hall fund to increase donations from alumnae of that school.[32]

Since Palmer's future was relatively secure, Frank Hobgood resigned as chairman of the school's board and was replaced by Edward P. Wharton, a well-respected businessman, in September 1917. E. D. Broadhurst of the Greensboro school board and Lunsford Richardson, a local executive of the Vick Chemical Company, also joined the board. Wharton was president of the Greensboro National Bank, and the bank cashier, A. H. Alderman, became Palmer's treasurer. Active in education for years, Wharton, along with Charles McIver, George A. Grimsley (a Greensboro educator and insurance company executive), and Charles Ireland, had founded the Educational Improvement Company to supplement public school funds. Brown was aware of Wharton's reputation in education and had asked for his aid as early as 1902. In early

Palmer baseball team, circa 1916. NCDAH.

1918, thrilled to be asked to serve on the board, he wrote: "I have been amazed at what you have accomplished."[33]

After a visit to the school, Wharton expressed delight in Brown's progress in education and race relations. He found her white neighbors to be very positive about Palmer and remarked: "I knew the prejudice you had to overcome," and "you seem to have overcome this prejudice entirely." Wharton apparently was correct because up to this point in the school's history there was no record of violence between whites and blacks in the area. Palmer had become a power for good within the African American community. The school had won the support of both races, in both the North and the South, and symbolized the best interests of Washingtonian blacks and progressive whites. Tuskegee's R. R. Moton commended Palmer's "spirit of cooperation, the spirit of racial goodwill and helpfulness," and described Brown as one who worked for, and "if necessary, would die for the best interest of the white and negro people of Greensboro."[34]

Since Palmer had gained a fine reputation and biracial support, its prospects were bright, and most of Brown's plans were being realized. Then catastrophe struck at the end of 1917. Palmer's Mechanical Hall (the industrial building) and adjacent commissary were destroyed by fire on December 29. The school lost its crucial stock of food for boarding students and its prized center of industrial education. But eventually Brown would turn this tragedy into triumph.

Chapter Five

FROM TRAGEDY TO TRIUMPH,
1918–1922

ALTHOUGH 1917 had begun as an auspicious year, it suddenly became a nightmare when fire destroyed the school's industrial building and the nearby commissary. Started by a student who carelessly struck a match near a gasoline tank, the fire caused losses estimated at $7,000. Neither the institute nor the community had a fire department, and a bucket brigade composed of teachers, students, and neighbors, black and white, failed to conquer the blaze. Everyone escaped without injuries. The school carried no fire insurance on either structure, and the loss of the industrial building meant that the elementary grades had no place to hold classes.[1]

The day after the blaze, Brown hurried to Greensboro to seek help. Charles Ireland appealed to the city's chamber of commerce for aid. The chamber responded by forming a special committee including Ireland, Thomas Foust, and Edward P. Wharton. Ireland and Foust also urged the county board of education to aid Palmer because they believed its closing would be "an industrial and educational calamity."[2]

As a result of such efforts, many local businessmen agreed to help Palmer. The *Greensboro Daily News* wrote that the community promised to provide $1,000 to enable Palmer to complete the term. This assistance by the white community of Greensboro was indeed welcome. The institution could have maintained itself on its excellent credit in Greensboro, but Brown wanted to avoid taking on additional fund-raising. Greensboro business leaders assured Brown that she would not have to bear new hardships due to the fire.

One reason Brown was able to gain the support of southern white community leaders was her persuasive salesmanship. She had the ability to win friends by describing the hardships she faced in her effort to educate African Americans. A Greensboro reporter lauded Brown's refined

New England background, bravery, selflessness, common sense, and talent in speaking convincingly of "entire nights spent upon her knees in the poor hut in which she first lived and worked."[3]

As surrounding communities collected whatever monies they could, friends in the North also began to rally behind Palmer. Mary Grinnell wrote encouragingly to Brown. As word of the catastrophe spread, contributions poured in. Brown's former high school teacher, Grace Deering, referred to the tragedy as a blessing. Among the gifts were contributions from such noted figures as Madam C. J. Walker, African American beauty products millionaire, and Julius Rosenwald.[4]

Donations to the fire fund came in at a remarkable rate. One contribution of $100 was very special to Brown—it came from George Palmer. After first advising Brown to close the school when he learned of the misfortune, he later had a change of heart and wrote, "Now that you have undertaken it, I want to have a share in it." Galen Stone also offered to help. Brown later recalled that after the fire both "Stone and his wife became loyal friends and supporters." Amazed at the overall response, Brown confided: "I have never seen people more deeply touched than the Greensboro people. I feel that my calamity has brought about a condition that nothing else could have produced."[5]

The African American community also supported Brown. James Dudley, president of the North Carolina Agricultural and Mechanical College for Negroes in Greensboro and an honorary member of Palmer's board since at least 1912, exemplified the black response. Along with the heads of most other well-established African American schools, he had personal knowledge of Brown's struggles, having faced many of the same obstacles. Having similar views on race and education, he was her mentor and friend.

James Benson Dudley (1859–1925) was born in Wilmington, North Carolina, to slaves of former governor Edward B. Dudley. After studying at a Freedmen's Bureau school and later in Philadelphia, he eventually received degrees from Shaw University, Livingstone College, and Wilberforce University. For fifteen years, he was a school principal. In 1896, he became president of the Agricultural and Mechanical College in Greensboro, a job he held for twenty-nine years. Dudley's ability to win biracial support saved the college from bankruptcy. Adept at making school industries self-supporting, he induced the white legislature to fund African American industrial education. He also replaced the primarily white faculty with African American instructors. He shared with Brown a Washingtonian faith in agriculture, industry, and public service as arenas of African American uplift. Like Brown, Dudley was deeply religious; he also was a founder of the state African American teachers association. Although both Dudley and Brown were concerned about social justice, they advised members of their race to be patient and non-resistant.[6]

Brown and Dudley were part of a national network of African American educators who had become close friends and allies. When Dudley learned of Palmer's misfortune, he generously delayed his own school's $1,000 fund-raising campaign. Other African American colleges in the area assisted Palmer. The secretary of the Greensboro chamber of commerce, in response to inquiries by African Americans, asked black college heads to inform African American preachers about the school's tragedy so that they could encourage their congregations to help Palmer.[7]

Brown was not content merely to accept charity. To show her gratitude, she arranged a concert by the Sedalia Singers at the Greensboro Municipal Theater in January 1918. The chamber of commerce sponsored the event. Brown received approval from the chamber for blacks to attend the concert along with whites, an unusual concession in the Jim Crow South that was a testament to Brown's influence.[8]

Many southern whites had never heard the Sedalia Singers, although they were well known in parts of the North. The weather that week was unseasonably cold, but the performance went on. The 1,500-seat auditorium was filled, and scores of people were turned away. Reporters described the music as "typically negro of the most enjoyable character." Songs included the national anthem, a powerful version of "America," "Swing Low, Sweet Chariot," and a variety of tunes familiar to southerners. The amazing attendance enabled Brown to collect more than the needed money. Although the concert was advertised as free, the chorus of fifty voices sang a "considerable part of $1,000 out of Greensboro pockets."[9]

This response to the fire inspired the institution's trustees to intensify their efforts to place Palmer on a more secure footing. Before the fire, Brown had received mostly moral support from the board. She seized the opportunities after the tragic fire to gain substantial publicity for Palmer and energize its new leadership and took advantage of the situation by expanding her goals. In fact, it seemed as if Brown was rejuvenated by the conflagration.[10]

Before the fire, the school had begun three fund-raising campaigns: an annual giving fund, a $30,000 building fund, and a $50,000 endowment fund. The endowment and building funds received the greatest gains in contributions after the fire, but the annual giving and fire funds also enjoyed increased donations. In the South alone, Brown felt that she could collect $2,000 per year after the fire, whereas before she had been able to raise only $200 to $300. Brown believed that the people of the South had experienced an awakening. Moreover, she thought that people who had become interested in the school would support it regardless of whether she was involved.[11]

Edward Wharton, a racial moderate, was one of the major advocates of southern support for Palmer. He commented in a Palmer brochure: "I am making the greatest personal sacrifice to contribute all I can to this institution. It has done more to bring about splendid feelings between the races than any institution I know of." Such an endorsement not only expressed approval of Brown's school but also indicated white acceptance of her Washingtonian views. Nevertheless, racial tensions in the area increased, primarily because of the growing unwillingness of African Americans to endure rising racist violence. African American soldiers returning from duty in World War I in western Europe, where they had observed little racism, were less inclined to tolerate such violence.[12]

After the armistice of November 11, 1918, hopes for total racial equality in America rose among African Americans. After all, they had helped make the world "safe for democracy." Such confidence in social justice was brief, however, because some whites were determined to contest the demands for full citizenship of returning African American soldiers. The Ku Klux Klan was reborn in the South by 1915. In less than a year, the membership of the violent white supremacist group grew to over 100,000. Many whites, in both the North and the South, thought it was necessary to put African Americans back in their place, and more than seventy blacks were lynched in the first postwar year. Ten were soldiers, several still in uniform. Eleven African Americans were burned alive. Some twenty-five race riots throughout the United States marked the Red Summer of 1918. Civil unrest, fueled by lack of federal protection, seized a large segment of the African American population. It became apparent that most whites sought to negate African Americans' small wartime gains in civil rights. For the first time, African Americans organized into large groups and defended themselves.[13]

In this racially charged climate, Brown remained a major proponent of racial goodwill. Perhaps her willingness to call for African Americans' greater endurance of oppressive and dehumanizing actions by whites was the result of her Washingtonian outlook, her personal success with local whites, and her belief in the middle-class-uplift ideology of her mother's generation. The actions of the Greensboro chamber of commerce and progressive local whites after the fire might well have strengthened Brown's faith in future racial tranquillity. Whatever her reasons, she was convinced that belief in African American inferiority and second-class citizenship could be overcome by appropriate education. Apparently this involved a return to the pre–Civil War attitudes of mutually supporting elite classes of southern blacks and whites. The degree to which Brown shared these attitudes is uncertain, but clearly most of her early supporters held similar views. Frances Guthrie, for example, thought there had been a bond during slavery between "*old time* colored people" and their masters.

The war had a negative effect on Palmer. Contributions were not as large as expected, and inflation made nearly everything more costly. Enrollment declined as students enlisted in the armed forces or left for jobs in factories because of the civilian labor shortage. Brown served on a statewide committee of black leaders that addressed wartime issues and spoke on the war work of the school and the state, emphasizing the unanimity of blacks and whites in supporting the war effort. By pursuing such activities, she demonstrated that African Americans were able to make significant contributions as first-class citizens.[14]

Her most forthright petition to whites to fulfill their obligations to blacks was her 1919 work, *Mammy: An Appeal to the Heart of the South,* a sentimental novella aimed at securing sympathy and support for blacks from white southern women. Brown believed that the image of the mammy aroused tender emotions in white southerners. The book encouraged readers to reflect on the "good ole days" when slaves and masters lived in supposed serenity. Based on a true story that occurred in North Carolina, it told the tale of a devoted former slave and her husband who honored a promise to their master to remain with his family until he returned from the Civil War. Although he never returned, Mammy faithfully served the wife and children of her deceased master for over fifty years without reward, living in a run-down shack while tending to their needs.[15]

After Mammy's own son grew up and moved to the North, where he became successful, he asked his parents to come live with him in comfort. Although she realized her years of service were not appreciated, Mammy refused because of her promise to serve her master's family "until death." She died tragically in a snowstorm while trying to carry a meal for one of the white children to the "big house."[16]

Although it was ignored by black periodicals, *Mammy* received mixed reviews from the public and from Brown's friends, with most negative comments coming surprisingly from northerners. Guthrie said that Brown had "opened an old wound, which you should have tried to heal," and she feared that it would discourage "less intelligent and fortunate colored people" from ever believing that whites might try to help them. Later, after *Mammy* became a success, Guthrie revised her views and congratulated Brown for a "splendid victory." Carrie Stone, Galen Stone's wife, wondered if Brown had written this story of a faithful African American more for her pupils than for the public. The book was dedicated to Lula McIver, who predictably praised it.[17]

In the tumultuous early 1920s, Brown found it necessary to go beyond merely publishing *Mammy* as a statement against racism. She was personally affected by the racial violence and discrimination of the postwar era. In the campaign for women's suffrage in 1920, for instance, Brown, who had worked on various projects with white clubwomen, became the target of a scheme in which a widely circulated letter intended to persuade white Tar Heel women to register as Democrats was forged in her name. In retaliation, she coordinated a campaign by black clubwomen to register black female voters. In her many travels, Brown was regularly "put out of Pullman berths and seats during all hours of the night." She often sued the offending railroads in protest, winning small settlements. In one case in 1920, after sleeping all night in a Pullman car, Brown was awakened by a dozen white men who ordered her to either move to the Jim Crow car or be put off the train at the next stop into the hands of an angry white mob. Humiliated and resentful, she was forced to march through three white coaches to the Jim Crow car. Brown was on her way to speak before the white Woman's Missionary Convention meeting in Memphis, the first convention of women's clubs to invite black speakers in Tennessee. Ironically, on her way to the "colored" section, she walked past white women en route to the same meeting, at which they would proclaim the goal of making "Negro women unashamed and unafraid."[18]

Brown did not let the matter rest and filed suit against the Pullman Company. The company offered a $200 settlement. Her attorney Frank Hobgood advised her to counter with a demand for $1,000 but to be prepared to take $500, half of which was his fee, rather than face costly litigation. Brown replied that the time had come for the courts to test the issue of "justice for Negroes." Nevertheless, she told Hobgood to ask for $1,500, reminding him that his fee was one-third of the award.

Brown pointed out that Mrs. Thomas Bickett, wife of North Carolina's governor, and about eighty other white women agreed that the company should pay for her poor treatment. She reiterated her great resentment at the insults and her willingness to become a "martyr for Negro womanhood."[19]

Because of such personal encounters with racism, Brown gradually moved away from strict Washingtonian principles of accommodation. In fact, she suggested to Hobgood during the Pullman case that times had changed substantially since Washington's day. Nonetheless, she was careful not to alienate white supporters. She told the press in 1921 that she "was not interested in racial equality" or in anything that might cause discord. Her one goal was to aid African Americans through education, and progressive southern leaders applauded that safe objective.[20]

Within five years, however, Brown would present an incisive speech, "Where We Are in Race Relations," at Berea College, an American Missionary Association school in Kentucky. Brown repeated the same themes in many other lectures. Her key point was that despite improvements in race relations, much remained to be done. Prejudice persisted and formed a patchwork of inconsistency. Blacks, except for prisoners, were not allowed to ride some city buses in North Carolina, but they were allowed to ride such buses in Alabama. Conditions in the North were not much better. Brown argued that if "staying in his place" meant "jim-crow cars, segregated districts, unpaved, unlighted streets in an isolated section of the city, doing all the menial tasks, the handing out of the back door of some restaurant a sandwich . . . , the willingness to be called by one's just name by those with whom one is not familiar . . . the Negro today will never find his place." Brown believed that very few white southerners supported progress in race relations and chastised them for lacking respect for blacks as thinking people. The average southern white man held African American women in low esteem, even though most young black women "would bow to the lust of no man." Northern prejudice grew as more African Americans moved there. Brown admitted that many blacks were "loud, boisterous, and untrained in habits of culture," which fed the growth of prejudice, "a malicious, malignant disease." Brown's greatest fear was the spread of the bitter attitude of African American youths who "no longer consider patience a virtue."[21]

Hoping to remedy such tendencies among African Americans, Galen Stone increased his support of Palmer. Shortly after the fire, Stone and his wife made their first visit to Palmer to assess the damage. Two months later, he helped arrange a meeting between Wharton and leading Boston businessmen in hopes of arousing their interest in the school. The following spring, the trustees, encouraged by Stone's participation, increased the building campaign to $50,000. He subscribed $10,000, on the condition that southern whites raise the same amount. In response, citizens of Greensboro, through the chamber of commerce, agreed to match Stone's offer.[22]

Recognizing that Brown had endured a great deal of stress because of the fire, Stone paid for a much-needed vacation for Brown in Denver, Colorado, in 1918. He gladly financed the trip since after more than sixteen years of selfless service she had only $25 in the bank. Stone also paid Brown's tuition for a course in physical culture at Harvard University. She had requested tuition for a class in music as well, but Stone asked that his gift be used solely for therapeutic physical culture.[23]

After Stone's visit, Brown began a series of calculated moves to ensure his continued support by suggesting that Stone and Daisy Bright meet with her to discuss the needs of the school. Brown insisted that she sought advice rather than money. Her monetary requests continued, however, and increased as time passed. Less than two weeks after her appeal for a meeting, she asked him to be a trustee. Stone refused but restated his interest in Palmer and its future. Brown persisted with her request. After numerous polite expressions of his unwillingness to join the board, Stone bluntly informed Brown of his wish to restrict his involvement.[24]

Nevertheless, Brown continued to cultivate Stone's interest. Little by little, he began to respond favorably to her incessant requests. She cleverly reminded him that he was "doing more than helping a negro school—you are helping the entire South for this effort, first of its kind in the state, is going to wake up North Carolina." Brown recognized Stone's importance as the first wealthy supporter who did not believe in limited education for African Americans. She spoke openly to Stone about her desire to educate students beyond Washingtonian limits to encourage him to increase his support. In the past, he had sent $500 each summer and each fall since 1915. In response to Brown's prodding, Stone's contributions increased. He also became more involved in Brown's personal life. Encouraged by Stone's aid and an increase in enrollment to some 200 students, after her well-deserved vacation, Brown pushed forward with plans to expand Palmer. With Stone's ongoing sponsorship of the new building campaign, Brown believed it was just a matter of time before the modern classroom building was completed.[25]

To accommodate the rise in enrollment, Brown hired more teachers.

Among them was Ola Glover, a nurse trained at Hampton Institute who began at Palmer in 1920 and became Brown's closest friend and adviser. Brown entrusted her with many responsibilities, appointing her as school nurse and director of the girls' dormitory and the dining hall. As Brown's private nurse, Glover saw Brown through several serious illnesses. Glover was not intimidated by Brown's dominant personality. From the beginning, the two women respected each other. Glover's own determination revealed itself in her tough negotiations over her initial salary at Palmer. In less than two years, Glover's annual salary rose from $500 to $1,080.[26]

During the 1920s and early 1930s, Palmer maintained a faculty and staff of about fourteen persons. Between five and nine were high school teachers, and the rest taught in the elementary and junior high school departments. By the end of the period, Palmer had sixteen employees with undergraduate or master's degrees mainly from about twenty black colleges. Some faculty members were involved in more than one department. A few, such as D. D. Scott, a graduate of West Virginia Collegiate Institute, worked in all three departments. Scott instructed students in the newly accredited high school department in science and was the director of manual training. Another valued employee was Mrs. M. L. Gullins, director of admissions. Gullins was responsible for assigning dormitory space for girls. She also served as a role model by overseeing the girls' cultural training.[27]

Brown expected teachers to work around the clock as instructors, chaperons, and campus residents. They taught Sunday school, led trips to Greensboro, and ate meals with students. Like other staff at black schools and at boarding schools in general, Palmer teachers often played the role of surrogate parents. Brown held faculty and students to the same high standards of decorum and appearance. Partly due to the tough working conditions, many teachers left Palmer, often moving on to black colleges. Of those who stayed, a few refused to be dominated. Palmer faculty socialized with colleagues at Bennett College and the renamed North Carolina Agricultural and Technical College. Brown provided transportation one night a week for teachers' recreation in Greensboro and reputedly expected full reports after their social forays. In the 1920s, young, single Palmer teachers received invitations to social events anywhere from Greensboro to Raleigh. Teacher Mildred Dudley traveled to one event in Greensboro with five young male teachers in their old car, the "hootwagon." Brown was not pleased when the six stayed out dancing until 2:00 A.M. or when Dudley and several teachers stayed out all night at a New Year's Eve dance.[28]

The most versatile member of the Palmer staff was Reverend John Brice (1877–1960), a graduate of Knoxville College in Tennessee who joined the staff in 1920 and served as chaplain and vice principal for more than thirty years. Brice was devoted to Palmer and the surrounding community. In addition to his duties as vice principal, trustee, farmer, mason, gardener, and teacher, Brice was pastor of Bethany Church. When Brown was away, he directed the school. In the summer months, aided by two men and a few boys, he managed Palmer's farm and woodlands. The strong, lanky preacher might be seen plowing a field one day and building a brick wall the next. During one summer, he held weekly community club meetings for local boys, and his wife canned around 800 quarts of vegetables and fruits for the school. Ella Hawkins Brice (1886–1947) was Brown's youngest aunt and a talented musician seeking a professional singing career. Her ambition frequently kept her away from the school and her four small children. When on campus, Ella, also a Knoxville graduate, taught history.[29]

Inflation and the expansion of the faculty and student body caused an increase in the school's annual budget from some $9,000 in 1914 to about $16,000 in 1921. After E. P. Wharton equipped a new science laboratory in early 1922, enabling Palmer to attain vital accreditation, the budget continued to increase because of the need to cover extra expenses for staff and equipment essential to maintaining an accredited high school. It is possible that the expenditure per student actually decreased over this time. Some questioned Brown's decision to expand student enrollment. She explained that she had made the decision expecting a new building to be ready by November 1919. When that did not happen, dormitories in Memorial Hall were converted to classrooms and a cheap, temporary dormitory was quickly built.[30]

Construction of the new classroom building was a priority of the Palmer board. Because of Stone's increased support, Brown suggested that the new structure be named in his honor. At Stone's request, however, the building was ultimately dedicated to Brown's New England benefactress Alice Freeman Palmer.[31]

The story of the funding and construction of the Alice Freeman Palmer Building demonstrates Brown's dedication, determination, and faith. The board approved plans for an administrative and classroom building in November 1918, by which time $40,000 of a projected

$50,000 had been pledged. The board expected construction to take about a year and authorized Harry Barton, a prominent Greensboro architect, to draw up plans for the building.[32]

Barton also designed central electrical, sewer, and water systems for the entire school. He estimated that these improvements would cost about $12,000. With the completion of these systems, Palmer would go from oil lamps to electric lights, from outside rest rooms to modern indoor bathrooms, and from hand-pumped water to indoor plumbing with hot and cold running water. The achievement made the school a small town in itself, an oasis of modernity in poor, backward Sedalia, which had no public utilities.[33]

The contract for construction of the Alice Freeman Palmer Building was awarded to J. T. Solomon, who bid $59,000 and promised to complete the structure by October 15, 1919. With the building already $9,000 over the $50,000 set as the capital fund goal, the board also needed $12,000 more for the new utilities. To oversee the development of the physical plant, Wharton became chairman of the building committee. The committee addressed the need to cover the $21,000 deficit. With the contracts awarded, it was critical for Brown to raise the remaining funds.[34]

To complete the construction, Brown began new campaigns. One was a drive to raise $25,000, soon increased to $35,000. To avoid imposing further on Stone, she decided to enlist Charles Eliot's help. Eliot had given Brown permission to use his name for endorsements, but she also asked to be allowed to list him as treasurer of the fund to attract New Englanders to contribute to an African American school in North Carolina. She explained that an assistant treasurer "would attend to all the detail work." Eliot had been a loyal friend since 1914 and had presided over a few fund-raising affairs in earlier years. As a result, Palmer had gained many supporters. On this occasion, however, he declined to cooperate, but he did accept the post of chairman of the fund's Reference Committee. Brown was satisfied because she could continue to publicize his ongoing interest.[35]

As committees in New England, New York, and North Carolina sought funds, the construction of the building proceeded. The dedication date was postponed to November 1, 1919, by which time the structure was still unfinished. Reasons for the delay are unclear, but Stone later asked Solomon to reduce his bill because he had not delivered the building on time, a request that Solomon denied.[36]

The builder now promised that the building would be finished by

September 1920, nearly a year later. Meanwhile, trying to cut expenses, Palmer's students made 225,000 bricks and milled 75,000 feet of lumber. By May 1920, the brickwork and roof were done. Realizing that Solomon would have to be paid in full before he would turn the structure over to Palmer, Brown asked the Stones for further support. The next month, they sent an additional $10,000. Brown was especially grateful for this gift because it arrived at a time when several other building-fund pledges were not honored.

Three major supporters of the school died without having settled their affairs during this period. The most important was Lunsford Richardson, president of North Carolina's Vick Chemical Company. Brown felt that his death was a great blow to Palmer because he had promised to stand behind the new building financially. Richardson died without fully paying his pledge of $5,000. His loss was all the more painful because he had voted to continue construction of the building despite rising costs. To compensate for such losses, Brown appealed again to Stone: "I am asking you (for I feel that my work for my people and my thoughts for my people are just as important as Dr. Washington's were) to make the Palmer Memorial Institute your special contribution to the education of the Negro race, as many others did Tuskegee twenty-five or more years ago."[37]

Work on the structure continued amid growing concern about paying the contractor. Stone hinted to Brown that he was considering providing further financial assistance. "I should like to know just how much money you owe [on the new building]," he wrote, and "would like to have that direct from the treasurer, himself." Stone learned that $12,000 was still due. Brown secured $1,700 through a letter-writing campaign, and Bright offered to sell her shooting club near the campus to get the rest. By the spring of 1921, the building was close enough to completion for the school to use the top floor.[38]

As plans to dedicate the structure during the school's twentieth anniversary celebration went forward, contributions began to dwindle due to a brief recession that beset the nation in 1921. The slowdown caused Brown to suspect that people around Boston had become discouraged. "I can't get any money to go ahead," she confided. To make matters worse, another fire on the campus in March 1921 destroyed the barn built in 1914. The fire caused a loss of $5,000, "a very hard blow to the school because all the farm implements were burned up at the time the students were preparing to use them." Unfortunately, there was no insurance on the barn or its contents.[39]

Among friends who expressed their support after the fire, Carrie Stone was the most comforting to Brown. "I know you feel like the burning of the Palmer barn is the last straw," she wrote, reminding Brown to "praise the Lord for all his goodness." Stone also used the tragedy to attempt to convince Brown to allow others to assist her in the management of Palmer. Brown thanked Carrie for her concern but asked friends not to let the fire divert their attention from the effort to complete the new building.[40]

Brown redirected her supporters' attention to the most important issue at hand: completion of the new building. Wharton informed her that only $11,000 more was due to the contractor and tried unsuccessfully to borrow the funds by taking out a first mortgage on Palmer property. Greensboro trustees Julius W. Cone, president of Proximity Manufacturing Company; Emanuel Sternberger, president of Revolution Cotton Mills; and Wharton were also personally carrying a $14,000 note on Palmer's behalf. That sum was almost a year's budget at Palmer. In the same spirit, Stone offered to sign a note for $11,000 so that the contractor would release the building. Meanwhile, Palmer's immediate need for funds was intensified by the school farm's crop failure of 1921.[41]

Amid Palmer's continuing challenges, another serious illness beset Brown. In the fall of 1921, she was diagnosed with the degenerative nerve disease neuritis. The condition progressed to the point that she needed surgery. As she prepared for the operation, the board assured her that the school would remain open. Brown underwent the operation in early November and during her recovery insisted on regular reports on the work at Palmer. In response to a flood of cards and letters from "her children," Brown wrote the entire student body that in her absence, "God sent His angel, Mr. Stone," to their rescue. The angel contributed $7,700 to the school in 1921—22, over one-third of Palmer's total income that year. Stone's gift exceeded the school's revenue from the farm and from tuition and board and was almost twice the sum of all other donations.[42]

Without Stone's help, Palmer would have been forced to close its doors at some point between 1917 and 1922. Furthermore, the new classroom and administration building, ultimately finished three years late, would have been completed even later, if at all. Stone's efforts to maintain Palmer during those troubled years were no secret to the Sedalia community and friends of the school everywhere. Moreover, his role as adviser, financial backer, and personal friend to Brown showed no sign of diminishing. By 1921, Brown was asking Stone for money almost monthly to keep Palmer afloat, and he nearly always responded favorably. In January, he sent $500. Brown then informed him that she needed at least $4,000 to continue until October 1 and reported that it took $20,000 a year to run Palmer. In return, Stone promptly sent a check for $2,000 but suggested that limiting the number of students would reduce expenses.[43]

An astute businessman as well as a philanthropist, Stone asked Brown if he could send someone to study her accounting methods. Shortly afterward, he arranged for his personal accountant, a Mr. Totman, to review Palmer's books. After the visit, Brown informed Stone that the school was following Totman's suggestions scrupulously. Satisfied, Stone increased his contributions but reminded Brown that he could not cover all of Palmer's debts and reiterated that she should stop spending money before she had raised it.[44]

Other major contributors also criticized Brown's premature spending of funds. Grinnell, for instance, informed Brown that because she disapproved of the school's extra expenses, she would not contribute as much as in the past. Amid such questions about how funds were being spent, one theme persisted: although they might complain about her spending, Brown's faithful supporters never failed to rescue her. When pressured by supporters to curb spending, Brown shrewdly replied that she had asked for money only because she could not buy food for the school. Stone's irritation was understandable since Brown received a great deal of support not only from him but also from his wife and several close friends and relatives.[45]

Carrie Morton Stone (1866–1945) was a major supporter of Palmer. She was born in Hyde Park, Massachusetts, and married Galen Stone in 1889. They had four children: Katharine, Margaret, Barbara, and Robert Gregg, who would support Palmer until its closing. Carrie was a Unitarian and, like Brown, a God-fearing woman. As with other key friends of the school, Brown established a close and enduring relationship with Carrie by writing personal letters that secured her interest not only in African American education but also in Brown's well-being. Carrie became so close to Brown that it was difficult to discover whether her primary concern was for Brown or for Palmer. In fact, it was almost impossible to differentiate the two; Brown was Palmer, and Palmer was Brown.[46]

In time, Carrie became a tireless advocate for the school. She encouraged prominent New Englanders, as well as her children and relatives, to contribute. She often urged her husband to do more for the school.

Carrie M. Stone, wife of Galen Stone, who became a close friend
and adviser of Brown. Courtesy of Ambassador Galen L. Stone.

In March 1921, for example, after he had written Brown that he did not
wish to give Palmer further aid at that time, Carrie explained to Brown
his current mood of restricted giving. She also warned Brown against
depending too heavily on her husband.[47]

In an attempt to overcome the constant shortage of funds, Charles
Eliot and others agreed to meet with Galen Stone to discuss ideas for
a national letter of appeal. Launching a national fund-raising project

in the immediate postwar period was particularly difficult because the country was still recovering from World War I and a reaction was setting in against the patriotism and idealism of wartime. After the paranoia caused by the Red Scare in 1919 and two years of severe inflation, in 1920 many people stopped buying goods, and industrial production began to decline. Unemployment increased from 2 percent in 1919 to 12 percent in 1921. Railroads, mines, and particularly New England textile companies were hit hard.[48]

Efforts by Brown and her supporters to raise money in that climate were an uphill battle. Nevertheless, volunteers continued to solicit contributions for the building, endowment, and other funds. Eliot wrote a national letter of appeal and Brown mailed out over 5,000 copies, but the response was disheartening, with returns barely paying for the postage. Nonetheless, instead of downgrading her fund-raising goals, Brown astonishingly suggested increasing them fivefold. She informed Stone: "I propose the raising of $250,000, ¾ of which [will be] for an endowment." She then began another letter-writing campaign to friends of the school and in response received numerous notes of regret from regular contributors.[49]

Shocked by Brown's impulsive attempt to begin a new campaign, Stone replied: "It is impossible for me to tell from your letter what campaign you are planning to undertake, whether it is for an endowment fund or for funds for current affairs of the school or for a building fund." He strongly cautioned Brown against using such unorthodox fund-raising techniques. Stone was not alone in questioning Brown's irregular methods. Caroline M. Caswell, president of a settlement house in Boston, wrote:

> May I call your attention to a sentence in your letter where you say, "we have no endowment." In your most excellent booklet it is stated that in 1910 you were given $1000 to start an endowment, that in 1911 $5000 was given conditionally for this purpose, that $500 was added in 1913, and that in 1920 $1000 was given for endowment—yet your letter says that you have no endowment. A critical person would at once raise some question about the truth of your statement. . . . Would it not be better to say "only a small endowment" or name the amount which is of course very small?[50]

The Sedalia Club also objected to Brown's solicitation style. Its second president, Louise Winsor Brooks, a prosperous unmarried woman from Boston, broke with the club's usual hands-off policy by questioning Brown's methods. Brooks initially backed Palmer's $25,000 campaign to finish paying for the new building, but she was concerned when the campaign grew to include equipping the building. Club members could find no discussion of such changes in fund-raising in the Palmer board minutes because Brown employed a change-it-as-needed style until influential friends demanded clarification of the use of money obtained for specific purposes.[51]

The Sedalia Club's concerns provided a focus for the issue. The confusion over fund-raising set off a series of events that challenged Brown's absolute control. The altercation began when the club hired professional publicist and fund-raiser Harry W. Merrill of Boston. His publicity campaign for Palmer proved, however, to be short-lived.[52]

Brooks then further challenged Brown's dominance of solicitation by inviting Galen Stone to attend club meetings. The two began to discuss their concerns over the management of funds. Inquiries to the Boston chamber of commerce by prospective donors further intensified the problem.

In an effort to address such inquiries, Brooks wrote a letter to Palmer's treasurer, A. H. Alderman, sending a copy to Brown. She noted that although she was a trustee, she never received any official information on finances. Brooks asked: "What is the annual budget?" "How much is it yet necessary to raise to complete the new building?" "How has the money already sent from the Sedalia Club been used?" "Have you an annual report?"[53]

Brooks's letter drew a response from Brown, not Alderman. In a separate letter written to Brown the same day, Brooks had told her not to approach Stone for more money until Alderman forwarded the requested financial information. Brown replied: "I had made up my mind not to bother him for at least a month and was about to say the same thing . . . to you but thought it seemed dictatorial." A few months later, Brown apologized, adding defensively: "I have learned through all struggles that when I have done my best whatever follows is God's solution."

Nevertheless, the club sought control of fund-raising in New England. Brown finally agreed to supply Brooks with monthly budget reports and to send the names of New England supporters, but she asked that she be allowed to correspond with some two dozen contributors who were personal friends. This uncharacteristic relinquishing of control was partly the result of Brown's upcoming operation. The compromise was probably traumatic for Brown.[54]

Brown in turn asked the club to guarantee that it would raise at least

$4,000 annually, telling Brooks that she usually collected about $8,000 of Palmer's $20,000 annual budget in New England. Leaders of the club believed they could secure more money in New England than Brown could raise. Because of Brown's health problems, they and the Stones were convinced that they were helping to lessen her burden. Brown had misgivings, however, and wrote to Carrie Stone to ask whether she thought the club's letters would be as effective as her personal letters. Carrie suggested that she try the club's idea for a year. Galen Stone advised Brown to meet with the club's leaders for instruction in fundraising. Brown also reluctantly agreed that the Stones should send their contributions to the club.[55]

Whatever agreement was made at Brown's meeting with club leaders is not fully known. Despite her growing health problems, Brown continued to write old New England friends. She had not changed her view of her role in acquiring money in New England. When Galen Stone finally expressed his resentment of her constant requests for money, Brown for the first time became aware of the alarming possibility of losing her most generous supporter, which surely would have meant the end of Palmer. In a matter of days, she became much more cooperative, but even in defeat she managed to win. The supporters she retained provided most of the $8,000 she hoped to raise in New England. Without them, the club would have great difficulty meeting its $4,000 goal.[56]

About this time, Galen Stone agreed to become a Palmer trustee, a major victory for Brown. His change of heart came about because of his tremendous financial investment in the school and his growing fondness for Brown. Brooks had counted heavily on the Stones' support for her challenge to Brown's authority, but when Stone joined the board, Brown gained more access to him. After recovering from her operation, Brown no longer allowed the Stones' contributions to go through the club. Brooks realized that without the Stones' influence and gifts it would be almost impossible for the Sedalia Club to raise its quota, but it continued to try. Still seeking clear information on the school's finances, the club made the error of requesting the exact amount of monthly salaries at Palmer, including Brown's.[57]

To Brown, that was the last straw. After over a year of squabbling, she insisted that her list of contributors be returned. She also informed the Sedalia Club that she had erred in allowing it to take over fund-raising in New England and that Bright, Stone, and Wharton all agreed with her. She hoped that the club would not disband but said that if the "folks up there who give are not satisfied with the management of things they can withdraw." Confidently, she continued: "I wouldn't be worried out of my life for the *little* $1500 or $2000 a year that the club *might* give. . . . I don't need anybody to help me."[58]

To firmly impress on the Sedalia Club her position of ultimate power at Palmer, Brown met in New York with the school's most important friends. The group decided once and for all that Brown should control all solicitation. It proposed a compromise to reassure the club that funds were being spent properly. Edith H. MacFadden of Cambridge, a member of the club, was voted a director of the board and given the position of controller for Palmer. MacFadden asked that requests for financial information from the club and the Boston chamber of commerce be addressed to her. The arrangement prevented the breakup of the club, which continued raising funds through bake sales, concerts, and other social functions. MacFadden remained on the board for several years. As paid controller for at least a few years, she personally oversaw Palmer's financial affairs. It is unclear how much she accomplished, however, for she became very frustrated with Brown, whom she described as "incompetent to run a school and a very dangerous leader of the negro race."[59]

As efforts to raise funds in the North continued, Palmer expanded its support among white southerners. To strengthen this link, the board formed the Southern Investment Committee. Leading members were banker Wharton and company presidents Cone, Richardson, Sternberger, and Ireland. The county public school system and the local press also supported Brown. During the campaign to complete the classroom and administration building, the *Greensboro Daily News* reported that Guilford citizens planned to raise $5,000. Lula McIver insisted that Brown deserved the assistance of Guilford whites. Southern whites pledged $15,000 to Palmer in less than two years. Although Brown built a broad local base of southern friends, she collected much more money in the North. But the moral and physical support of southern whites was as important to Palmer as economic assistance from the North.[60]

The same could be said of support from the African American community, which was limited economically but rich in elements essential to Palmer, such as a sense of determination and a spirit of self-improvement. Without such qualities, there would be no need for Palmer or for a leader such as Brown. When black families could save extra money, they often spent it on a deserving youth's education. Whether for tuition, food, books, or clothes, such support was hard earned. Nevertheless, African Americans who contributed to education considered it a worthwhile investment. The fact that the majority of blacks lived in poverty made their contributions more special.

The small, expanding group of African Americans who had raised themselves above poverty usually gave back more than their fair share to institutions that made it possible for blacks to escape the slavery of ignorance. Educators such as Howard M. Briggs, president of Straight College in New Orleans, and Mary McLeod Bethune sent modest contributions to Palmer. In many cases, such contributions were merely tokens of support, but they were welcomed all the more for that reason. African Americans from the business community gave as well. An excellent example was Charles C. Spaulding (1874–1952), who rose through the ranks of Durham's North Carolina Mutual Life Insurance Company to become its president in 1923 and built the company into the largest African American–owned business in the nation. He and his family were regular donors to Palmer, and Durham's black elite later sent several of their children to the school. Perhaps the most notable contribution by an African American society in the 1920s came from the Cambridge Charity Club, a group of women whose primary mission was to support deserving black organizations. The group sent $100, and Brown's response was as enthusiastic as it would have been if the society had presented $10,000. As emotionally encouraging as gifts from such groups were, African American charity had little impact on economic realities at Palmer. The school needed money to operate, and the gifts of wealthy whites alone could not ensure its existence.[61]

Brown and her trustees waged a continuing battle to acquire ongoing funding from the General Education Board (GEB) and other educational foundations. Early efforts to obtain major support from the GEB had failed because Palmer was a private rather than a public school. Another fault the GEB found was the limited production of graduates. In response to the latter criticism, Brown stated that Palmer aimed for quality, not quantity. As for private status, advocates of the institute made several proposals to Guilford County for public school programs at Palmer. Brown believed that endorsement by key persons could induce the GEB to offer permanent assistance. She asked Eliot, Stone, and others to write the GEB, and nearly all responded by sending impressive letters.[62]

Some Palmer supporters, such as influential New Yorker Carl A. de Gersdorff, who was a new trustee, believed that foundations did not contribute more to Palmer because the "school was without any backing—Municipal, State or Church." He based this opinion on information he obtained from Frederick Strauss, a trustee of the Rockefeller Foundation, and E. C. Sage of the GEB. Strauss cautioned his foundation that at Palmer a "new building has through the generosity of a Boston man, been put up,—a Building far too ambitious for the needs of the school. The School has a good intelligent head, but has no assurance of permanency." Sage had a similar view, and the GEB continued to refuse Brown's requests. GEB leader Jackson Davis also feared that a donation to Palmer would lead to the need to fund other similar schools, such as Bethune's school in Florida, and delay public acceptance of the responsibility for supporting African American education.[63]

Brown achieved better results with local school officials, whose endorsement de Gersdorff believed was crucial to gaining GEB help, than with national foundations. She was willing to do almost anything to receive stable county aid, except, of course, give up personal control of her life's work. One success occurred in 1920 when the county agreed to give a subsidy to Palmer for all Guilford students there. Brown saw the action as an endorsement of permanent cooperation that would ensure continuing federal, state, and county funds, which soon amounted to one-third of Palmer's salary budget. Palmer expanded its programs to receive increased funding and meet county academic requirements. The return was considerable; the following year, Guilford County agreed to pay the salaries of six of the school's teachers for six months. About the same time, after a meeting at the school with Brown and local school leaders, Jackson Davis of the GEB officially recommended to his employer that Palmer become a Guilford County high school and receive several years of diminishing GEB support to aid the transition. But again the GEB was unmoved.[64]

Assistance from county, state, and national organizations was certainly appreciated by Brown. Her own fund-raising campaigns also had been relatively successful. The building fund in particular was an excellent example, in Brown's words, of "what a young Negro woman can do." By 1922, it had mushroomed into a campaign seeking $150,000. To the surprise of many, the full amount was obtained, ensuring completion of the long-awaited administration and classroom structure.[65]

The dedication of the Alice Freeman Palmer Building on April 7, 1922, symbolized the diverse themes intertwined in Palmer's success—black and white, northern and southern, public and private, religious and secular. The event was a resounding success. Brown invited many promi-

Alice Freeman Palmer Building (completed in 1922), Palmer's administrative
and classroom facility, circa 1922. Courtesy of Maria Cole; NCDAH.

nent African Americans, Governor Cameron Morrison, and President
Warren G. Harding. Although the occasion drew half a dozen wealthy
northern board members, the only political leader to attend was faithful
educator Thomas Foust. The federal Bureau of Education was represented, and the state forestry agency supplied trees and shrubs to beau-
tify the school. The only major change in plans involved the date of the
event, which was postponed from March to April because of construction delays.[66]

The festivities began with the "national Negro anthem," "Lift Every
Voice and Sing," which Brown adapted as Palmer's song, after which
Reverend John Brice gave the invocation. George Palmer, one of the
main speakers, said his wife "never allowed any distinction of color to
enter into her relations." He commented that Brown was not the only
woman Alice Palmer helped to reach her full potential but that she
ranked as high or higher than most. Following Palmer, William J. Schieffelin spoke, comparing Palmer to Tuskegee and Hampton Institutes.
He urged Americans to live together in peace and to be an example of
equality for the world.

Edward Wharton and Carrie Stone then addressed the gathering.
Wharton discussed the financial status of the structure, stating that
Palmer still owed more than $14,000 on the building. He then intro-
duced Stone as someone with "a bit of good news" regarding the debt.
Stone said she was overcome by the affection of the students and fac-
ulty and offered to pay all of the building's remaining debt. Thus Carrie

Brown in faculty room at Palmer Building, circa 1930.
Courtesy of Maria Cole; NCDAH.

Students in library at Palmer Building, circa 1930.
Courtesy of Maria Cole; NCDAH.

Wellesley Auditorium, site of countless student assemblies,
at Palmer Building, circa 1930. NCDAH.

and Galen Stone generously assured that Palmer's handsome new cen-
terpiece would be free of debt and relieved Brown of an enormous burden. The dedication of the debt-free Palmer Building was one of the
highlights in the history of Palmer.[67]

The imposing Alice Freeman Palmer Building, a two-story Colonial
Revival brick edifice, would have been a welcome addition to any school
or small college in North Carolina. Similar to many new school buildings of its day, such as Raleigh's Murphey School building two blocks
from the governor's mansion, the Palmer Building had a dignified pedi-
mented portico featuring broad steps and four large columns. Inside the
building were offices; fourteen classrooms (five for high school); the
George Close Library, featuring a collection of reproductions of masterpieces; and the 230-seat Wellesley Auditorium. Brown had sold seats
in the auditorium for $3 each. The structure also had modern utilities —
the first indoor plumbing and electricity in Sedalia. Proud of her stylish
new headquarters with its student-made bricks, Brown insisted that it
and the entire campus be well maintained; as she put it, no "earmarks of

Agricultural and vocational classroom at Palmer Building,
circa 1930. Courtesy of Maria Cole; NCDAH.

color" should detract from an aura of propriety. The Palmer Building
clearly marked the beginning of a change in the appearance of the campus from an odd collection of frame houses to an orderly brick campus
suitable for a preparatory school.[68]

At this auspicious juncture, tragedy struck once again. The second
most important building on the campus, Memorial Hall, was destroyed
by fire on April 20, 1922, just thirteen days after the dedication of the
new building. The loss of classrooms and offices did not cause as much
mayhem as the destruction of dormitory rooms and the cafeteria. Sixty
girls lost their belongings and lodging. With the help of Ireland, cots,
mattresses, bureaus, tables, bowls, and pitchers were purchased, and a
section of the Palmer Building was converted into a temporary girls'
dormitory. An old barracks was transformed into a dining facility superior to the former one in Memorial Hall.[69]

Friends of the school responded quickly to Palmer's latest misfortune. Bright, thankful that the fire had not occurred while the girls were
sleeping, promised to do everything she could to get money for Palmer's
operating expenses the next fall. Brown, her staff, and her supporters,
black and white, northern and southern, struggled successfully to keep
the school on its promising course. Because at the time of the fire Brown
was still recuperating from her operation away from the school, Wharton initially suggested "closing school and helping only the graduating

class." This alternative was quickly dismissed, and regardless of the inconveniences caused by the loss of Memorial Hall, Palmer continued to operate. In fact, commencement that year was said to be one of the best in the school's history. Seven students were the first to graduate from Palmer's newly accredited high school, an uncommon status for a black school in North Carolina at that time. With the recognition of accreditation, a fine new building, and a growing corps of friends, Brown was ready to expand the school further. She and key members of the board recognized the importance of making recent gains permanent and secure.[70]

Chapter Six

THE NEW PALMER, 1922–1927

DURING PALMER'S first two decades, an overwhelming majority of white supporters believed in Booker T. Washington's concept that African Americans should accept second-class citizenship, social segregation, and limited industrial and vocational education. But in the 1920s, Brown, supported by such key philanthropists as Galen Stone, slowly began to move Palmer away from industrial training toward a curriculum that made Palmer arguably the finest preparatory school for African Americans in the United States.

Brown's early attempts to include more liberal arts in Palmer's curriculum were met with skepticism. One Greensboro corporate president, H. Smith Richardson, questioned the value of Brown's plan: "My experience with Bennett College and A. & T. scholars has been that by the time they have spent one year at either one of these institutions they are above all hard work." Richardson believed that most blacks required only a limited education that would train them to be good workers. Other Palmer supporters held similar views, including Frances Guthrie. Her approach to African American education was characterized by gradualism. Guthrie felt that Palmer's curriculum should focus on subjects that uplifted students "morally, mentally, and physically." She was convinced that even if Brown's students were taught only the domestic sciences, it would be "a great step in solving the 'great question.'" Brown nevertheless continued to incorporate the higher branches of learning into Palmer's educational programs. Outwardly, however, she seemed to agree with the proponents of limited education. The *Greensboro Daily News* reported that Brown said her objective was to "teach the negro [his]" place in the "industrial life of the south."[1]

By 1922–23, about forty students, mostly girls, attended high school at Palmer, where they enjoyed a solid education as well as extracurricular activities. The sixteen credits required for graduation included four credits each of English and mathematics and two each of science, history, and civics. Elective courses included physics, chemistry, French, and Latin. Classes were small, usually nine to twelve students. The day began at 8:30 A.M. with an hour of devotion and Bible study; academic classes ended before the midday meal at 2:30 P.M. In the late afternoon, pupils devoted ninety minutes to cooking, sewing, agriculture, sports, manual training, and/or dormitory work. Regular classes in manual training were suspended for three years for want of an instructor. Everyone was required to participate in physical exercise of some sort: football, baseball, and tennis for boys and volleyball and exercises for girls. The next year, boys also ran track and girls played basketball, and both attended special dances. Palmer's four years of high school included the ninth through twelfth grades rather than the state's customary eighth through eleventh grades. Brown chose the ninth grade as the first grade in the high school because she had found that many graduates of public grammar schools were not ready for high school, and she used the eighth grade as an intermediate level to enhance individuals' success in upper grades.[2]

Other improvements to the school included standardizing teachers' salaries to meet state requirements and lengthening the school year to nine months in 1921–22. As a result of such changes and the addition of the new science laboratory, Palmer became the only accredited rural high school, black or white, in Guilford County in 1922. Eighty-five of the state's 100 counties lacked accredited rural high schools, and thirty-five counties had no accredited high schools at all. Another addition to the curriculum was a prayer-and-decision week, a combined effort by Bethany Church and Palmer. The purpose of the program was to lead pupils to Christ.[3]

While enhancing Palmer's offerings in order to meet state standards, Brown found that the agricultural program was the most expensive program. Expanding the student body, however, would offset the extra costs. Besides offering new courses, Palmer hired several well-qualified faculty members, including three "A grade college men" for the high school. To receive needed public funds, Brown also asked Ella Brice to prepare a special curriculum for the primary and grammar schools that was acceptable to the Guilford County board of education. These improvements placed Palmer among the finest African American schools in the state.[4]

The 1922–23 academic year was one of the most outstanding in the school's history. The future of Palmer seemed full of promise. Average annual attendance rose to about 250 children, half of whom were board-

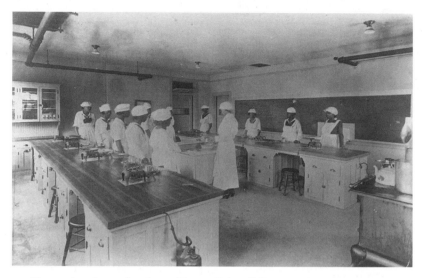

Domestic science class in cooking at Grinnell Cottage, circa 1930. NCDAH.

ers. The staff consisted of thirteen people; all but two did academic or industrial classroom work. The school boasted one of the most modern educational buildings in the state. The course of study covered twelve years, whereas the state only required public schools to provide eleven years of training until 1941. The institute offered elementary school work, a junior high school, and a senior high school. Special departments taught home economics, manual training, and agriculture.[5]

Accomplishing the transition to a liberal arts curriculum involved several steps, the most important of which was gaining the approval of the school's board. The board historically had been composed of a few progressive local blacks, white southerners, and liberal white northerners. Predictably, the African American board members believed that all students had the right to pursue whatever type of education they desired. Most southern white board members held fast to their belief in industrial education for blacks, but Brown with tact and persuasion was able to convince them not to thwart her plan to strengthen Palmer academically. Furthermore, although Galen Stone concurred with her, the bulk of Palmer's northern trustees continued to support educational gradualism.

By the early 1920s, Palmer had secured a reputation as a well-respected center of African American secondary education. To many, and especially to Stone, the only thing that Palmer needed was association with some organization that could assure the institution's future stability. By mid-1921, Brown had spent a great deal of time attempting to stabilize Palmer by associating the school with some funded educational group. Still finding her efforts to obtain funds from the General Education Board fruitless, she turned to the American Missionary Association (AMA). Since the AMA had operated the Bethany school that brought Brown to rural North Carolina, she hoped the organization had some personal interest in the success of her work. Brown informed Stone of her efforts to secure AMA backing. Stone welcomed the idea and agreed to attend a meeting to discuss how to facilitate that goal.[6]

At the meeting, Stone suggested that Brown draw up a proposal for AMA takeover of the school. When completed, she brought the plan before the board, and it was overwhelmingly approved. This set off a chain of events—not always met with enthusiasm by board members such as Edith MacFadden, who thought Brown's methods too abrupt—that eventually resulted in Palmer becoming an AMA school. The only concern was whether the AMA would allow Brown to remain in absolute control of the school. To discuss this matter, Una Connfelt asked that the board meet at her home in New York to determine what terms would be acceptable to resolve the issue.[7]

The AMA, fearful of taking on another school when its existing schools had great needs, agreed to accept the proposal if the school could raise enough money to ensure that no regular AMA funds would be needed for five years. The AMA insisted that in order for it to consider taking Palmer under its wing, a guarantee fund of $150,000 in addition to another $150,000 for operating expenses for a five-year period would have to be raised. After some hesitation, the board began planning how to meet the AMA's $300,000 requirement.[8]

The board's primary concern was the large amount of money the AMA requested. The board asked the AMA to reduce the amount, but no compromise could be reached. After much discussion, the board determined that if the people of Greensboro could raise an additional $2,000 per year for five years, the takeover fund could be completed. Greensboro friends Lula McIver, Edward Wharton, and others agreed to stand by Brown. Some members also suggested that the board employ professional fund-raisers. Stone asked the country's preeminent fund-raiser, John Price Jones, who had collected $10 million for Harvard University, to do a professional feasibility study for Palmer. Jones and his aides concluded that Palmer needed $500,000, including $150,000 for new buildings and equipment, but realistically could expect to get $250,000 or less. The consultants warned against southern resentment of northerners who tried to tell southerners how to handle blacks. Accordingly, Jones recommended different regional appeals: in the North, emphasis on regard for Alice Freeman Palmer and interest in uplifting African Americans; in the South, emphasis on local pride and support for industrial education. For unknown reasons, however, Brown and the board apparently did not continue to employ Jones. The board also considered what would happen to Brown and her position at Palmer after the takeover. Would the AMA treat her fairly? How could she be compensated for years of service without adequate pay? Brown's future treatment was an important issue, and Stone asked that a committee discuss the matter.[9]

At about that time, on October 1, 1923, Brown married her second husband, John William Moses. Details of Moses' life and their romance are sketchy.

Moses was born in 1898 in British Guiana. He enrolled in the agricultural program at Tuskegee Institute in late 1919, listing his occupation as "trading." Tuskegee records do not indicate what formal degrees he earned, if any, although Moses later claimed to have graduated from Oxford University. In any case, he studied at Tuskegee for about two semesters and then went to Palmer in 1921 to teach agriculture.[10]

Moses was described as a very handsome black man with a fondness for the opposite sex. Apparently he had been involved romantically with several women at Palmer and in the surrounding community. One person who had personal contact with Moses referred to him as a smooth-talking black man with much charisma. He dressed elegantly and had a refined taste in jewelry. His romance with Brown began during the summer of 1923 while most of the faculty were on vacation. When the faculty returned for the fall term, Brown told them that Moses had been promoted to business manager. This was astounding news in itself, but Brown's announcement that she and Moses planned to marry was even more of a surprise. Information from Tuskegee indicates that at the time of their marriage Moses was twenty-five years old, although the marriage license listed his age as thirty-six. Brown was forty. Reverend Brice performed the ceremony, with Brown's best friend, Ola Glover, as a witness. After they were married, Brown began to sign her last name "Brown-Moses" and changed her name on the school's letterhead.[11]

The marriage apparently came to an abrupt end after less than a year because of Moses' infidelity. Moses told Brown and a number of faculty members that he was part owner of a diamond mine in South America. After he left supposedly for a business trip to the mine, Brown decided to travel to New York with Glover to meet the ship on which she expected him to return. To her bewilderment, Moses was not aboard the ship. She shortly found out that he owned no mine and had gone to New York to visit another woman. Furthermore, the diamond jewelry he wore was on loan from a wealthy friend in New York. Brown despised dishonesty, and after returning to North Carolina, she never acknowledged Moses as her spouse again. Several months later, Moses had the marriage annulled.[12]

Brown's second divorce and her subsequent illness came at an unfortunate time because she needed all of her faculties to make the AMA campaign a success. Shortly after the marriage ended, Brown wrote: "I've had to abandon all my plans for the campaign and come here to Cambridge for treatment. An attack of ptomaine poisoning so undermined my whole system that the doctor discovered that I was on the verge of nervous prostration and ordered me here." Brown had again worked to the point of exhaustion.[13]

Another factor contributing to Brown's collapse was a fire that destroyed Palmer's Grew Hall on December 12, 1924. The two-story frame building, erected in 1905, housed thirty-one boys. The fire started in the dormitory's heating system and consumed all of the structure's contents, causing a loss of around $10,000. The new Alice Freeman Palmer Building also sustained some damage in the blaze. Citizens and school personnel bravely battled the fierce conflagration. The only injuries were caused by broken glass falling from the new Palmer building. The *Greensboro Daily News* quoted "Charlotte Hawkins-Moses" as saying that she had "never witnessed such heroic efforts as those made to save the main building." This was the fifth building on the campus to burn in recent years, three of which were major losses for the school.[14]

As unnerving as the Grew Hall disaster was, in less than two days, Brown began plans to rebuild. After the board held an emergency meeting, Wharton announced that a special fund had been started to build a new boys' dormitory. The disaster occurred at a time when all of the school's resources and energy were focused on meeting AMA requirements. A temporary structure was nevertheless soon built for some of the boys.[15]

While recovering in Cambridge, Brown continued her efforts to gain the AMA's support. Working despite her doctor's orders to rest, she wrote Charles Eliot: "You may be more interested in our plans to cooperate with the AMA when I tell you that we are to remain independent in a way much like Fisk. We shall retain our board of trustees and the control will be invested in them. The AMA will supervise the funds and make the apportionment. We shall not be bound by doctrines or creeds." After learning that Palmer would retain its independence, Eliot, initially opposed to the AMA idea, became more receptive.[16]

Eliot gradually increased his involvement in fund-raising to meet the AMA requirements. He accepted a position as chairman of a funding committee of Palmer's ten most influential directors. He also agreed to sign a fund-raising letter supporting the $150,000 endowment fund, along with five other longtime supporters and the director of the state's new Division of Negro Education, N. C. Newbold. With Eliot and Stone solidly behind joining the AMA, efforts to raise the various funds required by the association moved forward. The precise names and purposes of the different funds, however, are unknown. The confusion over fund names was perhaps caused by Brown's exuberance in raising the money and her tendency to neglect budgetary details. Such uncertainty persisted in many fund-raising campaigns throughout the history of Palmer and often caused even the school's strongest backers to seek clarification.[17]

A mid-1924 Palmer brochure titled *Some Interesting Facts about Our School* suggested that a "Foundation Fund" of $150,000 was mandated by the AMA. The brochure also stated that the AMA required that the school be free of debt. Stone pledged to match half of the foundation fund in three annual installments. To receive the $75,000, Brown had to raise an equal sum by July 1, 1925. Stone apparently made an identical pledge to the school's building fund during the same period, so it would seem that the foundation and building funds were two separate campaigns. The foundation, guarantee, or warranty fund was apparently a crusade to secure $150,000 to free Palmer from indebtedness and provide money for AMA operation of the school for a five-year period. The $150,000 endowment fund also included money for capital improvements such as in a building, construction, or physical plant fund. Thus, according to the *AMA Annual Report* for 1926, the building and endowment funds were probably the same thing. In fact, the Palmer board and the AMA agreed in late 1924 that the $150,000 could be applied either to structures or to the endowment in any proportion chosen by the board.[18]

Raising the $300,000 was not easy. Large cash donations from Stone and Daisy Bright went a long way toward completing the goal, but without the moral and intellectual support of men such as Eliot, it would not have been possible to collect such a huge sum. Brown requested that Eliot write influential men such as John D. Rockefeller. "Please express in strongest terms your faith in me and the work," Brown asked. After Eliot asked Rockefeller for $25,000, he informed Brown: "I have written Mr. Rockefeller about the merits and achievements of the Palmer Memorial Institute and yourself, and suggested that the Institute is an appropriate object for a gift from Mrs. Rockefeller, himself, or the Laura Spelman Rockefeller Foundation."[19]

By the fall of 1925, over 10,000 letters and 30,000 pieces of printed material had been distributed on behalf of the fund drive. In addition, 5,000 letters were being prepared as part of an intensive campaign in the Boston area to begin in December 1925. All was going well except for one problem: no plans had been made to cover the expenses of the fundraising effort, which had reached $7,500, or the withdrawal or reduction of pledges. Stone later donated an additional $16,500 to cover the costs of solicitation. With funds coming in at an unbelievable rate, Brown exulted in January 1926 in the success of the drive. The school had received more than $150,000 in cash and pledges, as well as pledges for operating costs of around $26,000 per year for five years.[20]

The ability to obtain more than $300,000 in charitable gifts in such a short time reflected not only Brown's remarkable talents and Stone's munificence but also the times. During the 1920s, the gross national product of the United States rose by 40 percent. Wages and salaries increased, while the cost of living remained about the same. Americans spent money as never before. Modern technology made numerous new goods available, and by 1929, around two thirds of all homes had electricity. From 1919 to 1929, the average American had more money to give to charities. Laissez-faire economics continued to be the rule of the day, and social Darwinism reasoned that people must be free to earn and give away wealth. Many contributors to Palmer also believed strongly that their wealth carried a moral imperative. John D. Rockefeller declared: "I believe it is my duty to make money and still more money and to use the money I make for the good of my fellow man according to the dictates of my conscience."[21]

The completion of the AMA campaign was a joyful occasion for Brown and her school. The elation was dampened, however, by the announcement of Stone's resignation as a trustee. Stone's departure, caused by his failing health, was accepted with great regret, and the board elected him an honorary trustee. He left confident that the school he had strengthened would outlast his own life.[22]

After Brown reported that the AMA's financial requirements had been satisfied, the board unanimously adopted resolutions conveying real estate, equipment, and money to the association. The AMA Executive Committee in April 1926 voted that receipt of an official deed would fulfill Palmer's agreement to join the association.[23]

The day after the AMA meeting, Palmer's trustees met to clarify the details of the arrangement. Brown stated that the school owned 250 acres, of which 100 had been promised to the association. Fred L. Brownlee (1883–1962), executive director of the AMA, reported that Palmer money held by the association amounted to $41,124.37 in cash and that Stone was ready to pay his first installment of $25,000. Trustees proposed that the 150 acres not deeded to the AMA be given to Brown and that the AMA purchase her campus home, Canary Cottage, then under construction.[24]

The next order of business was determining the relationship between Palmer and the association. Brownlee assured the board that the AMA takeover would not cause the school to lose its distinctiveness. Palmer Memorial Institute "would be the same, and what the trustees did would largely determine the future policies of the school." The AMA would serve as a "strengthening influence or balance wheel." Brownlee then joined Palmer's board. Other important issues addressed at this meeting were the commencement of a building program and further compensation for Brown's past service.[25]

Brownlee presented the board's recommendations to the AMA in May 1926. Its leaders proposed that a building program be approved and that a building committee be appointed. The AMA agreed to purchase Brown's home for $12,500 and grant her free use of it during her lifetime. The AMA chiefs also suggested that $5,000 be paid to Brown for land she had purchased for the school without compensation and that she be eligible for an annuity upon retirement. The AMA adopted these provisions as full settlement for Brown's prior service.[26]

With the passage of the Palmer resolutions, all that remained to be done was the legal transfer of property. The primary deed was recorded at the Guilford County courthouse on June 2, 1926. The amount of land transferred to the AMA was about 140 acres rather than 100 acres. The recording of the deed officially made Palmer an AMA school, ending several years of effort aimed at securing the future stability of the institution. Thus by mid-1926, the AMA framework was in place, with the understanding that Palmer would be a part of the association but at the same time self-supporting for the ensuing five years.[27]

As an AMA school, Palmer enjoyed the support of a mature organization that sponsored an impressive group of high schools, colleges, and universities. Like Palmer, those schools were maintained to meet the enormous demand for comprehensive education for African Americans. Although Palmer remained independent under its special agreement, the school fit well into the original plan of the association. That plan called for AMA sponsorship of at least one college or university in each of the larger states in the South, graded and normal schools in the principal cities, and common or parochial schools in small villages and rural communities. By the time of Palmer's acceptance by the AMA, the AMA's mission had broadened to include support of rural high schools if such institutions were not maintained by the state. The AMA gradually restricted this concept, however, as the southern states began to provide better public schools for African Americans. The association, not unlike a number of other private charities in various fields, encouraged local governments to expand and replace its programs with publicly funded education.[28]

During the twenty-five years since the AMA had closed Palmer's predecessor, Bethany Institute, many changes had occurred at Palmer and within the association, but similarities persisted. Both adhered to the New England system of education, which was based on academics, culture, and a strong faith in God. Both taught that social elevation and education went hand in hand with Christianity. W. E. B. Du Bois expressed these ideals when he wrote:

> This was the gift of New England to the freed Negro: not alms, but a friend; not cash but character. . . . The teachers in these institutions came not to keep the Negroes in their place, but to raise them out of the defilement of the places where slavery had wallowed them. The colleges they founded were social settlements; homes where the best of the sons of the freedmen came in close sympathetic touch with the best traditions of New England. They lived and ate together, studied and worked, hoped and harkened in the dawning light. In actual formal content their curriculum was doubtless old-fashioned, but in educational power it was supreme, for it was the contact of living souls.[29]

Palmer shared similar goals with other schools in the AMA system and had a comparable mission to promote racial goodwill through education. But Brown had been the lone guiding force in the development of Palmer, whereas other AMA schools had a heritage of generations of AMA-appointed principals. By agreeing to allow Palmer to remain virtually independent within the association, the AMA had cast its lot with one capable, strong, independent woman.

Prior to the AMA's takeover of Palmer, the board had resolved that "a homestead be provided for the Principal consisting of not less than fifty acres," including one acre of land on the "south side of the hard surface road and just west of the main school building."

That plan was amended to allow the trustees to construct Canary Cottage on that acre and give the home and the acre to Brown.

In her hasty fashion, however, Brown already had made arrangements to borrow $5,000 to begin construction. She informed the board that a $10,000 life insurance policy on her protected the school against any loss in case she was unable to fulfill her plans. Once again Brown had pursued an objective without properly consulting the board.[30]

Defending her actions, Brown told the trustees that she knew she could not legally borrow money on the land "until the title was hers, but contemplating this, she had it examined to see how much she could get on it." It was left to the trustees to approve her actions. Before the deed was conveyed to Brown, however, negotiations with the AMA resulted in resolution of the issue in an entirely different manner. Instead of paying Brown $5,000 and giving her Canary Cottage, the association proposed to grant 100 acres to Brown and purchase the principal's home using money from the building fund. Brownlee accepted, and the foundation fund paid $12,500 for that purpose. Most of the money went to the contractor for building the house.[31]

Canary Cottage was a one-and-a-half-story yellow clapboard house with a steep hipped roof, a screened porch at one end, and a rear kitchen. The house was situated about 100 yards west of the Alice Freeman Palmer Building facing the highway in front of the campus. The main entrance included a vestibule with classical details. On the first floor, a stylish living room stretched across the entire front of the house and included a handsome fireplace and a piano. Brown often entertained faculty, students, and visitors there. At various times over the years, a friend, such as Ola Glover or Cecie Jenkins, and children of friends or relatives lived with Brown. Among the children she cared for were her brother Mingo's offspring; Vina Webb; Hoyt Coble, who later ran Palmer's farm; and John Brice's children, whose mother was often away because of her career. Canary Cottage, then, was a lively home near the center of the campus.[32]

In addition to purchasing Canary Cottage, the AMA approved spending up to $100,000 to build a girls' dormitory and a dining hall on the campus. The board hired architect Harry Barton to design the two struc-

Brown in front of her home, Canary Cottage
(completed in 1926), circa 1935. NCDAH.

tures, and construction soon began. In January 1927, the board and the AMA agreed to cover an increased cost of $116,200 and chose May 12–15 as the date for the dedication of the buildings. Unlike the Palmer Building, which took years to complete, the two structures were finished in a matter of months because funds for construction were already in hand. The new dining hall was named Kimball Hall in honor of the Kimball family. Helen Kimball had supported Palmer almost from its beginning. Other members of the family who were honored were Mr. and Mrs. David Kimball of Boston. The girls' dormitory was named Stone Hall in honor of Galen Stone. At first, Stone rejected the proposal, but his wife persuaded him to allow the gesture.[33]

Unfortunately, Stone did not live to see the dedication of Stone Hall. With his death on December 26, 1926, Palmer lost its greatest friend, its largest contributor by an enormous margin, and one of Brown's wisest advisers. Carrie Stone faithfully supported Palmer until her death in 1945. The girls' dormitory became a memorial to Galen Stone, and Carrie Stone continued to work with Brown on plans to dedicate Stone Hall. She wrote: "Your card of invitation to the dedication exercises just received, and one thing about it disturbs me greatly. You have Mr. Stone's whole

Brown and friends at one of the numerous social functions
she held at Canary Cottage, circa 1940s. NCDAH.

name on the card, and I do hope and pray you haven't it on the building, as he would never allow me to use his middle name . . . , so I do hope
you haven't anything more than 'Stone Hall' on the building, or at most
Galen L. Stone Hall." [34]

Robert Gregg Stone attended to the settlement of his father's estate.
To fulfill his father's pledges to Palmer, Stone wrote within days of his
father's death to Palmer and the AMA confirming payment of the remainder of his father's pledge of "$75,000 on the FOUNDATION FUND,"
$25,000 of which already had been paid, and a pledge of "$5,000 per year
for five years on the Current Expenses Fund, $2,500 of the first annual
payment having already been made." His haste in addressing this matter
demonstrated that the Stone family gave Brown and Palmer top priority. Like his father, Robert remained a loyal friend to Palmer for many
years. [35]

Another great loss to Palmer occurred in September 1926 with the
death of Charles Eliot. Although Eliot had never been a large financial
contributor, his endorsement had secured hundreds of friends and
thousands of dollars. Fortunately, the deaths of Stone and Eliot did not
threaten the economic well-being of Palmer as much as the loss of major contributors in the early 1920s had. With funds committed or in

Galen Stone Hall (completed in 1927), the girls' dormitory, circa 1950. NCDAH.

hand, the school continued its projects with little slowdown, and Samuel Eliot and Robert Stone, like their fathers before them, played significant roles in the future of Palmer. Brown had lost two irreplaceable friends, but the growth of the school went on. Brown had apparently heeded Galen Stone's advice that she build an enduring institution not totally dependent on him or any other person.

Stone and Kimball Halls were dedicated in May 1927 during the celebration of the twenty-fifth anniversary of the school. Galen Stone Hall, a two-story Colonial Revival brick dormitory, had thirteen bays of large windows with granite sills. A two-story central portico with white Doric columns was flanked by classical entrance porches at both ends of the building. The building contained dormitory rooms, an office, guest rooms, matron's rooms, a lounge, and bathrooms. Stone Hall had a total living area of about 7,248 square feet on each floor and a full basement. In the basement were the furnace room as well as rooms for recreation, a beauty parlor, a laundry, and a storage area. Kimball Hall, also a Colonial Revival brick structure, contained about 4,735 square feet on the main level. It had a slate roof and a central portico with Doric columns. The main portion of the one-story structure was a large dining hall. For decades, students and faculty practiced their social graces there by having formal meals served by student waiters and hostesses. Many

Kimball Hall (completed in 1927), Palmer's dining
facility, after exterior restoration in 1997. NCDAH.

large parties and social occasions were held there, including staff mixers
with Bennett College. Finally for a time Kimball was the site of evening
glee songs three nights a week, vespers on Wednesdays, and programs
of "jollification" on Saturdays. Behind the dining hall were the kitchen
and serving areas, pantries, and storage rooms. The full basement contained an apartment, a workshop, a band storage room, and two kitch-
ens. To cut costs, Brown used student labor to clear the grounds and
make cement walks. Other physical plant improvements made during
this period included updating the school's water system to protect the
new structures against fire and installing a telephone system.[36]

By the time of the anniversary celebration, Palmer was flourishing.
Current expenses were being met, and although the Sedalia Club had recently disbanded, Palmer had not lost contributors. AMA support was in
place, and the addition of three brick buildings, Canary Cottage, a frame
faculty home for Reverend Brice, and modern utilities had increased the
value of the physical plant. At the end of Palmer's 1926–27 school year,
the AMA reported:

> The year just closed was the banner year for Palmer Memorial. It
> was the twenty-fifth year since the founding of the school and its
> second year under AMA auspices. . . .
>   Notable educators, white and colored, gathered at Sedalia from
> most of the southern states to hear tribute to the founder and
> builder of the Institute, Mrs. Charlotte Hawkins Brown. . . . As a
> cultural center of unusual religious, aesthetic, and intellectual in-

fluence no school is better than Palmer Memorial and few indeed are its equal.[37]

In twenty-five years, Palmer had evolved from a one-room rural school to a cultural center of exceptional intellectual impact. Its student population had increased from around 50 local boys and girls to over 200, including more than 80 boarders. Within a year, Palmer high school students would win a state baseball championship, an interscholastic debating meet, and first place in the state quartet contest. Furthermore, Palmer's faculty had grown from three to over fourteen full-time teachers and staff members.[38]

Not only had Charlotte Hawkins Brown built an impressive and sound educational institution from almost nothing, but she also received many honors and awards. Among them were honorary degrees from Cheyney Normal and Industrial Institute in Cheyney, Pennsylvania, in 1917; Livingstone College in Salisbury, North Carolina, in 1921; North Carolina College for Negroes (now North Carolina Central University) in Durham in 1921; and the National Training School for Women and Girls in Washington, D.C., in 1921. Brown also became one of only seven educators included in Philadelphia's hall of fame at the city's sesquicentennial celebration of American independence in 1926. As a result of her many accomplishments, she was listed in *Who's Who in Colored America* in 1927. Having received such honors and having placed Palmer, her life's work, in safe hands, Brown took a respite for recuperation from her continuing health problems.[39]

Chapter Seven

THE AMA YEARS, 1927–1934

BECOMING AN American Missionary Association (AMA) school placed Palmer on a more permanent foundation and provided stability for the school and its principal. Being relieved of fund-raising and operational responsibilities freed Brown to pursue other interests. At last, after years of self-denial and little financial compensation, Brown had time to rest and take a well-deserved vacation. Board members were very concerned about her health and gladly approved a one-year leave of absence for travel and study in May 1927.[1]

Financially, however, a vacation was not feasible. Brown had not taken much of a salary over the years and had very limited personal savings. Carrie Stone once again came to the rescue. As with her trip to Denver, Brown did not ask for money. Stone offered it after Ethel L. Williams, Palmer's secretary, wrote to her confidentially about Brown's situation.[2]

After much consideration, Brown chose Europe as her destination. Her ship sailed on her forty-fourth birthday, and she toured France, Italy, Germany, Austria, and Switzerland. After returning from Europe, Brown prepared to attend Wellesley College in the fall, where she would refine views about African American uplift that she shared with other well-known African American educators such as her longtime friend Mary McLeod Bethune.[3]

Mary McLeod Bethune (1875–1955) was born in Mayesville, South Carolina, the fifteenth of seventeen children. Unlike Brown, Bethune had no white blood. Bethune's parents and most of her siblings had been slaves. Her education began in 1885 at a local Presbyterian mission school. For six years, she attended Scotia Seminary in Concord, North Carolina, a Presbyterian school combining Christianity, culture, and industrial education. Bethune then went to the Bible Institute for Home and Foreign Missions in Chicago (now Moody Bible Institute), hoping to become an African missionary. After a year, however, she discovered that the organization did not employ African Americans abroad. Disappointed, Bethune nevertheless pursued her goal to teach African American youth, practically the only field open to an educated black woman. For the next five years, she taught in South Carolina and Georgia, closely studying the methods of Brown's heroine Lucy Craft Laney during a year at Laney's Haines Normal and Industrial School in Augusta. Laney was the only African American woman of that era who ran a school comparable in size and stature to the best southern institutions for African Americans.[4]

Like Brown and Laney, Bethune found little time for marriage and family. Although she remained legally married to Albertus Bethune until his death and they had a child, the couple lived together for only about eight years. Bethune's priority was education, which she saw as the best way to achieve racial equality. She founded a Presbyterian school in Palatka, Florida, in 1900 but in two years left to open an independent school there. Two years later, she established a third school for African American girls in Daytona, Florida. Daytona Educational and Industrial Institute (coeducational Bethune-Cookman College after 1923) opened on October 3, 1904, in a rented house. The school was modeled largely on Scotia Seminary. Bethune also operated a large farm to produce food and income. In 1905, Bethune, a black pastor, and several prominent white women formed a board of trustees. Like Brown, Bethune shrewdly gained the support of powerful white businessmen through their wives. Among them was James N. Gamble of Procter and Gamble, who was to Daytona Institute what Galen Stone was to Palmer. By 1922, some 300 girls attended Bethune's school. She stressed the "head-heart-hand" tradition, religion, and industrial education but gradually added courses in business, nursing, teaching, and high school subjects. Brown had her own triad; at Palmer, her educational philosophy encompassed a "triangle of achievement"—students were taught to be "educationally sufficient, culturally secure, and religiously sincere." Bethune was a superb role model, and like Brown, her accomplishments defied the theory of African American inferiority. Her achievements were all the more extraordinary because her very dark skin and notably black features conflicted with the concepts of physical beauty and leadership abilities held by most whites at the time.

Both Brown and Bethune hated racially based social, economic, and political injustice. But Bethune pushed for immediate reform, whereas Brown advocated compromise. Bethune rose above race and gender and overtly defied Jim Crow by insisting on desegregated seating at Daytona Institute. In spite of threats from the Ku Klux Klan, Bethune and her staff voted in elections in 1920 and afterward. But both women were fighting for the same goal—uplift of African Americans. Both sought better opportunities for their people and extended their influence widely in the black community. Aware of their parallel careers, each admired the other. Bethune placed Brown and herself among an elite group: "I think of you and Nannie Burroughs and Lucy Laney and myself as being in the most sacrificing class in our group of women. . . . I have unselfishly given my best, and I thank God that I have lived long enough to see the fruits from it."[5]

Nannie Helen Burroughs (1879–1961), the third of the "three Bs of education" (Brown, Bethune, and Burroughs), was born in Orange, Virginia. Like Laney, Bethune, and Brown, she was dark-skinned, had a commanding personality, and was a spellbinding orator. As a young girl, she moved with her family to Washington, D.C., where she graduated from high school. In 1900, she was instrumental in founding a women's auxiliary in the National Baptist Convention; as its secretary, she helped recruit over a million members in a few years. Burroughs founded the National Training School for Women and Girls in Washington, D.C., in 1909. Her school taught self-help, domestic science, vocational education, and some liberal arts. The institution began with about thirty students. Twenty-five years later, over 2,000 women had been educated in its high school and junior college.

Burroughs emphasized spiritual training at her "school of the 3 Bs . . . Bible, bath, and broom." Like Brown and Bethune, Burroughs played an active role in the African American women's club movement. She remained secretary of the Baptist women's auxiliary for almost fifty years (1900–1948) and then was its president until her death.[6]

By the mid-1920s, the friendship and competition of Brown, Bethune, and Burroughs were well established. The "three Bs," all disciples of Lucy Laney and founders of African American schools, would continue their relationship for decades. Like Laney, all three believed in education as the key to the uplift, Christian morality, and respectability that would empower black women. The trio had close ties to the middle-class African American women striving locally and nationally to improve their communities. All three established schools stressing morality, responsibility, and achievement modeled after Laney's work. All three struggled with race and gender. Never a strong fund-raiser,

The "three Bs of education" (left to right): Nannie Helen Burroughs,
Brown, and Mary McLeod Bethune in front of a statue of
Booker T. Washington at Tuskegee Institute, circa 1940s. NCDAH.

Bethune eventually left the full-time helm of her school to join President Franklin Roosevelt's "black cabinet" in the New Deal. Burroughs, wary of white domination, relied largely on African American support for years but during the Great Depression reluctantly began to court white supporters. Brown, more successful at fund-raising than at becoming the messiah of black America, edged toward the growing African American gentry and transformed Palmer into a cultured preparatory school for their sons and daughters. The "three Bs of education" had lives that were parallel in many ways, but Brown alone had a longtime fascination with elite women's colleges of New England such as Wellesley.[7]

Brown studied at the School of Education and Philosophy at Wellesley for a year after returning from Europe in 1927. She gained entrance to Wellesley mainly through the efforts of George Palmer, a trustee of the college, who wrote that she was "far too important . . . to be placed in a class with . . . immature minds in the graduate school" and requested that Brown be given special status. In response, Wellesley offered Brown a one-year scholarship of $1,000. Palmer also suggested that the college use Brown's expertise as a noted lecturer on education. Brown thus became the first African American to lecture at Wellesley on education.[8]

Brown's studies at Wellesley and her trip to Europe helped foster a change in emphasis at her school in rural North Carolina. After her experience at Wellesley, she brought some of its traditions to Palmer, such as the practice of students standing when instructors entered the room. Visits to schools in Europe also had an impact on cultural aspects of life at Palmer. During her trip, Brown benefited from having the opportunity to discuss her impressions of European education and culture with Bethune.[9]

Bethune was aware of Brown's success in raising funds to join the AMA and asked for her advice on acquiring increased contributions. Brown in turn received counsel from Bethune that was helpful to Palmer. Bethune informed Brown that she had dropped the lower grades at Bethune-Cookman, reducing enrollment by about 135 children. Bethune-Cookman then concentrated solely on its high school and junior college, a strategy similar to that of the evolving AMA. Subsequently, Brown would drop Palmer's elementary school department. Another concept Brown adopted from Bethune was the need to attract a "finer caliber of student" in order to raise scholastic standards. Bethune said she wanted her school "to be very efficient, rather than very large." As a testament of their mutual affection, Brown and Bethune even exchanged portraits, promising to hang them in prominent places to inspire African American youth. Although the lives of Brown and others in her small circle of intimate friends were great inspirations to African Americans, her speeches more than anything else endeared her to a broader public.[10]

By the mid-1920s, one observer considered Brown among "the most forceful, cultured and refined speakers on the American platform." At lectures, she displayed great skill in using language effectively, spoke with a flawless New England accent, and carefully enunciated each syllable. Her appearance onstage was highly dignified, and she captivated the audience with eager, bright eyes. Wealthy student Leslie Lacy later recalled Brown's characteristic presence at key chapel occasions: "From head to shoes she was dressed in perfect taste; even the carnation on her well-tailored white dress was still slightly dripping with dew." She generally addressed three main topics: culture, education, and race relations. Brown firmly believed that once African Americans had been educated in the best of middle-class American culture, the result—as shown by the example of her own life—would be greater acceptance by whites. In her mind, race relations would improve as African Americans learned the concept of doing one's best. Brown based her theory on her Christian principles and attacked segregation and hostile race relations in America. Writer Margaret Slattery called her the chief interpreter to northern whites of the hopes and interests of the educated African American women of America.[11]

In representing the goals of black people, Brown often spoke to white women's clubs. She maintained that white women's experience with African American women mainly was with untrained domestic workers. Through these women, many whites sought to understand all African Americans. But Brown argued that the inarticulate black woman was not "able to interpret the wishes and desires of the women of her race." In Brown's opinion, only educated black women could explain what African American women wanted. Such women, insisted Brown, "must be reckoned with as leaders . . . of their people before any amicable settlement of the trying problem of race" could occur. While informing white women of the existence of a large coalition of educated blacks, Brown demonstrated that African Americans had a rich society. That society, she said, was "not seeking social intermingling but social justice. . . . First, they want equal educational advantages for the children of the black race. Second, they want respectful recognition of their

womanhood . . . by members of the white race. Third, they want cooperation with the white women . . . to make it possible for their children
to have . . . a chance to be cared for while their working mothers are
nursing and caring for the children of the white race." [12]

Brown gained a reputation as an authority on race in America largely
because of her approach to the issue. Like Booker T. Washington, she
did not call for the overthrow of segregated society. She asked only that
African Americans be granted the right to obtain the full benefits of
being Americans through hard work and moral living. The first step was
to become educated; the next step was to become culturally aware. As
an advocate of social equality, Brown saw herself as a progressive American citizen.

Brown viewed culture as an expression of life at its best. Culture was
not a privilege of wealth; large numbers of white "newly rich" and "ignorant well-to-do" people did not have a trace of gentility. Many blacks
also showed little cultural or social refinement. But Brown insisted that
African Americans could acquire culture through study and application.
She felt that cultured whites rejected blacks in nonsegregated environ-
ments because blacks did not pay attention to social amenities. She was
convinced that culture arose from discipline manifested in "ease, grace,
and poise" that resulted in "development of the intellect and appreciation of the aesthetic." [13]

Brown believed that middle-class culture and propriety were attain-
able by all blacks and vital to the eventual resolution of the race question. She maintained that African Americans had not developed culturally because of the struggle for "industrial recognition; the incomparable
efforts to obtain educational advantages; and more than anything else,
the constant battle against race discrimination, unequal opportunity,
[and] unjust segregation." [14]

To Brown, blacks needed culture to attain the American dream. She
believed African Americans required art and asked: "Does the average
Negro have an appreciation for art?" Brown pointed out that copies of
masterpieces could be purchased for as little as two cents. Of music, she
inquired: "Are there many Negroes to whom a real symphony would be
a treat?" As for literature, Brown questioned: "Are not the books we
read a great index to our character, our culture?" Brown believed in the
uplifting power of culture and felt that men and women were the sum
of their habits. Cultural achievement was just another mountain for the
African American to climb. "Our quest," she wrote, "shall not end un-

til we possess the land of the beautiful in music, in literature and art—yea, emphatically, the art of living with one's fellows in the finest and best way." [15]

Brown's doctrine of culture was based on Christian principles. "A refined person," she explained, "is the Master piece of God. A well-seasoned, cultured, refined Christian gentleman or woman is the living statue of the Master Sculptor, God." But many whites did not share her theory of racial uplift and believed in the inferiority of African Americans. Furthermore, they thought God also held this view and did not expect whites to interact with blacks on an equal level. Even in supposedly biracial Sedalia, Palmer students did not see many whites, and little social mingling of the two races occurred. Brown was fully aware of whites' rigid beliefs and fought against discrimination on several occasions. On her own turf, she could be adamant, once upbraiding a white policeman for neglecting to remove his hat in her presence. [16]

According to Brown, the most tragic racial episodes she experienced occurred while she was traveling on Pullman Company trains. Including the incident that led her to sue the company in 1920, she endured much prejudice over the years. In 1936 while traveling in Texas as an officer of a national education association, Brown was again forced to move to the Jim Crow car. In this case, however, the white women with her offered their protection by attempting to pay for all of the seats in the car, but the railroad company refused. [17]

Despite such racist insults, Brown continued to hold up cultural education as a cure for the social ills of America. "I am by nature a fighter," she wrote; "I try to look everybody in the eye as an individual, the handiwork of a just God." She claimed to have no resentment against whites. Nevertheless, for the uplift of her people, she looked beyond segregation: "I have had to accept segregation because my people who need what I have to give live in larger numbers in the land of segregated ideals. But my philosophy is that position or place can never segregate mind or soul. I sit in a Jim Crow car, but my mind keeps company with the kings and queens I have known." As Brown's fame as an educator and lecturer grew, her standing as a proponent of interracial understanding through cultural uplift also increased. [18]

To clarify her approach to African American equality through culture and education, Brown outlined what she thought African Americans should be taught. In a speech to an interracial group in Kentucky, she revealed the concepts that would characterize the remainder of her career. She observed that no geographic utopias existed for African Americans since "our presence in large numbers always sets up a complex difficult to solve." Brown expressed her ideas in verse:

> Our aims are one, our hopes are one,
> And yet they many are;
> We meet to blend our efforts here,
> To view the coming star.
> Its radiance now we may not see,
> But hope on, trust will shine.

On the desire of blacks for education, she wrote:

> Out of the darkness and out of the night
> Has the black man crawled to the dawn of light,
> Beaten by lashes and bound in chains,
> A beast of burden with heart and brains;
> He has come through pain and through woe,
> Yet the cry of his heart is to know, to know![19]

Brown attacked the notion of Nordic superiority and argued that blacks and whites needed the same education. She criticized the public schools of her state for exhibiting substantial funding inequity. She insisted that youth of both races needed equal academic training and proposed various strategies, often centered on cultural correctness, for raising African Americans' self-esteem. At the same time, Brown maintained high educational standards and refused to value self-esteem more than academic accomplishment. She felt that young African Americans were at a point of revolt against un-Christian practices and values and appealed to educators to teach black youth enlightenment, righteousness, social mindedness, and brotherly love. To cultivate learning, discipline, and values at Palmer, she selected teachers with great care.

According to Brown, proper education must include recognition of the student's environment and an understanding of how the student has to adjust to the greater community. Students should be taught to widely apply knowledge gained in the classroom to realities of daily life. They should also learn the importance of self-control and respect for the rights of others. Brown insisted that African American youth had a reserve of power that would be a "veritable dynamo of patience and forbearance" and would one day "beat through chains of race" to break open the doors of opportunity.

Brown saw in African American youth a patience that if developed would result in greater authority. The black race would need such patience to obtain higher scholastic achievement: "To point to one *Carver* . . . will soon become monotonous. . . . One *Du Bois* will soon, having written, write no more." She also forecast a greater need for skilled mechanics and asserted that individual blacks should be educated in areas where they showed promise. Above all, African Americans must stop allowing white people to think for them.

Brown insisted that pride and knowledge benefited any group. She asserted that educators should teach fundamentals of black history and character to "help us to overcome the handicap of race and color in America and develop within the *blackest* youth a pride that no act of prejudice can abase." Brown exulted: "Thank God for [historian] Carter Woodson . . . for helping us find out that we came from somewhere." "Give them [youth] an idea of their capacity," she explained; "have a hall of fame in every Negro school house." Furthermore, blacks must understand the history of other races and know that slavery did not begin or end with them. She demanded "one standard of achievement, one standard of character for white and black alike." Brown advised African American youth to study the white man closely, "his habits of thrift, industry, his dogged determination." Above all, black youth must know God, follow Christ's example, and practice righteousness.[20]

At Palmer, Brown insisted that both students and faculty follow her personal example of emphasizing high standards in education, involvement in social groups, discipline, work, and morality. Energetic, motivated, and capable, Brown was known by midlife for her autocratic, no-nonsense rule of students and teachers. Dignified, stylish, and well dressed, she commanded attention. "You didn't even think, let alone say anything if you disagreed," recalled a student from the 1920s. An instructor of that era remembered that Brown was very strict and corrected even the smallest error on the spot; another colleague arrived for work around 1923 with a short dress and was promptly ordered by Brown to lower her hem. A third new teacher reported to Palmer with a warning from her mother (who knew Brown well) that no one could get along with Palmer's head. Students spanning two decades knew that when Brown adjusted her eyeglasses she was about to express herself forcefully; they recalled her as exceptionally "dynamic" and "very efficient, meticulous, and highly explosive." But Brown, whom the students variously nicknamed "the Big Wheel" and "the Madam," also had a sense of humor and a ready supply of jokes for those who knew her well. When appropriate, she used laughter, earnestness, music, and charm to influence others.[21]

Brown's philosophy also was spread by the Sedalia Singers, who used music to convey Palmer's message of religion and culture. From the school's earliest days, Brown had utilized song to attract people of means to her cause. Music was vital to Brown and very popular at her school. The importance of the Sedalia Singers for publicity and income became clear after their appearance at the Greensboro Municipal Theater in January 1918. As the years passed, their reputation grew in the eastern states. By the late 1920s, the group had raised enough money from concerts to pay for silver utensils for the new dining hall and a bus for travel.[22]

Each year, the singers held a popular spring musical and a Christmas program at the school, attended in later years by both blacks and whites. Among the most memorable special performances was a concert at the White House for President Franklin D. Roosevelt on December 5, 1933. The group also performed at Boston's elegant Symphony Hall and New York's Town Hall from the mid-1920s through the late 1940s. In 1928, one packed concert in Boston yielded over $4,000, four times the return Brown had expected from a dozen concerts at New England churches a few years earlier. Leading patricians in both cities publicly sponsored the events. Some students, such as Ezra Totton, took their first trips outside of North Carolina on buses bound for performances in New York or Boston.[23]

By her forty-eighth birthday, Brown had received national recognition for her efforts on behalf of African Americans. While influential in the North Carolina Federation of Negro Women's Clubs, she led a long drive to create a home for delinquent African American girls at Efland. At that time, the home was one of only a few successful joint efforts by black and white clubwomen in North Carolina. Mrs. T. W. Bickett, widow of the late governor, worked diligently to secure state funding for the home. By that time, Brown was encouraging various state officials to address the race problem. She served, for instance, on a committee planning interracial programs at forty summer schools in North Carolina and Virginia in 1933. In 1934, Governor J. C. B. Ehringhaus (who allowed Palmer to use his name in fund-raising) appointed Brown to a special biracial committee to investigate problems in black education. On such committees, Brown was not afraid quietly to draw attention to perceived injustice, such as when she asked that blacks be appointed

The Sedalia Singers, Palmer's famous singing group that performed
throughout the Northeast and South for many years, circa 1940s.
Courtesy of Bennett College Archives, Holgate Library; NCDAH.

to the state staff of the National Youth Administration, a New Deal
agency.[24]

Growing respect for Brown as an expert on racial affairs and as an ur-
bane, safe, nonradical African American enhanced her reputation and
kept her in demand as a speaker. By 1930, she had spoken in over thirty-
five states and lectured at Mount Holyoke, Smith, Radcliffe, and Wellesley Colleges. Brown at various times was a vice president of the National
Association of Colored Women and a member of the Southern Interracial Commission, the Interracial Committee of the Federal Council
of Churches, an advisory board of the National Urban League, and the
Executive Board of the National Association of Teachers of Colored
Schools. She was the first African American woman elected to the
Twentieth Century Club of Boston and a delegate for the Council of
Congregational Churches of America at a conference in Bournemouth,
England, in 1930. In 1932, Wilberforce University in Ohio gave her an
honorary doctorate. Her résumé of awards marked her as an example of
a highly successful educated African American clubwoman.[25]

Increasing recognition of Brown's achievements brought greater regard for Palmer as an educational institution. Following Bethune's example, Brown proposed adding a two-year college. The AMA had begun planning for higher academic offerings at its schools in the early 1920s and already was establishing a junior college at LeMoyne College (now LeMoyne-Owen College) in Memphis when Brown began seeking AMA support. Her plans matured in 1928 when she convinced James H. Dillard of the Slater Fund to support the creation of a model junior college at Palmer.[26]

Brown informed the AMA's Executive Committee that the trustees had voted to add a junior college. In response, the AMA reluctantly authorized the creation of a department of pageantry, drama, and fine arts. Brown declared that the purpose of the two-year college would be to provide art instruction and training for teachers. The AMA was concerned because Palmer was already $5,000 in debt, however, and the expansion would require at least $7,000 more each year. Thus, the AMA voted to postpone inauguration of the new department until Brown proved that she could secure the additional money.[27]

Patience, however, was not one of Brown's strong points. It was against her nature to put off anything that might increase her school's reputation, so she pushed the AMA for unqualified approval. Again, the association, because of Palmer's unique position, broke with custom and implemented a feasibility study. The AMA instructed Fred Brownlee to work sympathetically with Brown but to keep a careful eye on Palmer's finances. Before completion of the study, however, Brown simply expanded the school by establishing a one-year art program after high school.[28]

As in past years, Brown set out to complete her objective before funds or materials were available. Her faith in God led her to believe that if something was good for Palmer, God would find a way to accomplish it. Brown's preemptive action frustrated the AMA leaders, but they respected her vision and were willing to compromise. They agreed to allow the one-year postsecondary art program to continue.[29]

In 1930, the controversy became heated. Brownlee commanded Brown in April: "The committee *emphatically* instructed me to inform you that for the present promises should be made to *no* one that work beyond the high school grades will be offered . . . next year." By late May, it seemed that Brown and the AMA had agreed that Palmer would not offer courses beyond high school. Nonetheless, Palmer continued its postsecondary art program. Stalling, Brown informed Brownlee that no change could be made until the trustees met again, which would not be for some time because they met only once or twice a year.[30]

In the junior college, the school's musical groups had much success with productions such as the operetta *Betty Lou* in 1931. The college also offered instruction in public speaking and dramatics. The drama department's staging of *The Man Higher Up* in 1931 was well received by reviewers. The junior college gained the admiration of African Americans throughout the United States, and the board suggested that presenting plays and concerts in key cities would lessen the extra expenses of the college. Accepting the idea, Brown took various productions on the road; Palmer's troupe, for instance, performed *The Will and the Way* at Boston's Symphony Hall in 1928. The board also favored establishing a physical education program in the college. Although it generally disapproved of expanding the curriculum, the AMA allowed Palmer another exception since "practically nothing had been done by the other southern Negro colleges" in physical education.[31]

By 1930, the greatly expanded offerings in fine arts enabled Brown to recast Palmer as a finishing school as well as a budding junior college, and the new Palmer began to attract a different type of student. These students were better prepared academically and came from a wider area of the United States and the Caribbean. Brown emphasized culture because she believed that the previous education of blacks in the South lacked appreciation for "truth, beauty, and goodness." She wanted Palmer to be a pioneer in teaching refinement to African American students, a goal she had sought for over twenty-five years.[32]

By the early 1930s, the experience of Palmer students was crystallizing into a characteristic form that would be remembered by three decades of graduates. Brown billed Palmer as a unique preparatory institution, a "distinctive school of Christian culture," and "a little bit of New England in North Carolina." From architecture to academics, she imitated education in New England. The high school department offered a fully accredited course of study with special classes in voice, piano, orchestra, dramatics, and art. Palmer claimed an art collection larger than any similar school in the South. Quartettes and glee clubs for boys and girls sang throughout the state, and the Sedalia Singers performed regularly in northern cities. Students' character and faith were strengthened by weekly prayer meetings, Sunday school and church services, daily and Sunday vespers, and mandatory morning chapel attendance. All students participated in physical education. Boys' teams in

Students dancing a minuet, circa 1930s. Courtesy of Maria Cole; NCDAH.

basketball, football, and baseball competed with other schools' teams, and girls played basketball. Enrollment was deliberately restricted so that students would receive personal attention from advisers and teachers. Boys and girls participated in supervised hikes, parties and socials, and off-campus cultural outings, including a ten-day trip to a northern city for seniors. Although such offerings clearly catered to the growing black middle and upper classes, students who needed to offset expenses could work on campus up to four hours a day as groundskeepers, janitors, farmhands, or kitchen and dining hall help.

Undoubtedly, Brown added a fine arts program and a junior college partly out of sheer stubbornness—and her desire to keep up with Bethune and Burroughs—but her motives also were idealistic. Brown wanted to provide cultural training to select African American youth who would share that culture with other groups. Such a concept mirrored the social theories of W. E. B. Du Bois and others. Brown wanted to educate a "talented tenth" of African Americans so that they could train the masses in cultural matters.[33]

The issue of cultural training symbolized a broader dispute over who controlled Palmer, Brown or the AMA. In the end, Brown emerged as the unquestioned leader of her school, sacrificing Palmer's affiliation with the association to retain control. Why didn't the AMA want Palmer to establish a junior college? Besides factors involving power and personality, an answer can be found in the times during which the conflict occurred.

Students costumed for one of the numerous
dramas presented at Palmer, circa 1940. NCDAH.

The Pirates, Palmer's baseball team, circa 1930s. NCDAH.

The Great Depression, which began with the shocking stock market crash of late 1929, brought an end to much charitable giving and clearly influenced the AMA's decision. The depression hurt schools and other institutions across the country, but southern African American schools bore an especially heavy burden. Nearly all construction of new schools stopped, staffs were reduced, and salaries for survivors shrank. Already minimal resources were cut even further. When the depression threatened the existence of a number of its schools, the AMA no doubt felt justified in refusing to expand programs at Palmer. Brown faced serious financial challenges as well: by early 1933, spring contributions had decreased by half, and she shortly had to take out a $10,000 mortgage (for which a friend paid yearly interest) from Greensboro's Jefferson Standard Life Insurance Company.[34]

Although the association opposed adding new classes, it approved a small supplement to funds previously raised by Brown for the construction of more buildings. In 1928, Brown asked the AMA for permission to build faculty housing. The trustees requested $5,000 from the "foundation fund" to erect two cottages for married teachers. The AMA's Executive Committee asked that plans be drawn up and estimates secured. When actual expenses exceeded the original request by about $2,700, the association approved the additional funds. The new cottages were named Brightside Cottage in honor of Daisy Bright and Gregg Cottage in honor of Robert Gregg Stone.[35]

Brown continued to push for expansion of the physical plant. To finally fulfill her dream of having a school that taught academics, culture, and the dignity of labor as the prerequisites for living life at its best, Brown had to achieve two essential aims. The first was to build a boys' dormitory, which would be named for Charles W. Eliot. The second was to establish a $100,000 endowment fund to stabilize Palmer, the George Herbert Palmer Memorial Fund. To raise money for these two goals in New York and New England, supporters of Palmer (including old Sedalia Club members) formed the New England Committee.[36]

To spearhead her current campaigns and chair that committee, Brown recruited Samuel A. Eliot, son of Charles Eliot. She had approached Eliot in late 1927, but his response was tentative. Like his father, he declined to endorse Palmer publicly before seeing it. Brown arranged a visit, after which Eliot endorsed the school, accepted a five-year term as trustee, and began soliciting for the Charles W. Eliot Fund. In one of his first appeals to New Englanders, Eliot wrote that his father had been keenly interested in Brown's plans and had been her counselor in the early days of the school.[37]

Meanwhile, Brown announced in May 1929 that she had received over $10,000 in pledges toward the proposed $50,000 goal for the construction of the boys' dormitory. During the first year of the campaign, she increased the target to $100,000. In past years, Brown had notable success in fund-raising, but this campaign was decidedly different despite the greater stature of the school because of its AMA membership. From the beginning of the venture in 1928 until 1933, the association collected a mere $7,222 for the Eliot fund. This sluggish progress was the result of the onset of the Great Depression more than anything else; when jobs were scarce and people were hungry, capital campaigns were not attractive to donors.[38]

In addition to funds for the new boys' dormitory, Brown continued to collect money for other purposes. She was optimistic that she could complete the Eliot fund because the school continued to receive contributions from longtime supporters, including a contingent bequest of $100,000. She declared that "not withstanding the depression, I believe . . . the people of New England [will send] a few hundred checks of small denominations." Although many other schools were closing and facing increased problems with the AMA, Brown persisted in her struggle armed only with her strong faith that God would sustain the school. Relating to Eliot her financial troubles and growing problems with the association, Brown wrote confidently, "I've just passed my fiftieth birthday but I am . . . full of enthusiasm and can go on."[39]

Brown wrote these words a number of months after fire again struck Palmer and on October 31, 1932, destroyed its main residence for boys. Grinnell Cottage, originally the girls' home economics building, had been used as a dormitory for some boys since the Grew Hall fire of 1924. The eighteen-room wooden frame building housed forty students, three single teachers, and a married couple. The fire was discovered around 6:30 P.M. as students were leaving the dining room. Despite efforts by fire companies from Greensboro and Gibsonville, students, and community residents to contain the fire, the structure burned down completely in forty minutes. Brown's greatest fear was realized when wind began to blow flames toward Stone Hall. As workers began to wet down the girls' dormitory, it started to rain. Brown believed that the providential rain saved Stone Hall.[40]

Brown immediately took charge of dealing with the aftermath of the blaze. She was the only member of the board's depleted Executive Committee able to do so. Edward Wharton and Charles Ireland had passed away earlier that year, Daisy Bright was in New York, and Brownlee was tending to AMA business. Teachers went to town to purchase emergency supplies ranging from shoes and overalls to toothpaste and combs. Despite the great commotion, meals and classes went on the next day as scheduled; Brown had experience with fires and acted quickly to restore normalcy. Students remained undaunted, verifying Brown's claim that she had taught them "how to meet disaster with their head unbowed except to God." To create emergency living quarters, she moved girls and female teachers to the second floor of Stone Hall and housed boys and male teachers on the first floor. The Palmer Building also was used as makeshift housing, and the old barracks, about to be torn down, was remodeled for housing boys for about $650. Brown commended "young white men whose parents were my friends" for collecting clothing for the students. She asked the AMA for emergency aid, but before any funds arrived, she borrowed $500 from a local bank to buy supplies. At least $1,000 more was required, however, and she urged the AMA to send money from Palmer's building fund. This disbursement nearly consumed the rest of the $150,000 building fund.[41]

After the loss of the last remaining wooden building from the old campus, Brown recommended to the AMA that bills from the fire be paid out of insurance, that the remaining money be applied to the building fund for the boys' dormitory, and that the board of trustees, which had been dormant since the AMA took over control of the school, be reorganized immediately. She pushed for immediate construction of the new boys' dormitory and asked the directors to consult architect Harry Barton to see what could be built for $30,000. Remarkably, by the summer of 1933, Eliot Hall was already under construction.[42]

During this crisis, the relationship between the AMA and Brown continued to deteriorate. She confided to Eliot: "Well, the a.m.a. has closed some of its schools, discontinued others and cut us 41% with the understanding that if Sedalia is to go on it must find its [own] support. . . . I haven't been altogether happy under the [AMA] relationship, because they did not wholly fulfill their promises and I had to raise ⅔ of the budget."[43]

Brown had secured much of the money to begin construction of the boys' dormitory herself. She wrote Eliot: "By the way aren't you happy to know that $20,000 worth of Eliot Hall is being built this summer? . . . It will be complete enough to house 40 boys. Building is cheaper now and we are really getting fully half of it completed." During the depression, building costs were substantially lower than they had been before the depression. Brown expected to build two-thirds of the structure for approximately $20,000, about $7,700 of which she had raised. The AMA had pledged to cover the rest. It is not known whether any free labor or materials were used, as with the Palmer Building.[44]

The new structure was originally projected to be a mirror image of Stone Hall. Brown sent a copy of Barton's plans to Eliot, indicating that everything but the left (south) third of the structure "will be finished from exterior by October 1, 1933." Soon the new boys' home was ready for use. The two-story brick building with its slate hip roof, dormers, eight bays of windows, and classical portico with large Doric columns sat at the western edge of the main campus, separated from Stone Hall by Brown's home and several other structures.[45]

The dedication ceremony in April 1934 was part of Palmer's thirty-third anniversary celebration. Frank Porter Graham, president of the University of North Carolina at Chapel Hill, presided at the program. Mary E. Woolley, president of Mount Holyoke College in Massachusetts, was the keynote speaker. Woolley characterized Charles Eliot as a "cultured man with the power of great thought" and urged the students to see him as a role model and become "Enlargers of the Common Life."[46]

By this time, the conflict with the AMA appeared irreconcilable. Al-

Charles W. Eliot Hall (completed in 1934), the boys'
dormitory, in 1947. Courtesy of Griffith Davis; NCDAH.

though a variety of factors contributed to the split, Carrie Stone summed
up the key problem: the inability of the two major players, Brown and
Brownlee, to cooperate. Recognizing that both leaders had dominant
personalities and a need to be in control, Stone confided to Eliot that
"what Charlotte tells about the A.M.A. is not the story that I get from
them, and evidently they are not able to work together, which seems a
great pity. One can hardly blame her for wanting to run her school in her
own way, but if she is not able to raise the necessary funds, it might seem
wise to take another's advice."[47] Finally the AMA Executive Committee,
led by Brownlee, recommended that Palmer be separated from the AMA.

In February 1933, a special subcommittee of the AMA Executive
Committee reported "certain administrative problems" at Palmer, and
the Executive Committee asked Brownlee to confer with counsel on
how to restore Palmer to independence. Brown would not allow her
school to be controlled by the needs of other AMA schools. Because of
Brown's inability to develop a workable relationship with the AMA, the
AMA considered it "not only wise, but also just" to return Palmer to its
board. The AMA also saw Palmer as an unnecessary risk because of the
devastating effect of the Great Depression on the association. During
1933, the AMA's income dropped by nearly $350,000, a large percentage
of its budget, and it was forced to close some of its older, less trouble-

some schools for lack of funds. Brownlee tried to comfort Brown by reminding her that Palmer was not the only school affected by the depression.[48]

In May 1933, Brownlee informed Brown that workers at Palmer would not get new contracts from the AMA. Brown "didn't have a dollar for the next year's Budget" and asked the AMA to consider other options before withdrawing aid. The AMA reviewed the matter in June but decided to end support. To give Palmer special privileges would cause great misunderstanding within the AMA system, especially among other secondary schools, and the association's leaders felt it had been a mistake to take over Palmer in the first place.[49]

Although the AMA admitted its error, it wanted everyone to know that it had taken on Palmer with the best of intentions. In like manner, before deciding to return Palmer to its trustees, the AMA considered five alternatives:

1. Mrs. Brown might be removed from the principalship. This was dismissed as a procedure neither wise nor just.
2. The school might be closed. This procedure was also rejected on much the same ground.
3. The school might be returned to the Trustees. This action was, for the moment, set aside in face of the attitude which has been alluded to above.
4. A new basis of understanding between the principal and the a.m.a. Administrative Committee might be sought. This did not seem to offer a practical solution.
5. The school might be leased to Mrs. Brown for a nominal sum, to be conducted as might seem wise to her, the a.m.a. holding the property.[50]

During the June meeting, the AMA leaders agreed to lease Palmer to Brown. After the session, however, legal complications arose, and the AMA chose to return the institute to its trustees. To prepare for this, Brown called a meeting of the directors in New York. She also contacted major longtime contributors and former trustees and found some, particularly members of the Stone family, very amenable to independence. Regaining this status was not immediately possible, however, because the board had not met as a body for several years and was not prepared to assume such a large responsibility.[51]

Recognizing this situation, the AMA Executive Committee revisited the question of what was best for itself and Palmer in September. It

agreed to continue to operate Palmer for one more year while Brown reorganized the board and to allow Brown freedom to manage the school.
In that interim, it would contribute $7,000, about one-sixth of Palmer's
annual budget.[52]

To prepare for the break, Brown called on Frank Hobgood, her old
friend and attorney, and asked him to chair the new board. "I need you
as much now as I needed you in 1906," she implored, "for it seems that
I am starting all over again." She beseeched him to stand behind her to
show the AMA that she had support. What Brown needed most was a
large group of influential supporters to prove that she was not friend-
less. To increase this base, Brown asked Frank Porter Graham to join
the school's board and wrote: "The school was absolutely independent
over a period of twenty-seven years, but . . . at my suggestion the trustees . . . agreed to deed our property to the American Missionary Association . . . on the condition that they were going to assume largely the
financial obligations of the school." Brown had hoped to be released
from fund-raising activities once the AMA took over the school so that
she could strengthen Palmer's academics and work to improve southern
race relations. But this had not been the case, and during the years of
AMA control, Brown had lost several important contributors.[53]

Brown knew that to reestablish a credible board she needed influential men. In the South, Hobgood and Graham served as a firm foundation. In the North, too, a solid base was crucial. To rebuild it, Brown
wrote to her friend Eliot about the impending separation. In response,
he asked the president of the AMA, William Horace Day, to lend his
name to fund-raising efforts for the school. Fearing embarrassment to
the AMA, Day declined. Brown then gave Eliot a fuller explanation of the
break, admitting that the cause was more a matter of conflicting personalities than of finances. She implied that Brownlee resented her promi-
nence in public affairs.[54]

Despite the fact that the AMA had decided to withdraw its support,
Brown attempted to maintain good relations with the association as she
worked to rebuild a strong, effective board. The rejuvenated body included old friends such as Eliot, Hobgood, James Dillard, R. R. Moton,
Elizabeth MacMahon, Daisy Bright, Cyrus R. Wharton (Cyrus A.'s son),
John Brice, and Julius W. Cone. New additions, both African American
and white, included Graham; W. C. Jackson, dean of the School of Public Administration at the University of North Carolina at Chapel Hill;
Mordecai W. Johnson, president of Howard University; Oscar DePriest,
business executive and congressman from Illinois; May B. Belcher, ex-

ecutive secretary of the Young Women's Christian Association of Indianapolis; E. R. Merrick, executive officer of the North Carolina Mutual Life Insurance Company; James Weldon Johnson, author and professor at Fisk University; J. W. Burke, banker and Guilford County school board member; E. C. McLean, landowner in the Sedalia area; and Channing H. Tobias, senior secretary of the Colored Men's Department of the National Council of the Young Men's Christian Association. With much of the work of reorganizing the board behind her by early 1934, Brown trusted that Palmer's reputation would draw support from people all over the country.[55]

Many positive things had been accomplished during the AMA's control of Palmer. The school had survived the depression and actually had improved in a number of ways. All of the original wooden buildings had been replaced by modern brick structures. More than half of the 200 or so students were boarders, some from as far away as Massachusetts, New Jersey, and Pennsylvania. About eighty students were in high school, and over forty were in junior college. The Alice Freeman Palmer Building was still crowded with elementary school children, who comprised about three-fourths of the day students. By 1934, the school's property was valued at $500,000 and its annual operating budget was about $40,000. More than 75 percent of those funds had been raised by Brown and her trustees. In addition to this growth, Palmer enjoyed overall stability in its faculty population.[56]

With the new curriculum in place and the first junior college class about to graduate, Brown looked forward to institutionalizing Palmer's gains and becoming more involved in the wider world. She had many resources and supporters on which to draw, but Palmer's future stability was by no means assured in a changing, uncertain world.[57]

Chapter Eight

INDEPENDENCE AND STABILITY,
1934–1952

AFTER BROWN rebuilt Palmer's board in preparation for the American Missionary Association's (AMA) withdrawal of support, the school was ready for the return of its real estate. On November 27, 1934, the AMA conveyed all of its property in Sedalia, except for the Bethany Church lot, to the school's trustees.[1]

Although property ownership was a major part of independence, Palmer's survival hinged on Brown's ability to secure money to operate the school. Thus, long before the land transaction was completed, Brown began taking measures to ensure the future of the school. The Sedalia Singers increased the number of their performances, and Brown started to travel with them more often to take advantage of the opportunity to solicit contributions. But income from these performances alone was not nearly enough to operate Palmer. The school's proposed budget for 1934–35, although reduced from the AMA days, remained a substantial $31,292. Brown thus continued to rely on her remarkable ability to attract devoted and dependable contributors. Another source of modest additional revenue was investment in annuities. The board gave trustee Leslie R. Rounds, who advised the AMA regarding annuities, the responsibility for maximizing those investments. One more bright spot in the cloudy economic future was the fact that Samuel Eliot, chairman of the Palmer Fund, remained optimistic that the campaign for a $100,000 endowment would be successful.[2]

Eliot was so sure that Palmer would be able to count on income from the endowment as a continuing asset that he recommended setting up a committee to monitor the school's money. Aware of Brown's tendency to spend money but not wanting to cause hard feelings, he wrote Hobgood that he had "confidence in Mrs. Brown's integrity" but that he knew of the "temptation that a Head Master is under in the natural desire to strengthen the teaching body and to improve the plant." Eliot never doubted Brown's ability to raise funds, however, even during the Great Depression. In fact, he had witnessed Brown secure $5,000 in less than a month to clear up Palmer's current debt.[3]

Another method Brown used to increase donations was to enlist the support of national figures. The most notable were President and Mrs. Franklin Roosevelt, but that effort fell somewhat short of her hopes. Although the Roosevelts were willing to be honorary sponsors of the Palmer Fund and to permit the Sedalia Singers to perform at the White House, they declined invitations to attend public functions for Palmer to avoid any suggestion of their personal endorsement. Eleanor Roosevelt explained that she feared her participation at such gatherings would offend other deserving institutions.[4]

Among the important sources of income for Palmer were the Phelps-Stokes Fund and the Slater Fund. Although their contributions were small, they were an essential part of Palmer's budget. Over the years, such gifts, along with those of southern white supporters, totaled between $50,000 and $100,000. The Guilford County school board was also a dependable source of funding prior to 1937 and for several years paid Palmer some $3,000 annually.

Despite the problems that Brown faced during these years, life continued as usual on Palmer's campus. The school's academic reputation grew in North Carolina, in New England, and along the east coast. Increasing numbers of children from middle-class families added their names to the waiting list. The start of the 1935–36 school year, the first without the AMA, marked the beginning of a new era at Palmer. The institute boasted an impressive interracial board of trustees. Nine of twenty-six directors were black, and twenty were from outside North Carolina. Eight people, mainly older supporters such as Daisy Bright, Carrie Stone, and Lula McIver, were designated honorary trustees. Of some two dozen instructors, all were African American, nearly all were four-year college graduates, and eight held master's degrees. Most had studied at African American schools, but two held graduate degrees from the University of Pennsylvania.[5]

With AMA support gone and new directors, faculty, and staff in place, Brown felt that she was beginning her school all over again. This feeling carried over into her perception of Palmer's role in the uplift not just of the "talented tenth" but of all African Americans. Although in previous years she had acknowledged the importance of manners and cultural training in solving the "Negro question," Brown pronounced such beliefs much more forcefully after 1934. By this time, several conservative older supporters, such as Frances Guthrie, were merely honorary directors. Brown no longer tailored her views to the wishes of proponents of industrial education. At this point in her career, she felt comfortable about her approach to African American uplift and put into play her concept of uplift through cultural education. To announce the opening of the new Palmer, Brown advertised her school as the "School of Personal Charm."[6]

Palmer, however, was not merely a finishing school; it offered Brown's own mixture of Washingtonian and Du Boisian education flavored with a strong Christian emphasis and her version of New England preparatory training. Annual student costs were about $212 a year, in addition to $36 for optional music lessons, and all students worked one hour a day to "dignify toil of the hands." A few needy students did extra work for pay but did not carry a full academic load, some laboring on Palmer's 120-acre farm, which raised food for the school. The accredited high school had a term of 180 days and a curriculum that focused on classical and scientific subjects, recalling Brown's Cambridge schooling. Classes included Latin, French, and English; algebra and geometry; biology, chemistry, and physics; U.S. and world history; geography; agriculture; home economics; and industrial arts. The junior college offered classes in fine arts, history, science, math, English, French, education, and physical education. Elementary school training continued as well.

Resident students were required to attend weekly religion classes, church on Sunday, and daily chapel services. Faculty advisers aided students in developing knowledge, character, and cultural awareness. Brown, who shared her 1,000-volume library with the surrounding community and faculty members, periodically held open houses for the students and local residents. The school offered a wide range of clubs, athletics, and activities for its carefully chosen students.[7]

As Palmer students became increasingly upper class, Brown continued to push for adequate public education for all African Americans. She provided scholarships for a few local children at Palmer but encouraged the county to take on the responsibility of educating the masses. Since Palmer was becoming ever more selective and attracting an increasing number of students from out of state, a great need arose for a black public high school in rural Guilford County. This shortfall reflected a statewide paucity of good high schools for minorities, particularly in rural areas.

About a decade earlier, besides Palmer, there were only about eigh-

Reverend John Brice, vice principal of Palmer and pastor of Bethany Church, greeting students at the church door, 1947. Courtesy of Griffith Davis; NCDAH.

teen other private schools and colleges for African Americans in North Carolina, but only seven black high schools were accredited, four of them associated with colleges. The state set up a few normal school courses to train African American teachers at black state colleges and created a Division of Negro Education. Some private black colleges offered courses to train high school teachers. A few private black high schools offered a one-year course for elementary teacher training. To encourage such courses, the state paid the salary of one teacher at each cooperating institution. But most African American high school students were still enrolled in secondary departments of state colleges or private schools. Rural African American public schools doing secondary work at that time were called county training schools because one of their main purposes was to provide elementary teacher training. During the 1930s, citizens and school officials continued to request that the counties establish more and better high schools for blacks. Brown had been pushing the Guilford school board to do just that for some time.[8]

For four decades, starting in 1905, Guilford County supported only limited high school training for rural blacks. As early as 1909, Brown appeared before the school board seeking a rural black high school, but her request was "filed for future reference." Brown approached the board again in 1918, and it again promised to consider her plea. At that time, the school board paid for some teachers' salaries and school desks at Palmer. Eight years later, the board, still unwilling to establish a new school, agreed to pay transportation costs for a few students attending Palmer; before long, the board also covered their tuition. One excuse for the continuing inequality in black education was the declining percentage of African Americans in rural Guilford. The board had difficulty justifying the creation of a new segregated high school for such a dispersed population. By paying for a few students to attend such schools as Palmer, the high school branch of Bennett College, and public Dudley High School in Greensboro, the board could meet some of its responsibilities without incurring any capital expenses.[9]

As late as 1935, Guilford had not established a rural high school for African Americans and merely continued to pay tuition for some students to attend other black schools. Of the private schools, only Palmer was accredited, and it offered a better education than the white rural public high schools. Then the State School Commission notified Guilford that it would not continue funding for African American high school teachers in 1935–36. Brown appealed to the school board not to deprive black students of a full secondary education. Reviewing her petition, the board made an exception for Palmer. Although Palmer continued to receive county funds, Brown still insisted on the necessity of a public high school in Sedalia.[10]

Brown's efforts to secure a public high school for African Americans in Sedalia received little serious attention until the mid-1930s, when the State School Commission finally decided to establish rural high schools for African Americans throughout North Carolina. The school board chose Gibsonville in eastern Guilford County as the site for such a school. Learning of this, Brown used her influence with prominent whites to persuade the school board to recommend that the school be located in Sedalia instead. One such ally was J. W. Burke, a Guilford County commissioner and a resident of Gibsonville. Burke felt that Gibsonville was too close to Alamance County and favored Sedalia because of its more central location. Furthermore, he argued that black children would get a better education "in an atmosphere created by The Palmer Memorial Institute."[11]

Brown also enlisted the assistance of Frank Porter Graham, explaining that Palmer's atmosphere was "conducive to the best ideals in education." Graham immediately recommended Sedalia to the state commission. On August 9, 1935, after considering Graham's input and the comments of a delegation from Sedalia, the commission chose Sedalia as the site for the school.

Brown knew that her victory meant that Palmer would lose more than $3,000 in public funds after the new school opened. She recognized that some additional means of support must be found for Palmer, which, because of the continuing depression, would lose some 500 donors in the next three years.[12]

First Brown attempted to convince the Guilford board to contribute $10,000 toward Palmer's operating budget for the 1936–37 school year. The board rejected her plan. As a result, she was forced to find another means to fill the void in the school's budget left by the withdrawal of county funds. Acquiring a source of stable funding, advocated years earlier by Galen Stone, had become an obsession for Brown.[13]

Declining health and advancing age also motivated Brown in her ceaseless search for permanent funding. By 1936, she was fifty-three and faced repeated illnesses, typically following periods of great stress. Brown knew that she had been largely responsible for Palmer's progress and that without her guiding hand, the school would have closed. Brown thus attempted to develop strategies to guarantee that her "air castle" would remain firmly planted on its earthly foundation.

One proposal was that Palmer become the State College for Negro Women, which would be part of a black university system that paralleled North Carolina's white university system. The concept seemed so promising to Brown that she abandoned efforts to retain county school funds by providing agricultural and industrial training for the future public high school.[14]

Brown knew that segregation would continue for years and that institutions such as Palmer, with a reputation for interracial goodwill, would fare better than other less benign institutions in a segregated environment. She realized that she had to choose the people she shared her ideas with carefully. In a letter to state official N. C. Newbold, she wrote, "We had better get all of our institutions in line within the next four or five years." Brown believed Newbold understood the "Negro question" better than anybody she knew, except for James Dillard, and wanted to enact her proposed changes while Newbold was still in office.[15]

Brown suggested to Newbold that the black university system be composed of the North Carolina Agricultural and Technical College in Greensboro, the North Carolina College for Negroes in Durham, and the State College for Negro Women, which Palmer would become. Winston-Salem Teachers College and similar schools in Fayetteville and Elizabeth City would continue to train elementary teachers. By sharing this blueprint with Newbold, Brown hoped to place Palmer in a position of favor. She dreamed of Palmer's becoming the black counterpart to the white state women's college in Greensboro and of herself as its first president. Who would be better qualified for the position? Besides, Palmer was her school, and in what better way could she preserve its future than by transforming it into a state college?[16]

Brown thought of her vision of an African American university system as a prophecy and of herself as a founding pioneer. She wanted to ensure a place for herself in that vision. She believed that a black women's college would complete the program of African American education in North Carolina. Such a college was needed for the "exclusive development of the young women," she proclaimed to Graham. Brown hoped that Palmer's reputation for interracial goodwill, along with her personal influence, would convince Graham, Newbold, and other officials to support her proposal.[17]

Furthermore, Brown was so determined that Palmer become a state women's college that she attempted to prevent the selection of other African American schools. Brown warned Graham that although "Mr. Newbold is interested in me," he might prefer the Methodist Episcopal Church's Bennett College in Greensboro because it was at "this end of the state." Brown suggested that Graham respond that "all people do not want to send their children to denominational schools." She went on to point out that most African Americans were too poor to transport their children across the state to schools such as that at Elizabeth City.[18]

Brown was so excited at the prospect of transforming Palmer into a black women's college that she did not care precisely "what kind of state institution" it became. If it professed "high vocational ideals," she told Graham, she would compensate by providing a strong cultural background as its president for eight or ten years, after which she was confident that her influence would not be forgotten. Aware that she must have sounded egotistical to Graham, Brown explained, "I have just got to express out of my soul what I feel to somebody who knows that my whole life has been dedicated to my people."[19]

In the midst of these negotiations, however, a series of events interrupted Brown's professional life. The opening of the public high school in Sedalia in 1937 and the deaths of Brown's close friend, Ola Glover, and her mother, Carrie Willis, in 1938 reinforced Brown's conviction that Palmer needed institutional stability.[20]

The opening of the Sedalia public school, which actually incorporated eleven grades, had an immeasurable impact on Palmer. Prior to 1937, most children in the area had received their education at Palmer, where the student body had consisted of mostly day students. Once the new school opened, however, nearly all of the local children, generally in elementary grades, became pupils of the free public school. The Sedalia school, built next to Palmer and across from Bethany Church, initially had six teachers, including William Henry Lanier (1898–1975), valedictorian at Palmer in 1922. Lanier had earned a degree at Lincoln University in Pennsylvania and had taught school in Lexington, North Carolina. In Sedalia, he lived at Palmer and assisted its football coach while teaching science and math at the public school. Brown welcomed the new school, for she had long advocated public responsibility for education. The presence of the school changed Palmer into a boarding high school and junior college. It thus gave Brown the opportunity to offer students more personal support and guidance, college preparatory work, and cultural training.

Since Palmer students were under the supervision of the staff day and night, they were required to observe Brown's rules of social conduct virtually without interruption. Brown was also able to experiment with varied educational techniques for training future leaders from upper-class African American families. Field trips to mills and factories, universities, the state prison, banks, and housing projects enlightened students. Palmer became a small community where pupils and teachers experienced academics, religion, fine arts, athletics, clubs, and dormitory life together. Brown required memorization and practice in public speaking. Once, when she discovered that students were having problems

Brown and children at the piano in Canary
Cottage, 1947. Courtesy of Griffith Davis; NCDAH.

with high school–level work, she canceled classes for a day so that
teachers could test all pupils for competency in spelling, grammar, and
related subjects. Only 19 of 115 students passed. Consequently, Brown
suspended regular classes for two weeks of concentrated remedial work.
Later help was tailored to individual need. On another occasion, Brown
replaced seniors' regular schedule with three-hour classes in two subjects a day for nine-week periods. Clearly, the coming of the public school

Dance group in Wellesley Auditorium, 1947. Courtesy of Griffith Davis; NCDAH.

greatly affected Brown and Palmer and allowed the school to evolve into its final form.[21]

The other major events that occurred at this time were the deaths of two of the most important people in Brown's life: her close friend and companion, Ola Glover, and her mother, Carrie Willis. Glover had been a reliable, understanding, and unselfish housemate and associate on whom Brown had depended for many years. Although Glover had been ill for some time, her death came as a great blow to Brown. Brown's grief was compounded by the fact that her mother was critically ill in the same hospital.[22]

The death of Brown's mother was an irreparable loss. After Carrie Willis became seriously ill in the summer of 1937, Brown rushed to her bedside in Cambridge. She spent July and part of August taking care of her mother, whose condition began to improve. Willis's health deteriorated severely that fall, however, and Brown moved her to Canary Cottage. She continued to decline and was hospitalized in Greensboro during the Christmas holidays. On April 9, 1938, Brown's mother died at the age of seventy-three.[23]

These two deaths so close to each other in time left Brown lonely and

Orchestra practice, 1947. Courtesy of Griffith Davis; NCDAH.

without the moral, spiritual, and emotional support of her two best friends. With characteristic determination, however, Brown continued to fight for the survival of Palmer. As a result, Palmer's first years without county support showed promise. Brown's major concern was the ever-present need to expand the school's two primary sources of income: tuition and outside contributions. The former seemed promising since middle-class students were enrolling in record numbers from several states, and the school had reached its boarding capacity. Many qualified students were placed on a waiting list or rejected outright. From nearly 300 students, enrollment was cut by almost half as elementary students and teachers left. The remaining pupils, however, were able to pay the rising tuition.

As most other black boarding schools closed or became public schools, Palmer gained a reputation for being the only school of its kind in the country. Brown enhanced Palmer's emphasis on propriety, academics, and uplift. She constantly restricted mixing of the sexes. Boys and girls, even junior college students, studied on separate nights at the library. An invisible line divided girls' and boys' areas on campus. Boys and girls were separated at chapel, various assemblies, and trips off cam-

Brown making a point to a senior with characteristic
emphasis, 1947. Courtesy of Griffith Davis; NCDAH.

pus. Girls in particular were protected and restricted. They were not
allowed to enter the country store across the street from the school if
boys were there. Girls also were weighed regularly and examined by a
doctor at Brown's discretion to detect pregnancy. Kissing was a serious
offense, and perpetrators were reported to Brown. Personal appearance
was considered extremely important. The dress code, which was implemented as early as 1907 when Brown directed boys to wear suits and
girls to wear dark blue skirts and hats but "positively no silk," continued
for decades. Fridays and evening dinner were formal occasions. By the
1940s, boys were required to wear white dinner jackets on the opening
day of school, and girls also wore formal attire.

Groups of students (divided by age and sex) met on Monday nights
with faculty advisers for required weekly classes in decorum. High school
and junior college students received training in cleanliness, health and
hygiene, dressing neatly and tastefully, posture, and so forth. Brown required students to learn her rules of etiquette and what she considered
the desirable traits of ladies and gentlemen. Other requirements ranged
from memorization of ten psalms to attendance at all meals to visiting
hours during which boys could call on girls once or twice a month. Dormitory rules were posted in the rooms and on bulletin boards. In Stone

Posture and poise practice, 1947. Courtesy of Griffith Davis; NCDAH.

Hall, teachers supervised a mandatory two-hour study hall four or five nights a week, and playing cards was not allowed in the rooms. Mrs. Boulware, the matron in charge of boys in Eliot Hall, enforced rules on study hall attendance, card playing, use of the radio, and the 10:30 P.M. lights-out time.[24]

Despite such regimentation, students enjoyed a wide range of activities. Popular clubs included the orchestra, numerous singing groups, the Young Men's Christian Association and Young Women's Christian Association, the student council, and the literary society. Palmer students in such groups commonly attended programs and competitions at other schools such as Bennett College, North Carolina Agricultural and Technical College (A & T), and Dudley High School. After Brown first allowed dances to be held on campus in 1934 (except during Lent), closely supervised informal dances and proms became quite popular. At such social events, older high school and junior college students mingled with Palmer faculty members and students from schools such as Bennett. Other events included athletic games, an annual field day, card games, recitals, presentations by outside speakers, fashion shows, Friday night

Dormitory life in Stone Hall, 1947. Courtesy of Griffith Davis; NCDAH.

socials, "dean dinners" featuring speeches by black college deans, and cultural programs at nearby schools.[25]

Besides such school-approved activities, the young people engaged in the sorts of amusements common to people their age. Brown would not have sanctioned many of these activities if she had been aware of them, but student recollections make it clear that they occurred. Students sneaked out to play cards behind the dormitories and engaged in illicit kissing and petting. Boys cut off classmates' neckties and sent freshmen on snipe hunts. Daily chapel programs provided another opportunity for mischief. After Brown's dignified comments on social graces, pupils would often applaud and shout, "Dr. Brown! Dr. Brown!," for fifteen or more minutes to delay the start of classes. Some boys slept through the daily assemblies; others played games, such as betting on the number of hymns that would be sung or the number of minutes Brown would speak on a given morning. One boy who was assigned as the driver of Brown's early 1940s Buick was known to take corners quickly, causing the diminutive president to slide across the backseat. Since most students were allowed to go home only at Christmas and parents were discouraged from disrupting the Palmer routine by visiting students, Brown and the staff dealt with troublesome behavior as they saw fit. Despite Brown's reputation for discipline, she expelled only a handful of students during her long tenure at the school.[26]

Besides personally monitoring the activities of students, Brown focused on efforts to expand the student body to its optimum size and ensure the permanence of the school. She enlarged the high school and junior college faculty by adding better trained and more experienced teachers and continued her search for economic stability. When her attempt to interest Newbold and Graham in a State College for Negro Women at Palmer failed, she confronted the presidents of other African American colleges directly.[27]

First she sought in 1938–39 to join with the North Carolina College for Negroes in Durham. Its president, James E. Shepard, in turn presented the plan to the state Commission on Negro Education. Brown offered to deed Palmer to the state for $50,000, to be used to pay institutional debts and compensate employees not retained by the state. In the final analysis, the merger failed because of the distance between the campuses and the unwillingness of the state legislature to fund another African American school.[28]

Brown immediately put into effect a second plan of action—to merge with the Methodist Episcopal Church's Bennett College. Denominational affiliation troubled Brown, but she would accept it if it meant stability for Palmer. Bennett, ten miles west of Sedalia, shared Palmer's focus on cultural education. Originally coeducational, the school became a small junior college for African American women in 1926. A few years later, it became a four-year college. Bennett's president, David Dallas Jones (1887–1956), was born in Greensboro. He received his B.A. from Wesleyan College in Connecticut and his M.A. from Columbia University. Jones came to Bennett in 1926 and remained until his death.[29]

Brown approached Jones in 1938–39 with the same proposal she had made to Shepard. She felt Jones was suitable to guide Palmer in her absence. To make Palmer more attractive to Bennett's trustees, she decided to discontinue Palmer's small junior college to avoid redundancy with Bennett. The growing influx of high school applicants clearly offered a new opportunity for Palmer to excel as a high school rather than

Brown lecturing students (separated by sex) in Wellesley
Auditorium, 1947. Courtesy of Griffith Davis; NCDAH.

attempting to continue the small junior college program. Brown's board
approved her plan to enroll 150 students in the eleventh and twelfth
grades. However, the proposed merger with Bennett was not to be for
the Palmer-Bennett relationship over the years had been characterized
by not only similarity and cooperation but also competition and jealousy. Brown and Jones competed for funds from the same pool of northern donors and never became friends. The failure of the plan caused
Brown to reexamine her idea of union with one of the state-run segregated African American colleges and universities.[30]

Early in 1940, Governor Clyde R. Hoey expressed a strong personal
interest in Brown's women's college proposition. She had written him
two letters, the first of which explained that Palmer's board had voted
to give the school to the state to merge with either A & T or North Carolina College for Negroes. The board had also agreed to cover all of
Palmer's past debts and to guarantee to pay two years of operating expenses. A week after making this amazing proposal, Brown notified
Hoey that she would prefer that Palmer be a high school for practice
teaching as well as providing two years of women's schooling for one of

the state colleges and requested $50,000 (which was negotiable) from the state to straighten out affairs and supply annuities for veteran Palmer staff. She added her 100-acre farm to the package. Hoey replied that he would be glad to make arrangements to establish the school just as Brown suggested and expressed regret that she had not informed him about her plan before the previous legislative session had ended so that he could have implemented it earlier.[31]

Bursting with excitement, Brown sent an urgent letter to Graham informing him that although she would prefer to keep Palmer under her control, she was more concerned that it continue to serve African Americans. Citing her advancing age and strenuous workload, she explained: "I can help the state of North Carolina to develop fine womanhood. Please help me get the chance." Brown enclosed a letter she had written to M. C. S. Noble, the white president of A & T's board of trustees. Brown asked him to consider making Palmer a two-year women's college for A & T, with a high school department as a "finer practice school." Brown believed Noble could make her dream a reality. Graham expressed full support but cautioned that it took "considerable time for a proposal like this to get responsible consideration." Warning Brown not to be overly optimistic, he said the state was reluctant to take on the support of additional African American institutions of higher education besides those in Elizabeth City, Fayetteville, Winston-Salem, Durham, and Greensboro.[32]

Brown replied that the state would have to pay nothing for Palmer's physical plant and pointed out that girls would be much safer at Palmer than on the campus of A & T, where there were "four or five boys to every girl." She pleaded with Graham to inform Newbold and the governor of his personal approval of her plan. Brown closed by stressing her great desire to realize her goal but acknowledging that it would come to pass only if it was God's will.[33]

The merger with A & T, however, did not occur. Nonetheless, several months later, Hoey offered an alternative with guaranteed funding but questionable merit—the transformation of Palmer into a home for delinquent African American girls. Some state leaders reasoned that such a home was needed more than another college. Hoey's proposal was ironic because Brown, as president of the North Carolina Federation of Negro Women's Clubs, had been working to promote a home for delinquent girls. Thus, perhaps it seemed likely to him that she would accept the offer. However, although Brown first agreed to the proposal, she ultimately rejected it: "After forty years of trying to help boys and girls with a desire to do something to go forward, to start now at the age of fifty-seven to turn my whole attention to incorrigibles, was more than I could do. I have neither the strength nor ability to cope with the situation." The federation had purchased 140 acres in Efland as the site for a home, and Brown asked Hoey to reexamine the tract, which had been rejected by the state earlier because it was considered too near the main highway.[34]

Brown struck while the iron was hot, cleverly using the acceptability of the roadside Palmer property to negate objections to the Efland acreage. She succeeded, and the legislature provided $50,000 to establish the Efland home. Palmer's economic future remained to be settled, and Brown continued to solicit contributions from friends. In the meantime, the reputation of both Brown and Palmer continued to grow.[35]

Brown's continuing campaign to promote gracious living and fine manners was destined to have far-reaching effects on thousands of people. She believed that her own education, hard work, and social refinement would help other African Americans at Palmer and elsewhere win acceptance by whites. Her message was popular among accommodationist blacks and others struggling against negative stereotypes and seeking respectability. Former students remembered Brown, standing proud and distinguished in Palmer's chapel, telling students that she was about to speak on "a subject which is very near to my soul: the Negro and the social graces." Polite students greeted visitors to the campus, who were impressed by the students' cultural training and told others what they had witnessed.

The process continued as graduates became examples of the effectiveness of good manners. As Brown's "social graces" message gained popularity, she conceived the idea of publishing a book on manners and Palmer's cultural practices. Her objective was to teach the black and white youth of America the advantages of good manners in opening doors to advancement. Two months before the book was released, Brown gained national recognition as a cultural leader on the Columbia Broadcasting System's Sunday morning radio program, *Wings over Jordan*. A regular part of the program was a five-minute talk by a well-known African American. On March 10, 1940, Brown delivered the address, "The Negro and the Social Graces."[36]

Brown's radio speech advanced her career in much the same way that Booker T. Washington's 1895 Atlanta address aided his, bringing her message of racial understanding to a broad American audience, including many potential middle-class students. National interest in the sub-

ject was at an all-time high. The Commission on Interracial Cooperation of Atlanta asked for permission to print Brown's comments in
leaflet form. Shortly after the program, Brown enhanced her reputation
by writing a weekly column, "The Correct Thing," for the *Norfolk Journal and Guide.*[37]

Such publicity stimulated sales of Brown's new etiquette book, *The
Correct Thing to Do, to Say, to Wear,* which she published herself in 1940.
The slender volume contained rules Brown had acquired from her
mother, polite white society, Palmer instructors, and writers such as
Emily Post. Brown offered detailed guidance to children and adults on
the correct behavior for a variety of situations at home, school, church,
and various social occasions. Her rules ranged from the obvious to the
sophisticated and included twenty-four "Earmarks of a Lady" and
eleven "Earmarks of a Gentleman." Brown wanted her students, who
practiced her rules daily, and her school to shed any "earmarks of
color," as she put it. She advised, for instance, that "a lady . . . does not
mark tools, walls, or furniture" and a gentleman "lets no opportunity
whatsoever escape for improving himself."

During its first year, the paperback book sold well. Brown set up a
small office at Palmer to fill orders for the book, but she felt it would
reach a much larger audience if marketed by a well-known publishing
firm. The Christopher Publishing House of Boston agreed to publish a
revised, hardbound book and released the new edition in November 1941. In recognition of her book and her work, in 1944 Brown was
elected an honorary member of the International Mark Twain Society,
whose purpose was to "unite the whole world in bonds of cultured
peace." Among its members were such literary and political figures as
George Bernard Shaw, Robert Frost, Upton Sinclair, Winston Churchill,
Madame Chiang Kai-shek, H. G. Wells, and Margaret Mitchell. With
sales of *The Correct Thing* mounting and applications to Palmer at an all-
time high, things were looking up for Brown.[38]

It was during this period that the United States entered World War II.
While fighting to protect the free world against dictatorships, however,
it continued to deny full freedom to more than 13 million African American citizens. Brown and other notable Americans spoke out against
segregation in the armed services. As a result of such efforts, African
Americans made more gains in civil rights during World War II than in
prior wars.[39]

Along with most other American institutions, Palmer contributed to
the war effort. Students and faculty members left to join the fight, al-

though Brown helped seniors get deferments so that they could graduate before being inducted into the military. Dean Walter English and Business Manager Joseph Williams became army lieutenants, and two other staff members joined the navy. These departures possibly delayed the completion of a cheaply built wooden gymnasium that faculty and students had partially funded as a surprise for Brown's approaching fortieth anniversary at Palmer. Located near the southern end of Stone Hall and the baseball field, the gym was finished around 1943 and would serve Palmer through the next decade.[40]

Brown increasingly protested the wartime treatment of blacks in both the South and the North. She attacked Jim Crow in 1943 before 25,000 blacks and whites at New York's Madison Square Garden. There Brown claimed to speak for black women about "the four freedoms so eloquently voiced by our president [Franklin Roosevelt] especially in the application of these freedoms to the Negro people of America." In her opinion, all African American women would remain slaves until the unjust influences of discrimination were removed. Freedom was a concept for which lives would be lost. African American women continued to be the "burden bearers of the race" and demanded that their children have "the equality of opportunity to pursue their highest aims." Blacks were dying overseas, declared Brown, for the four freedoms denied them at home "because of the color of their skin." She remarked that many African Americans were driven to lament "I would rather my children would die unborn than be sacrificed upon the altar of prejudice and hatred to preserve white supremacy." True democracy could not exist in America until Roosevelt's freedoms were granted to minorities.

"We must be as one Negro moved by the suffering of all Negroes.... We are willing to lay our all on the altar of freedom to destroy Jim Crowism," Brown declared, in the "land for which our children are willing to spend their last drop of blood to defend." Brown concluded by calling on the mothers of America, both black and white, to abolish racist attitudes and teach children the finer things in life, including values such as honesty, hard work, and patience.[41]

Brown also spoke widely on promoting racial understanding through propriety and cultural training. In the summer of 1943, Frederick Patterson, president of Tuskegee Institute, organized a series of lectures entitled "Character and the Social Graces." That series enabled Brown to share her philosophy of cultural training and interracial goodwill with college and university students as well as teachers in isolated areas. Patterson wrote approvingly of her message in the *Pittsburgh Courier:* "Unquestionably Dr. Brown has a message that our youth needs today. . . . The moral laxity and lewdness of many of our youth are definitely to be measured in the number of broken lives; frustrated hopes, ambitions, and dreams; and in the high incidence of venereal disease." The following October, Brown was keynote speaker at the tenth Good Manners and Culture Day at Durham's North Carolina College for Negroes.[42]

Brown lectured throughout the United States on topics related to racial uplift. In the spring of 1943 alone, she received twenty-one requests to deliver commencement addresses, most of which she had to decline. Brown's efforts did not go unnoticed. She gained numerous honors and awards for her contributions to humanity. Among them were two honorary doctorates, one from Lincoln University in 1937 and the other from Howard University in 1944. Thereafter, Brown was addressed as "Dr. Brown."

One person who took note of Brown's achievements at Palmer was North Carolina governor J. Melville Broughton, a trustee of Shaw University and a Palmer sponsor. In May 1943, he delivered the keynote address to 500 people at Palmer's combination baccalaureate-commencement ceremony. After the governor's speech on Brown's life of service, John Brice led the audience in Palmer's fortieth mass singing of the Hallelujah Chorus. Thirty-eight graduates represented at least fifteen states. Three-quarters or more of the graduates during the previous half decade had gone on to African American schools such as Bennett College, Hampton Institute, and the North Carolina College for Negroes. Within a few years, many Palmer students would opt for nationally known universities such as Fisk and Howard, and Palmer would boast a total of 1,000 graduates, including fifty or more doctors and dentists and a host of teachers, ministers, and nurses.[43]

Brown's growing fame, hard work, and good luck resulted in increased stability at Palmer. By 1940–41, 60 percent of Palmer's income came from students' families, a record equaled by no other African American school in the South. The value of the school's physical plant and equipment exceeded $500,000, debts totaled only $15,000, and Brown borrowed no short-term money that year. By increasing the income from student tuition and board, Brown reduced the need for charitable gifts by nearly two-thirds. Student families supplied a sizable portion of those gifts through Brown's imaginative Roll Call Day, which had begun by the 1930s. Usually on January 1, after returning from the Christmas break, pupils each gave a dollar or more of their holiday money to the school. By 1939, the faculty contribution alone for the day reached

Palmer's graduating class in the school's traditional
"triangle of achievement," a symbolic formation
used for decades, 1943. NCDAH.

$200. After World War II, every member of the senior class gave at least
$5, and by about 1950, Roll Call Day had become an elaborate event, at
which total giving soared into the thousands of dollars. Classes competed in the giving by presenting dramatizations and dances. An auction
capped the day, and some students called home to ask their parents for
as much as $500 so their class could triumph in the auction and giving.

In 1942–43, for the first time in fifteen years, Palmer ended the academic year nearly free of debt. Brown credited four major factors for
this signal accomplishment. The first was the excellent management of
the school's farm by Charlie Maye. Second, because most students were
now from middle-class families, their ability to pay their tuition increased. An astonishing 800 applicants sought twenty-five or so vacancies at the school, which promised to build "sound character, mental
discipline, and a cultural approach to life." Third, the new wartime prosperity allowed former contributors and loyal friends to increase their
regular support. The fourth factor was the unexpected popularity of *The
Correct Thing,* for which sales reached 10,000 copies. Although she was
busy with outside activities, Brown somehow found time to run affairs
at Palmer so well that it reached a peak of efficiency. She also delegated

daily responsibilities to loyal, well-trained staff members such as John Brice, although she demanded that business affairs be carried out strictly according to her plan. The assistance of capable staff members enabled Brown to spend more time preparing Palmer for the future.[44]

One major project to ensure Palmer's future, after past debts were brought under control, was the creation of reserves to prepare for the time when Brown would no longer be able to raise money for the school. In 1943, Brown recommended that the school secure a $250,000 endowment. That idea received only limited attention for several years, possibly because the school collected substantial reserves due to wartime prosperity. The board did begin solicitation, however, for a $100,000 endowment fund by 1946. The trustees also began buying war bonds around 1943 and continued for several years. By 1946, Palmer's net worth was about $611,000, including $48,000 in a reserve fund, $10,000 in a special fund, and $51,000 in bonds. The cost per student to attend the "only finishing school of its kind in America" reached around $500 by 1946. Thus, the student population of 186 brought in $93,000. Palmer had low advertising costs since graduates and Brown's many appearances publicized the school at little expense.[45]

Carrie Stone, Brown's longtime supporter and close personal friend, apparently got the endowment fund off to a successful start. In the mid-1940s, she made two sizable contributions to help pay off Palmer's current debt. A few months before her death, Stone gave $2,500 toward the $10,000 needed to settle the school's mortgage. Upon her death in 1945, she left $5,000 to Palmer and $5,000 to Brown personally. Brown selflessly used her $5,000 to build a faculty cottage as a memorial to Stone. Over the years, the Stones' children continued their parents' tradition of generosity. In 1947, for example, Robert Stone paid for general repairs to Stone Hall.[46]

Besides Carrie Stone, others helped make the endowment fund a reality. One such person was J. Spencer Love (1896—1962), like Brown a graduate of the Cambridge English High School and the founder of Burlington Industries. Love and his wife were Palmer trustees and regular donors. Love was the largest contributor after the Stones, and his gifts far exceeded those of other southerners. Love subscribed $10,000 beyond his annual pledge of $2,000 to the endowment fund. Such a large sum helped Brown secure the entire $100,000 by the spring of 1948. Brown also raised another $10,000 to retire current debts. Confident in her fund-raising ability, Brown once wrote that there were "very few people who would turn me down personally." Once again, she had set seemingly unreachable goals and had surpassed them. By any standards, she was an outstanding fund-raiser. The only obvious obstacle now to Palmer's continued success was her advancing age and the lack of a chosen successor.[47]

As the 1940s closed, Brown and Palmer enjoyed national recognition for their contributions to African American uplift. Annually up to 1,000 students applied for about thirty vacancies. Brown kept enrollment small to enhance individualized teaching and personal relationships between faculty and pupils. At one point, Palmer had a waiting list three times as large as the student body. When asked how she selected students, Brown replied that she interviewed the students, their parents, their teachers, and their pastors and evaluated their ability to pay the tuition. Another question was how Palmer satisfied all of the people who wanted to attend. In her typical straightforward manner, she replied: "We do not satisfy them; they just have to take it or leave." Brown explained that students were selected by people in various parts of the country who investigated candidates' backgrounds, academic potential, and families. Once their character and scholarship were deemed acceptable, those able to pay full costs received priority, although Brown tried to provide some financial aid for gifted poor students. Although Brown imposed no age limits, she did not accept new students beyond the tenth grade because she believed that it took at least two years to absorb the Palmer experience. The few incorrigible children who somehow got into Palmer soon returned home again. In-state enrollment was limited so that the school could "reach people all over the country who support it."[48]

In 1947, students from twenty-four states and one foreign country (Haiti) attended Palmer. By 1949, the school registered African American and African youth from thirty-one states and four foreign countries. It had an average student body of 200, a jump of eighty or more since 1940 and the maximum size desired by Brown, and most students continued to come from North Carolina, with Georgia, New York, Virginia, and South Carolina high on the list. Some of the students at the finishing and preparatory school were from the country's wealthiest black families. For instance, pupils from nearby Durham—home of the nation's largest African American–owned business, North Carolina Mutual Insurance Company—included a Spaulding, a Kennedy, and a Merrick. Parents might typically be businesspeople, doctors, attorneys, undertakers, or clergy. Some Palmer girls wore fur coats, diamond rings, and prom gowns purchased in the North, flown to Greensboro, and delivered by limousine to the school. A few families had private planes, and the cars at one graduation ceremony were mainly Cadillacs driven by chauffeurs. One boy from Texas reputedly had a different shirt for each day of the school year. Palmer graduates became members of the best black private clubs in the North.[49]

During this period, another event—likely instigated by Brown— brought national attention: in October 1947, *Ebony,* the most influential African American magazine in America, published a feature on Palmer titled "Finishing School: Wealthiest Families Send Children to Palmer for Polishing." Griffith Davis, photographer-writer for *Ebony,* prepared the illuminating article on everyday events at Palmer. The article was written from the point of view of a female student, and Davis selected sixteen-year-old Henri Peyton as its central figure. She was the daughter of a Virginia confectioner, Emmet R. Peyton, and the second child in her family to attend Palmer. The story began by discussing Palmer's "high scholastic standard equivalent to a first class New England prep school." Davis then illustrated the high moral standard to which students were held by citing the suspension of eighteen senior boys because one of them used a profane word. That anecdote became a legendary example of Brown's strictness.[50]

The article followed Henri through an average day at Palmer. The day began when the bell rang at 6:00 A.M. During breakfast, Henri received etiquette training with "schoolmates who all practice the correct way to eat." Davis explained that "boys pull back the chairs for the girls next to them and sit only after the ladies are seated. All keep elbows and arms off the table." Dining etiquette was strictly observed; violators ate alone as punishment. After breakfast came the 8:30 morning chapel, followed by classes, lunch, and more classes until 4:00 P.M.; "then came study, socializing and chores." All students were required to work daily at the school, a carryover from Palmer's earliest days. Assignments, changed every six weeks, included "dish-washing for girls, janitor work for boys." Students served as waiters for two-week periods regardless of their financial status. In a well-done photo essay, Davis depicted Henri attending chemistry and sewing classes, studying at the library, taking music lessons, practicing modern dance, writing for the student newspaper, singing with the chorus, and attending church services with Reverend Brice. At lunch time, Henri sang grace, a custom before each meal. Recreation included movies on campus and chaperoned shopping trips to Greensboro.

The article also described student social life, which reflected Brown's serious view of Palmer's *in loco parentis* status. The Tea House, a snack

Students pausing for prayer before a meal in
Kimball Hall, 1947. Courtesy of Griffith Davis; NCDAH.

shop where students learned about running a small business, was a
favorite hangout. Hours were limited, and girls were not allowed to go
there after supper, a restriction that offered boys a chance to buy treats
for their sweethearts. Another favorite diversion was playing cards,
which Brown eventually permitted as long as the game did not involve
gambling.[51]

Students' favorite social affair was the annual junior-senior prom.
Girls were required to memorize the section from *The Correct Thing* on
proper behavior at dances before being allowed to attend. Students spent
many happy hours decorating the gym in preparation for the prom. Attendance (by invitation) was considered a great privilege. To prepare for
the occasion, students took special classes in ballroom dancing. At the
dance, students wore formal attire, and only formal dancing was permitted—jitterbugging was not allowed. Seniors performed graceful
waltzes during intermission.[52]

To educate and nurture Palmer's students, Brown trained new faculty
and staff members to replace such losses as her administrative assistant
Cecie Jenkins and Dean Charles A. Grant. Jenkins had become Brown's

Students taking a break at the Tea House, 1947.
Courtesy of Griffith Davis; NCDAH.

closest friend since the death of Ola Glover, and Grant had served Palmer for over twelve years. Brown had relied heavily on both of them for the past seven or eight years. After World War II ended, many new teachers joined Palmer; Brown and longtime faculty members attempted to instill in them Palmer's ideals. For Grant's job, Brown selected Donald J. Montague, a college graduate with six years' teaching experience. Montague arrived in 1946 and within a year took over the senior position of Palmer's administrative dean. Brown was so impressed with Montague that she recommended him as her potential successor. The following year, she even authorized him to sign checks in her absence. Montague resigned after only three years, however. The loss was a great shock to Brown, who had to begin a new search for a successor. This hunt led her to persuade Wilhelmina M. Crosson to take a leave of absence from the Boston public schools to teach at Palmer.[53]

While pursuing Crosson, Brown recruited several new board members. They joined forces with the corps of postwar teachers and a relatively affluent and geographically diverse student body. Among the new trustees was Robert Stone. Frank P. Hobgood, advanced in age and in

At the prom, 1947. Courtesy of Griffith Davis; NCDAH.

declining health, continued as chairman, with Cyrus R. Wharton as vice chairman. The two, along with treasurer J. W. Burke, another longtime director, continued to serve the board faithfully. Most newer directors were members of the growing African American middle and upper classes. Among such trustees were Channing H. Tobias, director of the Phelps-Stokes Fund of New York; Benjamin Mays, president of Morehouse College in Atlanta; and E. R. Merrick, vice president of the North

Carolina Mutual Insurance Company in Durham. Others elected to the board in the late 1940s were Mordecai Johnson, president of Howard University; Kenneth R. Williams, future president of Winston-Salem State University; Cecie Jenkins; and Wilhelmina Crosson.[54]

Along with changes in the board, students, and faculty came improvements to the school's physical plant. Proposals to upgrade and rehabilitate Palmer's buildings and grounds had originated soon after the start of World War II. But because of wartime demands, practically all plans to improve the school had been postponed. Included among them were the following projects and estimated costs: central sewage plant, $5,000; completion of Eliot Hall, $35,000; home economics practice home, $25,000; teachers' cottage, $15,000; grounds improvements, $3,000; general repairs, $5,000; and a new school bus, $3,000. After the war ended, Brown suggested that a $100,000 "reserve fund" be created for such improvements. In time, the fund was established and the suggested improvements were made, with the exception of the completion of Eliot Hall.[55]

The Carrie M. Stone Teachers' Cottage and the Massachusetts Congregational Women's Cottage were located at the northern edge of the campus adjacent to U.S. 70, the former next to Canary Cottage and the latter next to Stone Hall. Greensboro architect Charles C. Hartmann based the design of the identical one-and-a-half-story brick veneer Colonial Revival cottages with steep gable roofs on that of Canary Cottage. The Women's Cottage served as the girls' home economics practice house and was constructed primarily through the efforts of Brown's longtime friend, Daisy Bright, who had been associated with Palmer longer than any other living person except for Brown.[56]

The improvements in Palmer's buildings and grounds left the institute in good condition. Unfortunately, the same thing could not be said of Brown's health. Still energetic, however, she continued the search for a person to lead Palmer in the tradition that she had developed over nearly fifty years. The trustees, concerned about her future well-being, took additional steps to ensure that she would have a comfortable retirement. They planned to transfer to Brown the benefits of a $5,000 life insurance policy. The trustees in 1946 also promised to take care of her needs after retirement. In 1949, Brown asked that after her retirement Canary Cottage become a guest home for the institute. The board placed $5,000 in a retirement fund and also put the students' yearly "room fee" of $25 each into an account for her, renaming it the "opportunity fee."

Then the board established a trust fund of $10,000 to pay Brown up to $300 a month after September 1, 1951, until she died or the fund was exhausted. By then, Brown had convinced Wilhelmina Crosson, who already was serving on the board, to come to Palmer as an instructor and administrative assistant.[57]

Wilhelmina Marguerita Crosson (1900–1991), born in Warrenton, North Carolina, moved with her parents to New Jersey and then to Boston in 1906 in search of better educational and economic opportunities, continuing a string of parallels with Brown's youth. Crosson acquired her early education at Boston's public Hyde School and at Girls' High School, where she was an excellent student, a star player on the basketball team, and fully accepted by her white schoolmates. From an early age, Wilhelmina (Mina) had aspired to become a teacher, and after graduation from high school, she enrolled in the elementary education program at the Salem normal school.[58]

Crosson commuted sixteen miles to Salem daily, often after working at a part-time job. Although she attended Salem nearly two decades after Brown was there, like Brown, Crosson was the only African American in the elementary section. After graduating, without prior teaching experience or political connections, she found it difficult to obtain work as a teacher in Boston.

Crosson had known about Palmer since early childhood because each spring Brown, always dressed in white, spoke at the Ebenezer Baptist Church. As a result of those engagements, Brown came to know Crosson at an early age. While Crosson was in normal school, Brown sometimes took her out to dinner. Crosson hoped that Brown would interview her for a teaching position after she completed her training. When that did not occur, she worked as a substitute teacher to gain the experience needed for employment in the Boston public schools.

Crosson was finally offered a full-time position at the Paul Revere School in Hancock, an all-white district. Later she became one of the first teachers in Boston to employ remedial measures in teaching reading. Crosson was so successful that principals and supervisors asked her to explain her methodology to other teachers. When remedial reading centers were set up, Crosson became one of the first instructors, earning wide professional recognition. After being named one of the forty-eight best teachers in the Boston school system, she continued her education at various colleges. In 1934, she obtained her B.S. degree from Boston Teachers College. Later, Crosson taught at the Hyde School, the all-black elementary school she had attended as a child. There she conducted pioneer work grouping students by reading ability rather than by grade level.

Crosson, like Brown, was alert to community needs. Finding that African American youngsters in Boston were leaving school before graduation, she decided that they needed to know more about their own history to give them encouragement and hope. Crosson then founded the Aristo Club, a group of African American professional women who studied black history and provided scholarships to worthy children. She was a member of the League of Women for Community Service, the Boston League of Women Voters, the Alpha Kappa Alpha sorority, and the Charles Cox Fund Committee, which provided $32,000 annually to needy families.[59]

Finally, in 1949, Crosson accepted Brown's call to initiate a remedial reading program at Palmer. Although she was honored to receive the appointment, she had already earned an outstanding reputation and had obtained the experience she once had hoped to receive under Brown. Nevertheless, Crosson agreed to take a one-year leave of absence from the Hyde School to teach at Palmer.[60]

Crosson arrived at Palmer in August. After settling at Canary Cottage with Brown, she set up an effective program of remedial reading. She stressed grammar as well as reading because Palmer students had to pass an examination on grammar and writing to enter high school. Crosson also proved to be a good student, and Brown took every opportunity to instill in her the philosophy of Palmer.[61]

One of those ideals was the importance of cultural recreation, and Brown sent Crosson on outings with students to concerts, theatrical performances, and motion pictures. On these excursions, Crosson encountered Jim Crow, which she had seldom experienced in Boston. She later remembered that Jim Crow did not deter Brown. She recalled Brown saying, "Voluntary segregation is all right," then buying tickets for an entire section of a theater or renting the entire hall. Brown's stature in Greensboro made it possible for her students to shop in the best white department stores.[62]

In February 1950, Brown returned to Palmer from Boston, where she had just viewed the film *Pinky,* about an African American girl's attempt to pass as white. She felt that its message of the need to be proud of one's race would benefit the students. The entire student body attended the opening of the film in Greensboro on February 9. The students had

Students shopping in Greensboro, 1947. Courtesy of Griffith Davis; NCDAH.

been at the movie about half an hour when Brown, who had remained on campus, sent word that Stone Hall was on fire. Grateful for the safety of her students, Brown exclaimed: "It was an act of God that made me send the children to see *Pinky* this afternoon." In addition to various fire departments, residents of the surrounding community helped put out the fire.[63]

Brown estimated the total loss at around $150,000 and stated that it would probably take about $200,000 to replace the building and its contents. "The roof had vanished," and the interior was a rubble of "smoldering timbers, twisted plumbing, blackened bath tubs, and charred furniture and clothing." In the midst of this tragedy, however, Brown maintained a positive attitude for the benefit of the students and onlookers. But Crosson saw another side of Brown as she leaned against a tree: "I'll never forget it, because I think it was then that she showed her age."[64]

After the fire, Brown assured everyone that Stone Hall would be rebuilt by September. Doggedly continuing her duties in the face of disaster, she sent telegrams to worried parents: "Galen Stone Hall has burned down, . . . but the children are safe." With no loss of life, the real tragedy was that, despite all of Palmer's previous fires, Stone Hall carried only approximately $35,000 to $50,000 worth of insurance. Nevertheless, Brown maintained that she was not worried and that the dorm would be rebuilt.[65]

Immediately, the Executive Committee held an emergency meeting to discuss the devastation. Once again, Brown was appointed to head a campaign to rebuild the dorm, and once again, she was successful. Contrary to popular belief, Robert Stone did not provide the bulk of the funds used to reconstruct Stone Hall. Although Stone's generosity was considerable, J. Spencer Love was the largest contributor to the restoration fund. The board instructed Hartmann, architect of the Teachers' and Women's Cottages, to rebuild Stone Hall. In addition to approving restoration costs of more than $97,000, the board voted to install a sprinkler system. Pending completion of Brown's campaign for funds, money was available from fire insurance, the emergency fund, and a $40,000 loan.[66]

By September 1950, just as Brown had promised, Stone Hall was completely restored. The project had taken a mere eight months, but the disaster affected Brown's health much more than anyone suspected. She suffered delayed shock and became increasingly dependent on Crosson. During the following year, Brown spoke more and more of retirement. She was approaching seventy years of age and had served Palmer and African American education for fifty years. In a September 1951 letter to Wharton, acting chairman of the board, Brown stated that she would resign as president between May and June 1952.[67]

True to her word, in the spring of 1952, Brown asked Crosson if she thought she could take over Palmer. This question took Crosson totally by surprise because she had never thought of herself as anything other than an instructor and did not feel she would be an effective administrator. Moreover, she felt that the responsibility of becoming Palmer's second president would be simply too much for her to handle. The ultimate question in Crosson's mind was whether she would be able to fill Brown's shoes. In her heart, Crosson knew that she and Brown had different abilities and very different ways of doing things and that as long as Brown lived, she would impose her tremendous will on her replacement.[68]

Although Crosson did not want to take on the arduous task, she accepted out of respect for Brown. Therefore, on Sunday, October 5, 1952, just a few months after receiving an honorary doctorate from Tuskegee Institute, Charlotte Hawkins Brown stepped down as president of Palmer Memorial Institute after fifty years of loyal service. Wilhelmina Crosson, her handpicked successor, became the school's second president. A new era formally began at Palmer, although in some ways the change was largely superficial.[69]

Chapter Nine

IN BROWN'S SHADOW, 1952–1971

ON OCTOBER 5, 1952, during the ceremony that inaugurated Wilhelmina Crosson as Palmer's second president, observers could not help but notice that Brown's retirement was of more interest than Crosson's inauguration. For that reason, it would have been better if the two events had been held separately. Furthermore, many questions remained to be answered. Among those were whether Brown could leave the administrative operation of her school in another person's hands. How could anyone else do what Brown had done for Palmer? Hadn't all others, including the American Missionary Association and the state of North Carolina, failed to place the academy on a stable foundation? After several unsuccessful attempts to ensure Palmer's continued existence, before her retirement Brown had been able, through her own perseverance, skill, and determination, to leave Palmer in the best economic condition of its fifty-year history.[1]

While Brown was alive, however, Crosson never really saw herself as the head of Palmer and for several years allowed her mentor to make most decisions. Brown successfully transferred nominal authority to her former lieutenant, but Brown, Crosson, and the board were either unable or unwilling to allow the new leader to be what the institution needed—a president with full power. The founder could not foresee that within a few years her own doggedness and failing health would hobble her heir. Nevertheless, Brown's pride in her successor was evident as she introduced the institute's new president, whom she had known since Crosson was about nine years old. Brown then announced that she would remain at Palmer as vice chairman of the school's trustees and director of finances.[2]

At the time that Brown assumed her new role, Palmer was in solid economic shape. More than half of the $40,000 borrowed to rebuild Stone Hall had been repaid, and the Massachusetts Women's Congregational Society gave an additional $10,500 to retire the mortgage on the

Brown and new president Wilhelmina Crosson with
a bust of Brown, 1952. Courtesy of Alex Rivera; NCDAH.

new girls' practice home. Furthermore, in the year before she left office,
the school had received $126,400 in student tuition and fees, $20,500 in
contributions, and $5,700 in other income including earnings from the
farm. This added up to a total income of $152,600 for the 1951–52
school year. As a result, Palmer was able to make a $20,000 mortgage
payment, add $20,000 to its endowment fund, and still have a surplus of
$5,000. The value of the physical plant reached a new high. Buildings
and their contents had an estimated value of $626,500; land, $45,000;
water plant, $40,000; and farm and equipment, $10,000. This brought
the total estimated value of Palmer to $721,500. In all, the school's as-
sets, including the endowment fund, totaled $908,000.[3]

Brown's health, however, continued to deteriorate and prevented her

Brown and Crosson in center of receiving line on lawn
of Canary Cottage, circa 1952. Courtesy of Alex Rivera; NCDAH.

from preparing the budget for the 1952–53 school year. As time went on, diabetes and gradual loss of memory greatly weakened Brown, forcing Crosson and the trustees to take painful measures to prevent the administrative collapse of Palmer. Fortunately, during the early years of Brown's declining health (1952–55), Palmer's economic condition continued to improve.[4]

Despite the school's bright financial prospects, managing Palmer proved to be extremely difficult for Crosson, who felt a need to carry out Brown's wishes. This resulted in Crosson's complete loss of authority in administering the responsibilities of her office. On several occasions, she consulted with Brown and came to what she believed was a mutually satisfactory solution, but when it came time to implement the plan, Brown forgot their agreement and refused to cooperate with Crosson.[5]

This state of affairs continued until May 1955, by which time Crosson

Brown celebrating her birthday in Canary Cottage with Nat King Cole, Maria
Hawkins Cole, and "Cookie," circa 1953. Courtesy Alex Rivera; NCDAH.

no longer was able to tolerate Brown's irregular behavior. Because of
her devotion and respect, Crosson endured treatment from Brown that
she would not have tolerated from anyone else. The trustees, aware of
Brown's growing inability to analyze matters clearly, voted to give Crosson full authority over Palmer. The board also convinced Brown to give
up the demanding position of director of finance so that she might en-
joy her retirement years.[6]

Brown continued to refuse to give up absolute control of her "air
castle," however, and insisted on visiting classes and commenting on
their conduct. If something occurred on campus that displeased her, she
dismissed classes and ordered students and faculty to the chapel, where
she endeavored to explain her views. Her reputation and personality
were nevertheless so strong that students, faculty, staff, board members,
and, above all, Crosson continued to love and respect her. But her un-
predictable behavior, no matter how well intended, could not persist
without doing irreparable damage to her life's work.[7]

While living with Brown in Canary Cottage, Crosson struggled to
find a compassionate, workable, and just solution to the problem of the
founder's disruptive actions. Not wanting to be responsible for removing Brown from Palmer, Crosson in early April 1956 tendered her

own resignation. Crosson's decision forced the board to take immediate action.

Cyrus R. Wharton, board chairman, formed a special committee to meet with Brown to attempt to relieve the chaotic situation at Palmer. The committee advised the founder that the school could not operate if she continued to interfere with Crosson's authority. Furthermore, the delegation asked Brown to leave the campus and "sever any and all connection" with the management of Palmer. Brown rejected all overtures by the committee and proclaimed that Palmer was her school and that she was the final authority over it. After the meeting, the board (with faculty concurrence) asked Crosson to continue as president, assume full power, and obtain separate living quarters away from Brown. Crosson agreed, and for the first time in the history of Palmer, Brown was without legitimate authority.[8]

Although Brown remained a trustee in name, she was not on the Executive Committee, the primary body with full power to administer the school. Nonetheless, the board's actions did not deter Brown from continuing to attempt to run her school. It must have seemed to Brown that everyone suddenly had turned against her in a plot to take over her school. How much insight did Brown have into the effects of her declining health? The answer to this question will never be known. What is known is that Brown managed to retain enough control over Palmer to warrant further action against her. In late May 1958, the board held another emergency meeting. Wharton noted that "the interference of Dr. Brown . . . during the past two years had increased to the point that it would be impossible to continue the operation of the school unless something was done." To resolve the matter, the board voted to seek a court injunction restraining Brown from any interference in the operation of the school.

At the meeting, Brown reiterated that the school was hers to run as she pleased and that she was "elected President for life and that she proposed to run it." Despite frequent interruptions by Brown, Wharton called for a vote. Every trustee present, except for Brown, sorrowfully voted to remove her from Palmer's campus. After the resolution passed, questions arose as to Brown's future welfare. Wharton reported that her retirement fund amounted to more than $40,000.[9]

Before the injunction could be served, however, Brown's health suddenly deteriorated. At that point, Brown's niece Carol Brice and Crosson began to seek professional care for the ailing educator. Among those consulted was Boston physician Frances Bonner. After Bonner's examination, Brown was judged to be mentally incompetent, and a court appointed Brice to be her guardian. Bonner strongly advised against serving Brown with an injunction in her state of mind.[10]

Because of Bonner's efforts, Brown was spared the emotional stress of being forcibly taken from her life's work. Fortunately, Bonner convinced Brown to leave Palmer willingly to go to McLean Hospital in Belmont, Massachusetts, for treatment. Brice played an immense role in convincing Brown to leave Palmer for treatment. From the beginning of Brown's hospitalization, Crosson gave the welfare of Palmer's first president the highest priority and regularly visited her mentor. While under the care of Bonner, Brown began to show signs of improvement.[11]

After about a month, Jack Rice replaced Bonner as Brown's attending physician and recommended that she continue to have hospital care. He believed that a nursing home would not be able to provide appropriate care. The question of how Brown's health care bills would be paid then arose because the hospital's rate was $30 per day. Robert Stone intervened and convinced hospital officials to reduce the nearly $11,000 yearly fee.[12]

Brown's family pondered alternatives for her future care. Brice considered removing Brown from the facility and arranging for someone to care for her in more familiar surroundings. Brice, an accomplished professional singer, even suggested that she take Brown abroad with her on concert tours. Brice was convinced that it would be better for her aunt to be among loved ones for her remaining time. Many family members, however, felt that going to Europe would be too much of a strain on Brown's precarious health. Crosson recommended that Brown be returned to her home, Canary Cottage, but most trustees rejected that idea. They feared that if Brown returned to Palmer, they would be forced to have her committed to a mental institution to prevent her interference in school matters.[13]

Other board members, among them Robert Stone, believed the hospital's environment was good for Brown. After weighing all of the recommendations, Brown's family and associates chose interim care at McLean Hospital. Nevertheless, Brice and Crosson were skeptical. "McLean Hospital," wrote Brice, "though efficient, is remote, cold and I am sure very lonesome for Dr. Brown." Brice advanced a proposal by Brown's nieces Maria Hawkins Cole and Charlotte Hawkins Sullivan to move Palmer's founder to California to live with Sullivan.[14]

Brice and Crosson were convinced that Brown was unhappy living away from loved ones. Crosson again suggested that her mentor be returned to Palmer but not to Canary Cottage. The idea of moving Brown to California was rejected because of the same concern about her remaining in Massachusetts, that is, isolation from longtime friends and customary surroundings. The family agreed to allow Brown to remain at McLean until better accommodations could be found, and relatives and close associates continued their search for a lasting solution.[15]

A little more than a year passed before Brown was well enough to leave the hospital and return to North Carolina, the choice finally agreed on by her family. Her memory, however, was deteriorating with each passing day. In November 1959, Brown traveled to Greensboro, where she resided at the home of Mrs. Harmon Ivey, a former employee; Jessie Benton, a nurse, stayed with Brown around the clock. Brown's condition was not improving, and there was little doubt that the end was near. Realizing that fact, the Palmer trustees, as a symbol of respect, invited Brown to return to Canary Cottage to spend her final days. According to Crosson, Brown believed that Ivey's home was Canary Cottage, so she was content to remain there until she again had to be hospitalized. Brown died at L. Richardson Memorial Hospital in Greensboro on January 11, 1961, from complications associated with diabetes.[16]

Brown's funeral was held on Sunday, January 15, 1961, in the chapel of the Alice Freeman Palmer Building. Family and friends crowded into every available space to pay their final respects. Mordecai Johnson delivered the eulogy, an excellent recapitulation of Brown's role in uplifting educational standards for African Americans in North Carolina. Brown was buried on the campus in a place she had selected some ten years earlier: a slope between Canary Cottage and her office in the Palmer Building. She had chosen the site because of its central location on the campus.[17]

Six months after Brown's death, the trustees began to consider seriously a provision in her will that authorized the institute to use Canary Cottage for free for nine months, after which time the school was required to purchase it for $20,000. One major problem, however, prevented the action: an appraisal valued the home at only $14,500. Maria Cole and Crosson, Brown's two chief heirs, solved that dilemma by offering to donate the remaining $5,500 needed to buy the home. The trustees then proceeded with the purchase.[18]

The board also appointed a committee to draft a resolution in honor of Brown, who had worked selflessly without a commensurate salary for over thirty years. The committee placed a plaque commemorating

Brown's contributions to uplift through education on her grave. The inscription read:

> Dr. Charlotte Hawkins Brown: Founder and builder of the Alice Freeman Palmer Memorial Institute, leader of women in their quest for finer and more productive living—mentor, by her writing, of those seeking to live more graciously—by her eloquence, inspired youth to nobler achievements, by her vigor of mind and force of character, championed for a disadvantaged race in its striving for human rights and adult responsibilities. She gave 58 years completely of her unique energies and talents to the building of this institute from its humblest of beginnings in an old blacksmith shop. Her vision, dedication, singleness of purpose, and undaunted faith made this school possible in her native state—North Carolina. May her memory in turn lend inspiration always to this place and its people.[19]

In the year of Brown's demise, Crosson, her devoted disciple, wrote lovingly of the founder in the school's annual report. Reflecting on Brown's contributions, Crosson recalled her saying that the "first steps toward developing a high standard of life" for African Americans were "knowledge and time." Knowledge, Brown believed, was the "firmament" that "warmed our lives," and time was the "talisman that helps us to use knowledge." Throughout her entire life, Brown's thoughts were of Palmer. It was her personal hope and desire that her "air castle" would continue as a "beacon light to education and Christian living for our youth."[20]

After Brown's death, the financial state of the school under Crosson was very stable due to the continuing expansion of the African American middle class and the economic prosperity of postwar America. Economic conditions seemed to be steadily improving. Along with time-tested methods of fund-raising and donating a fourth of her modest salary to the school for several years, Crosson employed various methods to enhance contributions. Among other strategies, she suggested that a professional fund-raising firm be retained. Crosson also received approval from the trustees to travel, as Brown had done, in search of contributors. Moreover, the school still had a long waiting list of applicants, which offered Crosson the freedom to admit a select group whose parents were willing and able to pay the high cost. Aware that a growing number of middle-class African Americans could afford boarding school for their children, the trustees (as Brown had done earlier) counted more and more on student fees as a dependable source of income. In fact, in later years, charitable contributions comprised only a small fraction of the school's annual budget, a decided contrast to Brown's peak fund-raising years.[21]

By the mid-1960s, fund-raising among private individuals had been replaced in part by increased efforts to obtain funds from various corporations and foundations. But securing grants from such sources had its problems. Crosson found such agencies more interested in supporting colleges than in funding private secondary schools. She also realized that many northern contributors questioned the fact that Palmer was an "all Negro school." Many liberal northern foundations thought this type of school impeded integration, which had been ordered in public schools by the Supreme Court in 1955. As integration of schools slowly advanced across the nation, able African American youth increasingly enrolled in the best formerly all-white public schools.

In response to such criticisms, Crosson stated that in the past Palmer had been forced by law to be a segregated private school and therefore since its inception had been a traditionally all–African American institution. She made it clear, however, that Palmer's doors always had been open to persons of any race, creed, or color and that only southern doctrine and race relations in the state prevented whites from enrolling. Nothing in the school's charter or bylaws prohibited the enrollment of white students. Several southern foundations, however, had no objections to contributing to a segregated school. Leaders at Palmer in the early and mid-1960s therefore primarily targeted foundations in the South.[22]

Other attempts to increase Palmer's annual income included offering special programs during the summer months. One such program was a night school for adults that provided instruction in languages, math, science, and typing. Another more traditional summer school program for young people was considered a great success. During its first year of operation, the venture brought in $4,912 in student fees alone, $1,400 of which was net profit.[23]

Along with the extra income from the summer programs, the institute anticipated receiving an equal sum from an increase in student fees in the 1960–61 academic year. The estimated budget for the next year was approximately $203,600. Of that amount, $152,000 was projected to come from student tuition, room, board, and fees. Contributions were running at an annual rate of some $15,000, and income from investments amounted to $6,000. The remaining $30,600 needed to balance the budget would come from the reserve fund surplus. Palmer was on the road to maintaining itself as a financially sound institution with a sizable reserve fund and a stable endowment. The endowment principal of $120,000, established in 1952, was still intact. The reserve fund, which had peaked at about $144,000 in early 1959, remained in the $100,000 range after covering several annual operating deficits and major capital expenses such as a new sewage system. Surely Brown would have been proud of the financial achievements of her successor.[24]

In 1962, Palmer's yearly budget rose to $221,000, a jump of $17,400 caused primarily by an increase in faculty salaries to bring Palmer in line with rates of pay at public schools. To offset the growth in expenditures, Crosson proposed a million-dollar capital campaign to secure Palmer's future. But she was unable to convince the board to begin such an enormous undertaking, which would have been far larger than any of Brown's campaigns.[25]

Crosson continued the founder's practice of encouraging the regional diversity of faculty and students. Most faculty came from North Carolina, with Massachusetts ranking second and Virginia third. In 1960, the largest number of students (28) came from New York, followed by Virginia and then Georgia. North Carolina ranked fourth, with 22 of some 180 students. In 1961, the same student enrollment pattern persisted. The most common age of students in attendance at Palmer in 1961 was sixteen. Fifteen-year-olds were second, and fourteen-year-olds third. Only four students were eighteen, three of them boys. In 1961, most students were in the eleventh grade, with the twelfth grade second and the tenth grade third. The apparent discrepancy between a lack of eighteen-year-olds, the normal age of high school graduates, and the sizable number of students in grades eleven and twelve might have been the result of the then common practice of skipping grades.[26]

Crosson also faithfully sought to perpetuate the educational and cultural programs and philosophy of Brown. Student academics, activities, and life continued much as before. To ensure the future of the school and its culture, Crosson recommended that Palmer expand to achieve greater stability. She requested that the trustees appoint a cross section of professional and lay persons to a committee charged with ensuring the school's future independence and academic and financial integrity. Crosson also asked that a development committee be established to map out plans to increase Palmer's physical plant to accommodate up to 300 students. This enrollment, while far smaller than many public high schools, would have been in the same range as enrollment at such institutions as the prestigious Groton School in Connecticut. Finally, she asked that a national fund-raising campaign be started to safeguard Palmer's current endowment. But neither Crosson nor the board had the leadership gifts of Brown or Galen Stone to bring such a vision to fruition. Perhaps, too, as integration accelerated and customs changed, Palmer's philosophy became outdated.[27]

Crosson also introduced a number of nontraditional programs (by Brown's standards) at the school. Under her administration, students had more personal freedom on and off campus. Pupils in turn demonstrated their acceptance of more responsibility by conducting themselves as proper Palmerites. Students traveled to New York and Washington, D.C., to absorb the finer aspects of urban culture as part of their educational development. One highly successful program was the training of Peace Corps volunteers for work in Liberia. Crosson also expanded instruction in African American history at Palmer. Students were reluctant to choose the course initially, but after a stimulating "Negro History Week," many students manifested interest in the subject. Crosson correctly predicted that in future years black history would be a popular subject.[28]

Perhaps the most tangible of Crosson's later accomplishments was the addition of two major buildings to Palmer's campus. She achieved this despite ongoing difficulties in securing grants from large corporations and foundations. Two prominent Winston-Salem foundations responded to her appeal for help in funding a new boys' dormitory in 1964: the Mary Reynolds Babcock Foundation provided $100,000, and the Z. Smith Reynolds Foundation awarded $150,000. Construction began in 1967, and the foundations gave an additional $50,000 to complete the project. The handsome two-story brick structure, Reynolds Hall, was finished in 1968. It evoked the image of substantial edifices built by Reynolds family money on the new Winston-Salem campus of Wake Forest University. The second structure, completed in the same year, was a smaller brick science building, paid for primarily with a gift of some $39,000 (later supplemented by $10,000) from Mrs. Frank Forsyth, also of Winston-Salem. Stouffler Hall contained laboratory and educational space as well as a small greenhouse.[29]

Crosson remained president of Palmer and struggled with raising money until the summer of 1966. For fourteen years, she prolonged the existence of the $120,000 endowment. That task was difficult, primarily because of dwindling contributions from former supporters. In many cases, the reason for shrinking individual donations was unavoidable. Several longtime friends had died, although a few of their younger relatives and close friends continued to aid Palmer. In the absence of Brown, however, campaigns aimed at specific individuals and families were not as effective.[30]

The family with the longest history of continued financial and personal service to Palmer was the Wharton family. The contributions of Jessie R., Edward P., Cyrus A., and Cyrus R. Wharton have been noted in earlier chapters. Another member of this progressive, broad-minded, and apparently racially unbiased family also deserves a place in the story of Charlotte Hawkins Brown and Palmer Memorial Institute: Richard L. Wharton (1921–), son of Cyrus R. Wharton and grandson of Cyrus A. Wharton. Richard Wharton's grandfather had been one of Palmer's original white trustees. His father then became a trustee and was elected chairman during the 1950s. Richard joined the board in 1964 and succeeded his father as chairman in 1966.[31]

Wharton received his education from the University of North Carolina (1942), Harvard Business School (1943), and Yale Law School (1948). After returning to Greensboro, he joined his father's law firm. Wharton was continually exposed to Brown and Palmer as a youth. One of his early memories of Brown was as a guest in his father's home during a concert by the Sedalia Singers. Wharton remembered Brown as "an animated, dark-skinned person with a great deal of energy, outspoken and on the whole a very charming person . . . not someone having met that you would forget."[32]

Wharton also recalled that Brown opposed all racial discrimination, especially forced social segregation. According to Wharton, Brown sought total equality for blacks and wanted to "equip young Negro people to rise in the society that existed" rather than "revolutionize it." There was no question in his mind that "she would have been a major activist" had she been born later.[33]

On the decline of Palmer, Wharton later surmised that it began with the illness and subsequent death of Brown but also was a product of the end of legal segregation. He believed that the 1954 *Brown v. Topeka Board of Education* decision led to the creation of more nearly equal schools at the secondary level. As a result, Palmer and other similar schools were no longer the only institutions offering a solid education for African Americans. Wharton believed that Palmer might have weathered integration if the school had lowered its tuition. Such a decision, however, would have required amazing foresight.

Richard L. Wharton, the last of a line of Whartons who served loyally on Palmer's board of trustees. Courtesy of Richard L. Wharton; NCDAH.

By the 1960s, the trustees had become accustomed to existing conditions at Palmer. The board contained no visionaries with a "great sense of mission" to suggest that Palmer might have had another alternative: to become an integrated preparatory school. Believing that such a school was not feasible, the board did what it could to preserve the status quo. By that time, black private schools in the state had all but disappeared, with the exception of Palmer and Laurinburg Academy. Before long, with the continuing expansion of integrated public education, only Laurinburg would survive.[34]

It would have taken a very dynamic person such as Brown to even acquire enough money to continue Palmer as in former years, Wharton believed. Even she, however, would have needed a "much broader range of vision than she would have been able to have . . . at that time." Lacking a board with such insight and imagination, Wharton's primary concern as chairman was "keeping the ship afloat and/or preserving a nucleus from which hope might evolve." He later recalled his own "much more limited view . . . in the mid 60s. To the effect that what we should do was live within our means, demonstrate our financial need, and go to the public for assistance in maintaining Palmer more as a tradition than an expanding institution pending the time when a more vital approach may be possible." How to keep Palmer afloat became a major concern after Crosson's retirement in 1966.[35]

Crosson's successor, the school's third president and first man in that office, was Harold E. Bragg (1939–). Bragg was born in Birmingham, Alabama, and educated in Ohio, receiving an undergraduate degree from Kenyon College and a master's degree from Kent State University. His wife, Linda Brown, was the youngest niece of influential Palmer trustee Willa B. Player, formerly president of Bennett College. Bragg's wife graduated from Bennett and obtained a master's degree from Case Western Reserve University. When the Braggs came to Palmer, Harold was just twenty-seven years old. He had been a teacher in the Cleveland public schools and had taught history briefly at Kent State. A teacher for only three years, he apparently had neither administrative proficiency nor teaching experience. Nevertheless, Bragg arrived at Palmer in August 1966 to assume his duties as president.[36]

Bragg's selection for the post was an unfortunate one. It is not clear how the choice was made, who supported the nomination, and what role Crosson and the board played in making the decision. Obviously Bragg had none of the experience or dedication of his predecessors. At least two other candidates received interviews. One, Rudolph D. Artis, held M.S. and Ed.D. degrees from Cornell University.

The other was Charles W. Bundrige (1921–1997), business manager and a teacher for over ten years at Palmer. Bundrige, born in Georgia, was raised in Pittsburgh. He received a degree in business administration at North Carolina Agricultural & Technical College (A & T). Bundrige then began graduate work in counseling at Duquesne University in Pittsburgh. While there, Brown interviewed him, and he began teaching at Palmer in 1953. Bundrige continued to study at A & T and acquired a master's degree in education. When Crosson retired, he applied to become Palmer's third president. The board reportedly turned down Bundrige, recently widowed, because it wanted a young, progressive married man who could serve as a positive black role model.[37]

Bragg was young and married, but at a critical time in the history of Palmer and African American education, the school did not have a chance under his immature and fiscally foolish reign. Between 1966 and 1969, his administrative inexperience and persistence in unsound spending ruined Palmer economically. At the end of his first full year as president, the institute reported an astonishing operating loss of $149,038. In 1968 and 1969, the school again reported deficits of $95,097 and $93,117, respectively. To offset those striking shortages, immense amounts were transferred from the previously restricted reserve and endowment funds. In 1967, $115,208 was taken from those funds; in 1968, $95,226; and in 1969 (his final year), $1,100, or all that remained. Those actions totally exhausted the school's reserves, which Brown and Crosson had worked so hard to build and preserve. In three short years, Bragg took over $211,000 from Palmer's most important emergency accounts, and the school found itself burdened with an estimated $100,000 in new debt.[38]

Although Bragg bears primary responsibility for critically weakening Palmer, the board watched the decay for almost three years without taking effective remedial action. According to Wharton, the trustees tried to preach to Bragg about conservative spending and the need to stop "spending money that the school did not have." Bragg reportedly never listened to their pleas, and Palmer operated on "annual deficits and eroded its assets to the point where at the time of its dissolution it was heavily in debt." The trustees, meeting only once or twice a year, did not maintain adequate oversight or direct supervision of spending at Palmer on a daily, weekly, or even monthly basis.[39]

Without question, Palmer ultimately was forced to close because of a lack of funds and heavy institutional debt, and the board must share the blame for allowing Bragg's excesses. One trustee later commented that "no sufficient respect was given to financial reality. The motivation for it I won't speculate about." Bundrige maintained that Bragg's lack of economic sense was the major factor in Palmer's financial problems. The trustees must have been aware of Bragg's unreasonable spending habits, but they permitted them to continue; the alibi of lack of data and infrequent meetings is not sufficient to fully exonerate them.[40]

Wharton attempted to rectify the situation by resigning as board chairman because he believed the last thing Palmer needed in the turbulent 1960s was a "white chairman." He secured as his replacement Julius Douglas, a retired African American Presbyterian minister, hoping that he could curb Bragg's uncontrollable spending habits. Several other board members, who had experience "almost certainly more appropriate than Douglas, were unable or unwilling to accept the position." In the end, Douglas had very little effect on Bragg's continued spending.[41]

As a result of his poor performance as head of Palmer and his professed love for the institution, Bragg resigned shortly after the conclusion of the 1969–70 school year, leaving an enormous deficit and a diminished student population. Bragg's official explanation for leaving was to accept a better position at Bennett College as dean of student affairs.[42]

Thoughtful observers at Palmer who painfully watched young Bragg's profligate spending and immature judgment must have yearned for the sort of successful leadership once provided by Brown and to an extent by Crosson. Brown too had spent money she did not have, but she focused on improving Palmer's physical plant and instructional programs. Filled with selfless missionary zeal, she had the determination and the talent to raise large sums of money in emergencies. Tireless, committed, articulate, and extremely persuasive, Brown reached out skillfully to influential black and white Americans. With a clear image of what she believed a solid Christian education for promising young African Americans ought to be and how to provide it, she placed the highest priorities on character, discipline, and academics. Sadly, such qualities were not paramount during Bragg's tenure. After he departed, Palmer's directors belatedly tried to retrieve those traditional emphases.

The reshuffled board named Bundrige interim president of the school, and in the midst of almost overwhelming financial hardships, Palmer struggled to survive. Determined to begin the school's sixty-eighth year of operation, Bundrige assured all parties that the school would open as scheduled. He confirmed that students were enrolling in sufficient numbers to keep the school afloat. The enrollment for the 1970–71 school year was 150 students, an increase of 15 from the previous year. Repeating the cry for help made after the disastrous industrial building fire over half a century earlier, board members received aid from Greensboro's business community. Bundrige subsequently announced that Palmer would be able to operate during the next academic year as a result of new support from Greensboro financial institutions.[43]

Although fiscal problems critically plagued Palmer during its final years, other misfortunes of the late 1960s complicated continued operation. Because of rising annual student costs, which reached $1,750 per person by 1970, and the need to maximize enrollment, acceptance was based increasingly on ability to pay rather than desire to learn. Some parents could not afford to send their children to Palmer; others no longer perceived it as a special place. As a result, discipline problems became commonplace. The change in student attitudes accompanied Bragg's administration. He revoked many policies that had been traditions at Palmer, including classes in the social graces. He also expanded privileges for younger students.

This new laxity fostered a breakdown of discipline. One extreme example of a repercussion from abandonment of traditionally strict guidelines occurred in 1969. Seven girls were charged in juvenile court with intentionally setting fire to Stone Hall. Five of the girls were under sixteen. Damage to the dormitory was estimated at about $3,000. The blaze was the third to erupt during a twelve-hour period at the building.[44]

Another reason for some of the rowdiness and social and political protests at Palmer was that African Americans discovered that demonstrations could be effective when all else failed. Like black and white citizens throughout America, students pressed for what they believed was true equality. The most well-known protests were led by Martin Luther King Jr. and the Southern Christian Leadership Conference. Protesters demanded equal employment opportunities, desegregation of public facilities, and dropping of charges against King and hundreds of others arrested during demonstrations.

After King's murder in 1968, African Americans rioted for several days in more than a hundred cities across America. By that time, the sometimes violent opposition to large-scale American military intervention in Vietnam helped promote a disrespect for authority and order in society, especially on college campuses. Seeds of change and revolution found a few fertile minds in which to flourish on the Sedalia campus.

But incidents of student unrest, protest, and violence at Palmer were insignificant compared to confrontations at other institutions in Greensboro, Winston-Salem, Durham, Chapel Hill, and Raleigh.[45]

In the traditional spirit of Brown, in the face of adversities and hardships and under the leadership of Bundrige, Palmer began its sixty-eighth year in the fall of 1970. Surprisingly, things started off well for the troubled institute. Enrollment was up, and plans were under way to expand fund-raising. Crosson delivered the main address at the Founder's Day celebration in hopes that former contributors would rally to Palmer. "Take your inheritance in this school," she proclaimed, "as a trust from the founder, Charlotte Hawkins Brown, and the world will be reborn. It is your world." She declared that Palmer's continuance would take "wisdom, understanding, and love." Crosson stated that she had made changes that had allowed Palmer to continue to be useful and emphasized that further changes were required for the school to survive. To be effective, she declared, they would have to be based on Palmer's founding philosophy.[46]

Supporters attempted to obtain money to free the school from its financial predicament. But before any substantial permanent support could be found, a final catastrophe occurred. On Sunday, February 14, 1971, at around 3:30 A.M., Bundrige spotted flames "shooting skyward out the top of the [Alice Freeman Palmer] building." When the conflagration ended, only "the tall, thick walls and four huge colonial columns" stood intact.[47]

Fire had been no stranger to the Palmer campus. Large and small blazes had visited the school in previous years, but the damage they caused had been overcome eventually by the dynamic and spirited leadership of Brown. Bundrige's reaction to the disaster was reminiscent of Brown's actions under similar circumstances. He announced that in the aftermath of the fire classes would be held as usual. The faculty, staff, and students utilized space in various buildings for makeshift classrooms. The Sedalia community, officials and educators from other institutions, and church groups offered assistance. Many students rallied behind Bundrige and did whatever they could to make sure that they could continue their education.[48]

To overcome the loss of the school's central building, which included classrooms, a chapel, offices, the auditorium, and the library, an intensive but unsuccessful national fund-raising campaign was begun almost immediately. No rebuilding was attempted; the financially strapped, indebted school carried little or no insurance on the building. Without an endowment or other suitable collateral, further borrowing was virtually impossible. As in former years, the Greensboro chamber of commerce and others organized efforts to try to keep Brown's dream alive. One extremely essential element, however, was missing from the apparently well-conceived plan: Brown. In addition, Palmer lacked an angel such as Galen Stone and a clarity of mission and purpose. In the Bragg years, the institution had neither maintained its former mission nor developed an effective replacement. In such straits, within six months, failed attempts at fund-raising and continuing debts forced the board of trustees, by then under the chairmanship of Elworth E. Smith, to close the school and place Brown's "air castle" up for sale.[49]

IN LATE AUGUST 1971, only a few days after the trustees decided to close Palmer, they tentatively approved the sale of the campus to Malcolm X Liberation University (MXLU), a black separatist organization founded in Durham during the turmoil of the 1960s. This action caused an uproar among the institute's friends. MXLU, the prospective buyer, had been established by a $45,000 grant from the Episcopal Church in 1969. In 1971, the group moved to Greensboro and sought the Palmer campus for its permanent headquarters. Under the proposed agreement, MXLU would receive title to the campus in exchange for paying Palmer's outstanding debt of $250,000. Several trustees on principle opposed the idea. Among them was the chairman, Julius Douglas, who resigned in protest. Nevertheless, a majority of the board present favored the measure and elected Elworth E. Smith, a Palmer graduate and Greensboro funeral director, as the new chairman.[1]

Charles Bundrige called the planned sale "the worst thing that could happen" and condemned it as "a complete reversal of what the school stood for." He had devoted all of his professional life to Palmer in the belief that the school would continue. Discovering that it was going to close made his duties for the next few weeks the "hardest job of his life."[2]

To alumni, Sedalia residents, and friends of the school, the idea of a separatist sect on the very campus where Brown had fought so hard to end forced segregation was inconceivable. Residents met at Bethany Church to discuss ways to block the sale. They formed the Citizens for Palmer Committee and circulated a petition urging that Palmer be kept open or at least be sold to an organization more in keeping with Brown's principles. Resentment grew and citizens blamed the school's financial problems on the trustees' failure to plan for the future. Petitioners also pointed out that the campus was worth $1.5 million and that trustees were using poor judgment in selling it for a mere $250,000. Vina Wadlington Webb, leader of the citizens committee, urged that Palmer remain open by recalling the dying words of its founder: "Vina, Palmer must live. If just one of you will hold onto the principles I have tried to teach, then Palmer will live." Such increasing public disapproval caused an unexpected response from the separatist group, which stated that its objective was unity among all African Americans and therefore to avoid destructive controversy it would withdraw its offer to purchase Palmer.[3]

Citizens for Palmer, while successful in blocking MXLU, fell short of their second goal, reopening Brown's school. In spite of efforts by various parties, the board, led by Smith, continued to review bids to purchase the property and received eight legitimate offers. In November, the trustees heard various proposals, including presentations by George Simkins, local National Association for the Advancement of Colored People president, for a nursing home; Robert Hannon of Fayetteville for a similar school; W. C. Donnell of the United Holiness Church for a black preparatory school, junior college, and seminary; Bennett College; and the North Carolina School for the Deaf.[4]

Of all of the proposals, that of the United Holiness Church appeared most compatible with the traditions and values of Palmer. The church called for continuing Palmer's traditional mode of schooling and retaining Bundrige and as many staff members as possible. Although none of the other proposals offered such a wide range of concessions, the trustees in a closed-door meeting unanimously accepted Bennett's offer instead.[5]

At the time of Bennett's takeover of Palmer, the women's college had no firm plans for its use. Moreover, Bennett clearly lacked the resources for any substantial rejuvenation of the school and subsequently did little with it. In 1982, Bennett trustees abandoned ideas of reestablishing any permanent educational programs at Palmer and voted to sell the forty developed acres of the property to the American Muslim Mission (AMM).[6]

The AMM, formerly the Nation of Islam and commonly called the Black Muslims, had evolved from several black nationalist groups. Many of them had been founded in the early twentieth century in northern cities with large African American populations. The chief founder of the movement was Elijah Poole (Elijah Muhammad), who by the end of World War II had a large following as the result of the growing spirit of black nationalism. The Nation of Islam offered a militant yet traditionally nonviolent means of protesting discrimination. During the 1960s, the Muslims received national attention through the speeches of Malcolm X on racial pride and Muslim principles. Following Malcolm X's assassination in 1965, disagreements within the sect led to major changes.

These shifts, in the late 1970s under Warith Deen (Wallace D. Muhammad), included repudiation of racial precepts and the deification of M. Fard Muhammed, founder of a Black Muslim sect in Detroit. With new concepts came the name American Muslim Mission and the emphasis on religious propagation, education, family, community, and economic development.[7]

In 1982, the sect established the American Muslim Teachers' College on the old Palmer campus. The forerunner of the teachers' school was the so-called University of Islam. Such "universities" were in fact primary or secondary schools. By 1980, students from these schools were graduating, so in 1981, the AMM established its first college in Chicago for the study of Islamic scholarship, principles, and philosophy. Officials of the AMM came to believe, however, that the rural campus in Sedalia would be a better environment for students.[8]

The AMM purchased Palmer's fifteen surviving buildings from Bennett College for approximately $500,000 and opened a school with about thirty students. AMM leaders found that some members of the Sedalia community were upset that Palmer had been purchased by a group whose principles were at odds with Brown's Christian and integrationist legacy. Local parents feared that the new neighbors would attempt to convert their children to Islam, but after residents met with officials of the AMM, most were impressed by the sect's actions and goals. The AMM's plans to operate a college and boarding school somewhat reminiscent of the old Palmer were nevertheless destined to fail. The organization's misfortune, however, made possible the acquisition of the campus by North Carolina as a state historic site depicting Brown's life and legacy as well as other contributions by African Americans to the state's educational history.[9]

Although Palmer had closed in 1971, alumni, friends, and staff continued to commemorate Brown's life. One such effort was a twenty-five-minute videotape that traced the school's history, produced in 1981 by the University of North Carolina at Greensboro, *Palmer Memorial Institute: The Mission and the Legacy*. Widespread distribution of the video greatly helped publicize Brown and her work.[10]

The idea of a memorial to Brown arose in 1982 when two Palmer alumni, Maria Hawkins Cole, Brown's niece and the widow of singer Nat King Cole, and Marie Hill Gibbs, were visiting the educator's grave site. Cole and Gibbs made a covenant to convince the state of North Carolina to designate Canary Cottage and the grave site a historic site. They organized meetings of alumni and friends of Brown, and a delegation met with officials of the North Carolina Department of Cultural Resources.[11]

In 1983, William "Bill" Martin (1945–), then a freshman state senator from Greensboro, sponsored a bill to establish a memorial to "honor Dr. Brown's accomplishments and be a repository for black culture and history in North Carolina." Martin, the only African American in the North Carolina Senate at the time, requested $67,377 for planning the memorial. To his surprise, the senate approved the full amount. Interest in a memorial continued to grow along with recognition of the need to acknowledge the contributions of African Americans to the state's history. As word spread of the legislature's intentions, citizens began to rally support for a Brown memorial.[12]

As endorsements mounted, state officials took an increasing interest in the matter. Larry G. Misenheimer, then assistant administrator of the Historic Sites Section of the Department of Cultural Resources, reported that his agency was excited about the proposed memorial, which would be the first state historic site to honor either a woman or an African American. Initial plans for the Charlotte Hawkins Brown Memorial included restoration of Canary Cottage and development of a black history center.[13]

Marie Gibbs (1924–1986) was the dynamo in the crusade for a memorial to Brown. Born in Greensboro, she was educated at the public schools there and at Palmer. Gibbs received a bachelor's degree in elementary education from Bennett College and a master's degree from North Carolina Agricultural & Technical College (A & T). Her life was committed to the educational, religious, and civic improvement of her community. Like Brown, she attempted to instill that commitment in students by her example of Christian leadership. For twenty-three years, she taught elementary students in the Greensboro schools.[14]

Once Martin's bill became a law, Gibbs and other supporters formed the nonprofit Charlotte Hawkins Brown Historical Foundation. The foundation elected Gibbs as president and Burleigh Webb, dean of A & T's School of Agriculture, as vice president. With the foundation and state funds in place, Misenheimer hired two staff members to plan the memorial and study Brown's life and Palmer's history. L. Annette Gibbs began work as project director, and Charles Wadelington became its historian.[15]

On March 18, 1985, the AMM agreed to sell the Palmer property to the state at its appraised value. To obtain the funds, foundation leaders called on Senator Martin and Representative H. M. Michaux Jr., a Palmer

Left to right: Maria Hawkins Cole, state representative H. M. Michaux Jr.,
L. Annette Gibbs, and Marie Hill Gibbs at Canary Cottage, circa 1985. NCDAH.

graduate. The two legislators introduced companion bills for $500,000
in 1985–86 to purchase the land and for the same amount in 1986–87
to operate the memorial. The legislature approved $400,000 for land ac-
quisition and site development. Martin stated that by the spring of 1987
the former campus would be opened as the Charlotte Hawkins Brown
Memorial State Historic Site.[16] Problems in arranging the sale delayed
the transfer for more than a year. Just as plans were being made to dedicate the memorial on March 28, 1987, the state announced that acqui-
sition would be delayed because the AMM had declared bankruptcy. The
bankruptcy was settled within a few months, however, and the campus
was transferred to the state for $417,000.[17]

The dedication of the Charlotte Hawkins Brown Memorial on November 7, 1987, culminated a four-year effort. Speakers at the event
hailed Brown as "a woman and educator ahead of her time" and cited
creation of the memorial as a "sign that exclusion is giving way to in-
clusion, a change for which Brown so long had struggled."[18]

Since the state opened the memorial as a developing historic site,
progress has been sporadic. Although funds have been inadequate to restore all campus buildings, over the years the state has restored Canary
Cottage and Carrie M. Stone Teachers' Cottage. Other buildings, such

State senator William Martin of Greensboro, who in 1983 introduced the first bill for the preservation of Palmer, 1997. Courtesy of Senator William Martin.

as Kimball and Stone Halls, have received exterior stabilization. Activities have included annual African American History Month banquets; civic, educational, and religious workshops; and educational programs with area colleges. The memorial hosts an annual African American Heritage Festival. Exhibits highlight the contributions of African Americans to the educational and social history of North Carolina.[19]

At present, efforts to develop the memorial into an African American cultural center are continuing. Supporters are endeavoring to strength-

Dedication of the Charlotte Hawkins Brown Memorial as a state historic
site, November 7, 1987. *Left to right:* Jeanne Rudd, James R. McPherson,
L. Annette Gibbs, Harold H. Webb, and state secretary of cultural resources
Patric Dorsey. At far right is Governor James G. Martin. NCDAH.

en bases of financial support among the local populace and throughout
the private, philanthropic, and governmental sectors. New wayside exhibits are in place at major points on the campus. But much remains to
be done: the memorial's historic physical plant is far larger than that of
most other state historic sites, and several buildings remain unrestored.

Although the most expansive plans for the historic site remain unfinished, much has been accomplished at the memorial honoring Charlotte Hawkins Brown, women, education, and the African American
presence in North Carolina. All of Brown's dreams for Palmer Memorial Institute were not fulfilled, but through faith, determination, and
hard work, she redefined directions and tactics and for years made a
significant contribution to the development and education of African
Americans in North Carolina and the nation. Consequently, those who
seek to improve the lives of all Americans and those who search for creative ways to educate America's children more effectively today would
do well to consider Brown's experience at Palmer and her emphasis on
her triangle of achievement to make youth "educationally sufficient,
culturally secure, and religiously sincere." Just as her accomplishments

produced over a thousand well-educated graduates despite a penniless beginning, so can Americans and educators today, with far more substantial resources, envision the means to transcend contemporary conditions. Just as she labored to unite the races in a common pursuit of educational and cultural excellence, so can educators and educated citizens of all colors today be vehicles for greater racial unity and understanding. Just as she encouraged both philanthropy and increasing governmental responsibility for educating all citizens, so can modern philanthropic and governmental support foster innovative, effective public and independent education. Just as she maintained the values, standards, and independence of her school despite challenging odds, so must all citizens today cherish and encourage individual freedom, responsibility, and morality. In remembering her contributions, we realize what one young African American woman could do despite the restrictions of the racist environment in which she lived.

Appendix One

CHRONOLOGY

June 11, 1883	Lottie Hawkins is born in Henderson, North Carolina.
1888	Brown and nineteen members of her family move to Cambridge, Massachusetts.
1895	Brown organizes kindergarten class at Union Baptist Church in Cambridge, Massachusetts.
1897	Brown is principal speaker at her pastor's fifteenth anniversary celebration, attended by the governor of Massachusetts.
1900	Brown meets her future benefactor, Alice Freeman Palmer (second woman president of Wellesley College), for the first time.
1900	Before graduating from the Cambridge English High School, Brown changes her name to Charlotte Eugenia Hawkins.
1900	Brown enters the state normal school at Salem.
1901	Brown accepts a teaching position at the American Missionary Association's (AMA) Bethany Institute in Sedalia, North Carolina.
October 10, 1901	Brown begins teaching at Bethany Institute.
Spring 1902	The AMA closes Bethany Institute.
Summer 1902	Brown begins to raise money to open her school.
October 1902	Alice Freeman Palmer Memorial Institute opens.
Spring 1905	Palmer has its first graduation exercises.
Summer 1905	Brown becomes ill in Boston from overwork while raising funds for Palmer.
Fall 1905	Memorial Hall, Palmer's first major building, is opened.

November 23, 1907   Brown, John Smith, and Cain Foust sign the formal charter of Palmer.

1909   Brown becomes a founder of the North Carolina Federation of Negro Women's Clubs. In 1912, she becomes president, a post she will hold for two decades. The national club's motto is "Lifting as We Climb."

July 1909   Brown introduces the School Improvement League, inspired by Virginia Randolph, in Sedalia.

July 1909   Mary R. Grinnell becomes the primary benefactor for the construction of Grinnell Cottage, the new girls' domestic science building.

1910   Greensboro banker C. A. Bray is named treasurer of Palmer.

June 14, 1911   Charlotte Hawkins marries Edward S. Brown. They separate about a year later and divorce in 1916.

1913   Galen L. Stone becomes interested in aiding Palmer. The Stone family will be among Palmer's greatest supporters.

1916   The total number of Palmer graduates reaches fifty-five. The campus contains four main buildings: Memorial Hall, Grinnell Cottage, Grew Hall, and Mechanical Hall.

1917   Greensboro banker Edward P. Wharton accepts chairmanship of Palmer's board of trustees.

December 29, 1917   Fire destroys Mechanical Hall and the commissary.

1919   Brown publishes her first book, *Mammy: An Appeal to the Heart of the South.*

1922   Palmer's high school department is accredited.

April 7, 1922   Alice Freeman Palmer Building is dedicated. The final cost of construction is $150,000.

April 20, 1922   Memorial Hall is destroyed by fire.

October 1, 1923   Brown marries John W. Moses. The marriage is annulled in less than a year.

December 12, 1924   Grew Hall is destroyed by fire.

1926   Longtime Palmer supporters Galen Stone and Charles Eliot die.

1926   Brown is one of seven educators honored at Philadelphia's sesquicentennial celebration of American independence.

June 1926	The AMA assumes operation of Palmer.
1927	Brown moves into her new home, Canary Cottage.
1927	Galen Stone Hall and Kimball Hall open.
1927	Brown is listed in *Who's Who in Colored America.*
Summer 1927	Brown travels to Europe. She is impressed by the importance of culture in European schools.
1927–28	Brown studies and lectures at Wellesley College.
1930	Palmer opens for the first time as a finishing school.
1930	Brown is a delegate of the Council of Congregational Churches of America at a conference in Bournemouth, England.
1932	Palmer opens a junior college department against the wishes of the AMA.
1932	Wilberforce University of Ohio honors Brown with the LL.D. degree.
October 31, 1932	Grinnell Cottage is destroyed by fire.
December 5, 1933	The Sedalia Singers perform at the White House.
April 1934	Charles W. Eliot Hall is dedicated.
November 27, 1934	The AMA withdraws aid to Palmer.
1935–37	Brown serves as president of the North Carolina Teachers Association (now the North Carolina Association of Educators).
1937	The county establishes the first public school for blacks in Sedalia. Palmer receives no public funds for the first time.
1937	Lincoln University of Pennsylvania honors Brown with the LL.D. degree.
January 4, 1938	Brown's close friend and companion, Ola Glover, dies.
April 9, 1938	Brown's mother, Carrie Willis, dies after a long illness in Greensboro.
1939	Palmer's junior college closes.
March 10, 1940	Brown attracts national attention by speaking on the Columbia Broadcasting System's *Wings over Jordan* radio program.

1941   The Christopher Publishing House of Boston publishes Brown's *The Correct Thing to Do, to Say, to Wear.*

1943   Brown receives $50,000 from the North Carolina legislature to open the Efland Home for Wayward Girls.

Summer 1943   Brown delivers a lecture series at Tuskegee Institute entitled "Character and the Social Graces."

1944   Howard University in Washington, D.C., honors Brown with the Ed.D. degree.

February 9, 1950   Fire nearly destroys Stone Hall.

September 1950   Total renovation of Stone Hall is completed.

1952   Tuskegee Institute of Alabama honors Brown with a Litt.D.

October 5, 1952   Brown relinquishes her duties as president of Palmer; Wilhelmina Crosson of Boston becomes second president of Palmer.

January 11, 1961   Brown dies from complications associated with diabetes at L. Richardson Memorial Hospital in Greensboro.

1966   Crosson retires; Harold E. Bragg becomes Palmer's third president.

1968   Reynolds Hall and Stouffler Hall open.

Summer 1970   Bragg resigns as president of Palmer.

Fall 1970   Charles Bundrige becomes acting president of Palmer.

February 14, 1971   Alice Freeman Palmer Building is destroyed by fire.

August 1971   The board closes Palmer and soon sells the campus and surrounding property to Bennett College in Greensboro.

1982   Bennett College sells the Palmer campus to the American Muslim Mission.

June 1987   The state of North Carolina purchases the Palmer campus for development as the state's first historic site commemorating contributions of African Americans and women to its history.

November 7, 1987   The Charlotte Hawkins Brown Memorial State Historic Site is dedicated.

SELECTED NEWSPAPER ARTICLES
ON CHARLOTTE HAWKINS BROWN AND
PALMER MEMORIAL INSTITUTE

"Commissary Burned at Sedalia Negro School," *Greensboro Daily News,* December 21, 1917.

"Negro Singers to Appear Here for Benefit—Palmer Memorial Institute Which Must Raise Emergency Fund," *Greensboro Daily News,* January 1, 1918.

"Greensboro Will Aid," *Greensboro Daily News,* January 2, 1918.

"Concert Sunday Will Be Worth Attending," *Greensboro Daily News,* January 3, 1918.

"Big Concert Is on for Sunday in City," *Greensboro Daily Record,* January 4, 1918.

"Ministers to Help with Concert Plan," *Greensboro Daily News,* January 4, 1918.

"Be There," *Greensboro Daily Record,* January 5, 1918.

"Chance to Hear Real Music at Concert Tomorrow," *Greensboro Daily Record,* January 5, 1918.

"Negro Singers Will Give Concert Today," *Greensboro Daily News,* January 6, 1918.

"Fund of over $1,000 Subscribed to Palmer Memorial Institute in Meeting in Theater Yesterday," *Greensboro Daily News,* January 7, 1918.

"The Greensboro Way," *Greensboro Daily Record,* January 7, 1918.

"Sedalia Quartette at Jordan Hall," *Boston Globe,* April 1918.

"Plan to Raise $5,000 for Palmer Memorial," *Greensboro Daily News,* March 2, 1921.

"Sedalia School Barn Is Destroyed by Fire," *Greensboro Daily News,* March 3, 1921.

"Palmer Memorial Institute Celebrates Twentieth Anniversary," *Greensboro Daily News,* April 10, 1922.

"Sedalia Dormitory Destroyed by Fire," *Greensboro Daily News,* December 13, 1924.

"Start Fund for New Sedalia Dormitory," *Greensboro Daily News,* December 14, 1924.

"Seventy-Five Thousand Dollar Gift Offered to Palmer," *Greensboro Daily News,* January 14, 1925.

"Palmer Memorial Institute Wins Praise in N.Y.," *Norfolk Journal and Guide,* May 4, 1929.

"Mrs. Brown," *Roanoke Rapids Progressive Herald,* March 15, 1930.

"Negro Teacher Founded School," *New York World,* March 30, 1930.

"Dormitory Is Burned at Palmer Institute," *Greensboro Daily News,* November 1, 1932.

"Palmer Memorial Institute Unique," *Charlotte Observer,* March 10, 1940.

"Charlotte Hawkins Brown—Pride of New England," *Boston Chronicle,* December 21, 1940.

"Southern Viewpoint," *Pittsburgh Courier,* April 17, 1943.

"Dr. Brown to Talk at Philadelphia," *Greensboro Daily News,* January 20, 1944.

"One Hundred-Forty Nine Receive Degrees at Howard U.," *Norfolk Journal and Guide,* June 10, 1944.

"Elected to Wellesley Alumnae," *Philadelphia Inquirer,* September 17, 1944.

"Mrs. Galen L. Stone," *New York Times,* July 30, 1945.

"Tribute Paid to Dr. Brown," *Greensboro Daily News,* November 17, 1945.

"Brown Gets Ovation at World Conference," *Norfolk Journal and Guide,* December 22, 1945.

"Columbia University Women Cheer Dr. Charlotte H. Brown," *Norfolk Journal and Guide,* February 23, 1946.

"'Twig-Bender' Airs Women of Tomorrow for Two Clubs," *New York Amsterdam-News,* July 20, 1946.

"Dr. Brown Passes Her $5,000 Share in Estate to Institute," *Greensboro Daily News,* August 5, 1946.

"Palmer Institute Head Will Get Racial Award," *Greensboro Daily News,* April 10, 1947.

"Award Will Go to Dr. Brown," *Greensboro Daily News,* April 16, 1947.

"People of Henderson Present $1,400.00 to Institute at Sedalia," *Greensboro Daily News,* April 21, 1947.

"Palmer Memorial to Honor Founder," *Greensboro Daily News,* November 2, 1947.

"Dr. Charlotte Hawkins Brown," *Pittsburgh Courier,* September 11, 1948.

"Flames Raze Dormitory at Sedalia," *Greensboro Daily News,* February 9, 1950.

"Test by Fire," *Greensboro Daily News,* February 11, 1950.

"Dr. Brown Rounding Out Fifty Years of Service," *Greensboro Daily News,* July 8, 1951.

"Wilhelmina Crosson Named President of Palmer Memorial Institute at Sedalia," *Greensboro Daily News,* August 25, 1951.

"Dr. Brown Quits School Position after Fifty Years," *Greensboro News and Record,* October 6, 1952.

"Lottie Brown Wouldn't Disappoint Her Friends," *Greensboro Daily News,* December 27, 1953.

"Dr. Brown Selected Woman of the Year by New York Group," *Greensboro Daily Record,* February 21, 1955.

"Honor Accorded to Dr. Brown," *Greensboro Daily News,* August 26, 1955.

"Charlotte Brown Dies at Seventy-seven: Founded Negro Junior College," *Boston Herald,* January 12, 1961.

"Longtime President of Palmer Memorial Institute Dies," *Durham Morning Herald,* January 12, 1961.

"Palmer Founder Succumbs at Seventy-seven," *Greensboro Daily News,* January 12, 1961.

"Charlotte Hawkins Brown," *Greensboro Daily News,* January 13, 1961.

"Dr. Charlotte H. Brown," *Greensboro Daily Record,* January 14, 1961.

"Fifty Years with Dr. Charlotte Hawkins Brown," *Washington, D.C., Afro-American,* January 21, 1961.

"Palmer Institute Gets Brown Land," *Greensboro Daily Record,* October 4, 1961.

"Addition Is Building New Hope," *Greensboro Daily News,* August 8, 1965.

"H. E. Bragg Named Head at Palmer," *Greensboro Daily News,* August 27, 1966.

"Palmer to Remain Principally Negro," *Greensboro Daily News,* June 18, 1967.

"Seven Girls Are Charged in Blaze," *Greensboro Daily News,* December 16, 1969.

"Palmer Alumni View Campaign to Raise Funds," *Greensboro Daily News,* April 21, 1970.

"Palmer Institute at Crossroads of Its History," *Greensboro Daily News,* May 17, 1970.

"Rouson Will Speak at Palmer Institute," *Greensboro Daily News,* May 29, 1970.

"Pan-Africanism Is Commended to Palmer Grads," *Greensboro Daily News,* June 1, 1970.

"Palmer Head Takes Job at Bennett," *Greensboro Daily News,* June 23, 1970.

"Palmer Will Start Sixty-eighth Year," *Greensboro Daily News,* August 29, 1970.

"Bethany's One Hundredth Year: Church Born in Foundry," *Greensboro Daily News,* September 6, 1970.

"Palmer Notes Founder's Day," *Greensboro Daily News,* October 8, 1970.

"Palmer Institute Marks Sixty-eighth Year," *Greensboro Daily News,* October 12, 1970.

"Dolly Madison Award," *Greensboro Daily Record,* January 6, 1971.

"Fire Marshal Probes Palmer Institute Fire," *Greensboro Daily Record,* February 15, 1971.

"Fire Ravages Palmer Institute Main Building," *Greensboro Daily News,* February 15, 1971.

"Aftermath of Two Big Fires," *Greensboro Daily News,* February 16, 1971.

"Fire Investigation," *Greensboro Daily Record,* February 18, 1971.

"Palmer Directors Will Meet Today," *Greensboro Daily News,* February 20, 1971.

"Fund Drive to Be Started for Rebuilding at Palmer," *Greensboro Daily News,* February 21, 1971.

"Institute Planning Nationwide Drive (AFP Building Fire)," *Greensboro Daily Record,* March 3, 1971.

"Palmer's Forward Movement," *Greensboro Daily News,* March 3, 1971.

"Palmer Institute Funds Sought," *Greensboro Daily News,* April 11, 1971.

"Palmer Alumni Make Gift to School," *Greensboro Daily News,* May 30, 1971.

"Former School Head to Teach at Bennett," *Greensboro Daily Record,* August 27, 1971.

"Palmer Institute Closes Its Doors," *Greensboro Daily News,* August 27, 1971.

"Palmer Institute Closing," *Greensboro Daily Record,* August 27, 1971.

"Malcolm X University May Buy Palmer Site," *Greensboro Daily Record,* August 31, 1971.

"Palmer Sale Tentatively Approved," *Greensboro Daily News,* August 31, 1971.

"Sedalia Area to Discuss Ways to Block Palmer Institute Sale," *Greensboro Daily News,* September 3, 1971.

"Sedalia Protest to Halt MXLU?" *Greensboro Daily Record,* September 3, 1971.

"Malcolm X University Would Retract Offer," *Greensboro Daily News,* September 4, 1971.

"MXLU Withdraws Proposal," *Greensboro Daily Record,* September 4, 1971.

"New Study Suggested for Deaf School Site," *Greensboro Daily News,* September 9, 1971.

"Site to Use Less Funds," *Greensboro Daily Record,* September 9, 1971.

"Deaf School Site Committee to Investigate Sedalia Land," *Greensboro Daily News,* September 21, 1971.

"Masons Bid for Palmer Property," *Greensboro Daily Record,* September 24, 1971.

"Malcolm X Renews Palmer Land Bid," *Greensboro Daily Record,* October 14, 1971.

"Intrigue, Melodrama Envelop Palmer Tract Bidding," *Greensboro Daily Record,* October 15, 1971.

"Trustee Chairman Denies Receiving New Palmer Bid," *Greensboro Daily News,* October 15, 1971.

"Deaf School, Church Bids Ready," *Greensboro Daily Record,* October 22, 1971.

"Church, State Offer Palmer Bids Today," *Greensboro Daily News,* October 23, 1971.

"Palmer Tract Bidders Air Plans to Trustees," *Greensboro Daily Record,* October 23, 1971.

"Trustees Delay Palmer Decision," *Greensboro Daily News,* October 24, 1971.

"Palmer Board Leaves Bidders in Air," *Greensboro Daily Record,* October 25, 1971.

"Decision on Palmer's Future Set for Twenty-seventh," *Greensboro Daily News,* November 9, 1971.

"Palmer Trustees to Meet," *Greensboro Daily Record,* November 26, 1971.

"Trustees of Palmer to Air Bids," *Greensboro Daily News,* November 27, 1971.

"Bennett College Will Take Over Palmer Institute," *Greensboro Daily News,* November 28, 1971.

"Palmer Site Uses Studied," *Greensboro Daily News,* April 2, 1972.

"IRS Alters Palmer's Tax Status," *Greensboro Daily News,* May 13, 1972.

"Sedalia Is Site of Migrant School," *Greensboro Daily Record,* October 5, 1972.

"Great Plans Rising from Palmer 'Ruins,'" *Greensboro Daily News,* December 18, 1972.

"A Second Chance for . . . Palmer," *Greensboro Daily News,* December 18, 1972.

"Bennett Plans to Renew Unit," *Greensboro Daily Record,* June 25, 1973.

"Renovation Planned at Palmer Institute," *Greensboro Daily News,* June 25, 1973.

"Her Dream Became a Reality," *Greensboro Daily Record,* August 13, 1977.

"Palmer History Filmed," *Greensboro Daily Record,* March 17, 1981.

"Videotape Seminar Focuses on Palmer Memorial Institute," *Greensboro Daily News,* April 2, 1981.

"Rural Heritage Rots under the Sun," *Greensboro Daily Record,* July 3, 1982.

"Muslim Group Occupies Sedalia School," *Greensboro Daily News,* August 11, 1982.

"Muslims to Open N.C. College for Teachers," *Philadelphia National Leader,* September 2, 1982.

"Charlotte Hawkins Brown: Pushing for Academic Excellence," *Chicago American Muslim Journal,* November 1982.

"AMTC: On the Threshold of Great Challenge," *Chicago American Muslim Journal,* December 3, 1982.

"School Said Not to Be Just for Muslims," *Salisbury (N.C.) Sunday Post,* March 13, 1983.

"Stamp for Institute Founder Sought," *Greensboro Daily Record,* May 10, 1983.

"Memorial to Brown Probable," *Greensboro Daily News,* July 13, 1983.

"Charlotte Brown Memorial," *Greensboro Daily Record,* July 14, 1983.

"Palmer's New Future," *Greensboro Daily News,* July 15, 1983.

"Friends of Palmer Move Closer to Goal of Brown Memorial," *Greensboro Daily News,* July 28, 1983.

"Historic Site Plans Going Forward," *Greensboro Daily Record,* November 3, 1983.

"Historic Site Honoring Black Moves Forward," *Greensboro Daily News,* November 4, 1983.

"Foundation Set Up to Support Charlotte Brown Mem. Site," *Raleigh Carolinian,* November 21, 1983.

"Annette Gibbs to Speak," *Greensboro News and Record,* November 27, 1983.

"Charlotte Hawkins Brown Project Seen as Likely to Win State's OK," *Greensboro News and Record,* December 2, 1983.

"Support Group for Palmer School Set," *Greensboro Peacemaker,* December 3, 1983.

"Charlotte Hawkins Brown Foundation Inc. Is Set Up," *Raleigh News and Observer,* December 11, 1983.

"Ms. Brown Hailed in Biography," *Raleigh Carolinian,* December 29, 1983.

"The Historic Contributions of Black Women," *Greensboro Peacemaker,* January 21, 1984.

"Palmer Institute: Most Significant Experiment," *Raleigh Carolinian,* February 16, 1984.

"Passing Scene," *Greensboro Peacemaker,* February 18, 1984.

"Educator's Impact on Their Lives," *Durham Carolina Times,* June 2, 1984.

"Muslims, Legislators Hold Key to Black History Project," *Durham Carolina Times,* June 2, 1984.

"200 Honor N.C. Black Educator," *Raleigh Times,* June 11, 1984.

"Widow of Nat Cole Visits Guilford," *Greensboro News and Record,* June 11, 1984.

"Black History Center in Sedalia to Be a First for State," *Raleigh News and Observer,* January 28, 1985.

"Honors for First Black Historic Site Scheduled," *Raleigh Carolinian,* January 31, 1985.

"Historic Site to Highlight State's Black History," *Greensboro Peacemaker,* February 16, 1985.

"Bill to Set Funds for Museum of Black History," *Greensboro News and Record,* July 6, 1985.

"Martin, Gist Net Funds," *Greensboro Peacemaker,* July 13, 1985.

"Palmer Institute Campus Expected to Be Open as Historic Site by 1987," *Greensboro News and Record,* July 25, 1985.

"Educator Vina Wadlington Webb, Longtime Sedalia Resident, Dies," *Greensboro News and Record,* June 11, 1986.

"Educational Taskmaster Won Students' Respect, Admiration," *Greensboro News and Record,* June 16, 1986.

"Memorial for Dr. Charlotte Hawkins Brown a Reality," *Durham Carolina Times,* July 25, 1987.

"School's Dignity, Memories to Be Restored," *Greensboro News and Record,* August 7, 1987.

"Relative Visits First Historic Black Site," *Wilmington Morning Star,* August 9, 1987.

"Charlotte Hawkins Sullivan Visits Historic Black Site," *Raleigh Carolinian,* August 13, 1987.

"History Embraces Palmer Institute," *Winston-Salem Journal,* August 30, 1987.

"Black History," *Burlington (N.C.) Daily Times-News,* September 20, 1987.

"First Black State Historic Site Opens," *Greensboro Peacemaker,* November 7, 1987.

"Memorial 'Dream Come True' for Former Palmerites," *Greensboro Peacemaker,* November 7, 1987.

"N.C. Dedicating First Site Honoring Black Today," *High Point Enterprise,* November 7, 1987.

"Black History: Palmer Site Is Dedicated," *Greensboro News and Record,* November 8, 1987.

"Brown Foundation Receives $50,000 Grant," *Rocky Mount (N.C.) Telegram,* December 27, 1987.

"U.S. 70 Stretch Named for Black Educator," *Greensboro News and Record,* February 16, 1988.

"Chapters in Herstory," *Greensboro News and Record,* March 23, 1988.

"Black Educator Gets New Honor," *Greensboro News and Record,* April 23, 1988.

"Wilhelmina M. Crosson at Ninety-one: A Pioneer in Remedial Reading," *Boston Globe,* May 31, 1991.

NOTES

Unless otherwise noted, unpublished materials cited in the notes are in the Charlotte Hawkins Brown Papers, Arthur and Elizabeth Schlesinger Library on the History of Women in America, Radcliffe College, Cambridge, Mass. A microfilm copy of these papers can be found in the North Carolina Division of Archives and History, Raleigh, N.C. The North Carolina Department of Cultural Resources, Historic Sites Section, Raleigh, N.C., has assembled a significant amount of material on Charlotte Hawkins Brown and Palmer Memorial Institute, including unpublished documents and taped interviews. Interviews cited in the notes are from that collection unless otherwise noted.

ABBREVIATIONS

The following abbreviations are used throughout the notes.

AMA	American Missionary Association
"AMA Action"	"Action of the Administrative Committee of the American Missionary Association concerning Palmer Memorial Institute," 1933, American Missionary Association Papers, Amistad Research Center, Tulane University, New Orleans, La.
AMA Annual Report	American Missionary Association, *Annual Report of the American Missionary Association* (New York: American Missionary Association, 1892–1933)
AMA Papers	American Missionary Association Papers, Amistad Research Center, Tulane University, New Orleans, La.
Brice Papers	Carol Lovette Brice Papers, Amistad Research Center, Tulane University, New Orleans, La.
Brown	Charlotte Hawkins Brown
Brown Collection	Charlotte Hawkins Brown Collection, North Carolina Department of Cultural Resources, Historic Sites Section, Raleigh, N.C.
Davis Papers	Griffith Davis Papers, Charlotte Hawkins Brown Collection, North Carolina Department of Cultural Resources, Historic Sites Section, Raleigh, N.C.
C. W. Eliot Papers	Charles William Eliot Papers, Harvard University Library, Cambridge, Mass.

S. Eliot Papers	Samuel A. Eliot Papers, Harvard Theological Library, Harvard University, Cambridge, Mass.
GEB Papers	General Education Board Papers, Rockefeller Archive Center, North Tarrytown, N.Y.
Graham Papers	Frank Porter Graham Papers, Southern Historical Collection, Wilson Library, University of North Carolina at Chapel Hill, Chapel Hill, N.C.
Hoey Papers	Clyde R. Hoey Papers, Governors' Papers, North Carolina Division of Archives and History, Raleigh, N.C.
McIver Papers	Charles D. McIver Papers, W. C. Jackson Library, University of North Carolina at Greensboro, Greensboro, N.C.
NCDAH	North Carolina Division of Archives and History, Raleigh, N.C.
NE Papers	North Carolina Department of Public Instruction, Division of Negro Education Papers, North Carolina Division of Archives and History, Raleigh, N.C.
G. Stone	Galen L. Stone
C. Stone	Carrie M. Stone

INTRODUCTION

1. The only African American boarding school remaining in North Carolina is Laurinburg Academy, which was founded in 1904. This school has never gained the height of Palmer Memorial Institute's reputation and barely survives with a handful of students. In rural Mississippi, however, a thriving black boarding school with some 300 students, Piney Woods Country Life School, seems almost a mirror image of Palmer three generations ago. See *USA Today,* May 7, 1997.

2. See, for example, Frazier, *Black Bourgeoisie;* Gaines, *Uplifting the Race;* Gatewood, *Aristocrats of Color;* Gilmore, *Gender and Jim Crow;* and Neverdon-Morton, *Afro-American Women.*

3. Brown was one of only a handful of black women to found schools in the South. See McCluskey, "'We Specialize in the Wholly Impossible,'" 403–27.

4. Powell, *North Carolina,* 22–24, 42, 104–5, 112–13, 246–52; Lefler and Newsome, *North Carolina,* 319. The English sea dog Sir Francis Drake may have left captured slaves at Roanoke Island in 1586. A rich Spaniard was reportedly living with several Africans among the Native Americans in 1654. North Carolina's Fundamental Constitution of 1669 gave slavery legal status.

5. Cooke, *White Superintendent,* 4–8; Coon, *Beginning of Public Education,* 290–95; Dickens, *History of Negro Education,* chap. 1; Commissioner of Education, *History of Schools for the Colored Population,* 368. Nat Turner (1800–1831) is the most well known African American antislavery revolutionist of the pre–Civil War period. See Rayford Logan, "Nat Turner," and Styron, *Confessions of Nat Turner.*

6. Coon, *Beginning of Public Education,* 536–38; Cooke, *White Superintendent,* 8–9; Woodson, *Education of the Negro,* 116–17. Woodson revealed that the government of

North Carolina did not provide any educational opportunities for slave or free African Americans before the Civil War.

7. Cooke, *White Superintendent,* 8−11; Commissioner of Education, *History of Schools for the Colored Population,* 369; Knight, *Public School Education,* 279; Noble, *Public Schools,* 420−21.

8. Johnson, Williamson, and Hotchkiss, *Our American Missionary Association Heritage,* 9, 20−24, 40, 60.

9. Ibid., 30.

10. Ibid., 35, 39−40; *American Missionary* 16 (May 1872): 97−103, AMA Papers. See also Perkins, "Black Female A.M.A. Teacher," and Stanley, *The Children Is Crying,* 42−44, 64−66, 81−85. For a discussion of AMA work in the state prior to 1870, see Zipf, "'American Heathens,'" 111−35.

11. James Cooper, *North Carolina,* 6−8. Although the influence of the AMA might have waned after 1870, the group was still a major player in education in 1900. On African Americans in North Carolina, see Edmonds, *The Negro and Fusion Politics,* 58−179; Powell, *North Carolina,* 436−37; "The Field," *American Missionary* 38 (February 1884): 45, and *Carolina Hall at Peabody Academy, Troy, North Carolina,* brochure, 1923, both in AMA Papers; and *Dictionary of North Carolina Biography,* s.v. "Faduma, Orishatukeh."

12. James Cooper, *North Carolina,* 8. By 1901, the AMA had over fifty-five churches of this type serving African Americans in North Carolina. Before 1901, Bethany was listed by the AMA as a "common school" allowed to teach twelve grades. See *AMA Annual Report* 46 (1892): 58; Beard, *Crusade of Brotherhood,* 117; and Stanley, *The Children Is Crying,* 39−43. Although North Carolina had more AMA elementary, secondary, and normal schools than any other state, it had no AMA colleges.

13. Charles L. Smith, *History of Education,* 158−62.

14. Dabney, *Universal Education,* 2:432−33. Numerous studies have recounted the rise of the social gospel and philanthropy in American life. See Bremner, *American Philanthropy;* Hopkins, *Rise of the Social Gospel;* May, *Protestant Churches;* Woodward, *Origins of the New South;* and Tindall, *Emergence of the New South.* On Slater, see Dabney, *Universal Education,* 1:98−131, 2:433. Slater founded the fund in 1882. On philanthropy, see Franklin and Moss, *From Slavery to Freedom,* 239−44. On Jeanes, see Dabney, *Universal Education,* 2:445−46, 449, and Harlan, *Wizard of Tuskegee, 1901−1915,* 194−96. Jeanes made this first gift in 1905. President William Howard Taft was an original member of the Jeanes Fund along with Washington. See Grace L. Deering to Brown, July 8, 1908. On the GEB, see Dabney, *Universal Education,* 2:123−52, 449−50. On Phelps-Stokes, see ibid., 455−57. Rosenwald announced his plan for African American uplift in 1912 and eventually gave some $4 million to aid African Americans. See ibid., 464−74. North Carolina received over 800 Rosenwald buildings, more than any other state. See Hanchett, "Rosenwald Schools"; Embree and Waxman, *Investment in People;* and Cooke, *White Superintendent,* 53−57, 65−66.

15. Dabney, *Universal Education,* 2:17, 132. The SEB was composed of superintendents, principals, teachers, college men, and other friends of education. See ibid., 54−73, and Leloudis, *Schooling the New South,* 146−49, on the formation of the SEB.

16. Prather, *Resurgent Politics,* 10; Edmonds, *The Negro and Fusion Politics,* 3–5; Powell, *North Carolina,* 427–44.

17. Edmonds, *The Negro and Fusion Politics,* 5–6; Prather, *Resurgent Politics,* 12; Leloudis, *Schooling the New South,* xii–xiii, 107–41.

18. *Dictionary of North Carolina Biography,* s.v. "Aycock, Charles B." Aycock secured the first direct state funding of public education in thirty years. His inaugural address stressed education and the race problem. See Leloudis, *Schooling the New South,* 178–80.

19. *Dictionary of North Carolina Biography,* s.v. "Aycock, Charles B." See also Orr, *Charles Brantley Aycock;* Powell, *North Carolina,* 444–48; and Batchelor, *Guilford County Schools,* 42–43.

20. North Carolina Superintendent, *Biennial Report,* 1902–4, 22–23, 52–53, 66–67. The other three schools before consolidation were at Salisbury, Goldsboro, and Plymouth. See ibid., part 2, 550–59. White illiteracy and nonattendance were high during this period: 19.5 percent were illiterate and 43.1 percent did not attend school.

21. *Dictionary of North Carolina Biography,* s.v. "Joyner, James Y." Joyner was superintendent from 1902 to 1919. He believed the "old southern negro" was superior to the "modern negro." In 1903, P. W. Moore, principal of the normal school at Elizabeth City, wrote, "We have taught no Latin because the Board said not to teach it." See North Carolina Superintendent, *Biennial Report,* 1900–1902, 6–12; 1902–4, 73–75, 82–83, 535. See also Hall, *Revolt against Chivalry,* 81–82.

CHAPTER ONE

1. Record of marriage of Charlotte Eugenia Hawkins to Edward S. Brown, June 14, 1911, 603:402, Massachusetts Department of Public Health, Registry of Vital Records and Statistics, Boston, Mass.; license of marriage of Charlotte H. Brown to John W. Moses, October 1, 1923, Guilford County Marriage Books, p. 1025; Charlotte Hawkins Brown, death certificate, January 11, 1961, North Carolina Board of Health, Office of Vital Statistics, Certificates of Death, book 113, p. 120, Raleigh, N.C. Other sources confirming that Brown was born in 1883 are in the Brown Papers at the Schlesinger Library and elsewhere. See Jenkins, "Life and Story"; Brown, "Biography," 1; Daniel, *Women Builders,* 133–63; Brown, "Some Incidents," 1–3; Brawley, *Negro Builders,* 282–84; Jenkins, "Early Life," 3–5; Blackburn, *Heritage of Vance County,* 39–40; and Ruth Anita Hawkins Hughes, interview by C. W. Wadelington, Henderson, N.C., July 27, 1984. Twelfth Census of the United States, 1900: Middlesex County, Mass., Population Schedule, National Archives, Washington, D.C., states in error that Brown was born in June 1882. Although various theories and rumors exist, no one has verified conclusively the identity of Brown's natural father.

2. Jenkins, "Early Life," 6. Brown assisted Jenkins with the biography.

3. Ibid., 6–8. Brown claimed that her grandmother was the daughter of planter John Davis Hawkins.

4. Ibid., 8; Woods, *Marginality and Identity,* 33–34; Tera Hunter, "Biographical Study of Charlotte Hawkins Brown," 3–4; Ninth Census of the United States, 1870: Vance County, N.C., Population and Agricultural Schedules, National Archives, Washington, D.C. From 1880 to 1900, the percentage of southern farms operated by tenants and sharecroppers rose from 37.9 percent to 48.4 percent. See Fite, *Cotton Fields No More,* 5.

5. Gladys Hawkins, interviews by C. W. Wadelington, Henderson, N.C., July 11, 1984, August 21, 1990, October 24, 1991; Hughes interview; Charles Hawkins, interview by C. W. Wadelington, Henderson, N.C., July 11, 1984; Tera Hunter, "Biographical Study of Charlotte Hawkins Brown," 3.

6. Blassingame, *Slave Community,* 261, 304–5, 316; Tera Hunter, "Biographical Study of Charlotte Hawkins Brown," 4.

7. Peace, *"Zeb's Black Baby,"* 383–84; Ashe, Weeks, and Van Noppen, *Biographical History,* 5:160–61.

8. Peace, *"Zeb's Black Baby,"* 387–89; Watkins, *Vance County,* 39; *Dictionary of North Carolina Biography,* s.v. "Hawkins, John D."; Ashe, Weeks, and Van Noppen, *Biographical History,* 5:160; Cheney, *North Carolina Government,* 278, 302–10. John Hawkins, his wife, and at least seven of their children are buried in Raleigh's Oakwood Cemetery.

9. Peace, *"Zeb's Black Baby,"* 390–92 (see also 231–34); *Dictionary of North Carolina Biography,* s.v. "Hawkins, William Joseph"; Gladys Hawkins interview, August 21, 1990. The Raleigh home of William Hawkins was the office of the Historic Sites Section of the North Carolina Department of Cultural Resources for several years. If the alleged kinship is true, the memorial to Brown that the section developed began in the very home of her grandmother's half brother. The pre-1914 graves index in the NCDAH cites a Rebecca Hawkins who died in 1901 and was buried in Blacknalls Cemetery, an African American cemetery in Henderson.

10. Brown, "Biography," 17.

11. Caroline F. Willis, death certificate, April 8, 1938, North Carolina Board of Health, Office of Vital Statistics, Certificates of Death, book 2020, p. 332, Raleigh, N.C.; Tera Hunter, "Biographical Study of Charlotte Hawkins Brown," 4–5; Brown, "Biography," 1.

12. Brown had a brother, Mingo, who was several years younger. See Ruth Totton, telephone interview by C. W. Wadelington, June 11, 1997.

13. Brown, "Biography," 14. Brown's autobiography covers her life to 1901.

14. Tera Hunter, "Biographical Study of Charlotte Hawkins Brown," 5; Hughes and Gladys Hawkins interviews; Tenth Census of the United States, 1880: Granville County and Wake County, N.C., Population Schedules, National Archives, Washington, D.C.; Brown, "Biography," 1, 12–13; Jenkins, "Early Life," 1–4; Roell, *Piano in America,* 1–15.

15. Franklin and Moss, *From Slavery to Freedom,* 212, 214, 224–38. See also Powell, *North Carolina,* 416–18.

16. Peace, *"Zeb's Black Baby,"* 288, 291–93; Watkins, *Vance County,* 7, 36–39; Du Bois, *Black Reconstruction,* on black codes in North Carolina, 176–77; on politics,

526—27. See also Gutman, *Black Family,* 365, and Franklin and Moss, *From Slavery to Freedom,* 206—9. On Brown's ties to Henderson and Vance Counties, see Peace, *"Zeb's Black Baby,"* 443—45.

17. Woodward, *Strange Career of Jim Crow,* 97, 100—102; on public accommodations, 28, 39; on attitudes, 51; on African American legislation, 54; on disfranchisement, 84—85; on Supreme Court rulings, 157—58, 162; Franklin and Moss, *From Slavery to Freedom,* on education, 360—68, 445—48; on transportation, 380, 414, 437, 442—43; Edmonds, *The Negro and Fusion Politics,* 189—92; Daniels, *Freedom's Birthplace,* 141, 81—87; Peace, *"Zeb's Black Baby,"* 293.

18. Peace, *"Zeb's Black Baby,"* 310, 357—63, 440—43. The Glass House was the first winter resort in North Carolina. Most cooks, attendants, domestics, and "hunting boys" were African Americans.

19. Daniels, *Freedom's Birthplace,* 140—41, 461—62, 468. The population of the greater Boston black community increased by 3,905 people from 1865 to 1875; 2,341 from 1875 to 1885; 6,466 from 1885 to 1895; 4,929 from 1895 to 1905; and 1,981 from 1905 to 1910. This resulted in a total African American population increase of 19,622 from 1865 to 1910. In Boston, blacks were 1.2 percent of the population in 1865, 1.6 percent in 1880, 1.8 percent in 1890, 2.1 percent in 1900, and 2.2 percent in 1920. See Thernstrom, *Other Bostonians,* 179.

20. Daniels, *Freedom's Birthplace,* 314, 323, 326, 343. See also Pleck, *Black Migration,* 2, 7—12, and Thernstrom, *Other Bostonians,* 214. Thernstrom, *Other Bostonians,* 184—214, and Pleck, *Black Migration,* xvi, 3, 40, 128, argue that discrimination held blacks back economically and that little real progress was made until World War II.

21. Hornsby, *Black Almanac,* 37; North Carolina Superintendent, *Biennial Report,* 1902—4, 82—83.

22. Hall, *Revolt against Chivalry,* 78—79, 133. Between 1882 and 1930, ninety-nine lynchings were recorded in North Carolina. No lynchings were recorded in Massachusetts during that period. See Marks, *Farewell—We Are Good and Gone,* 17.

23. Brown, "Biography," 1, 12; Jenkins, "Early Life," 4; Tera Hunter, "Biographical Study of Charlotte Hawkins Brown," 6. Nineteen family members made the move, including Brown's grandmother Rebecca, aunts, uncles, and her younger brother Mingo. Later some returned to North Carolina. Carrie, Lottie, and others made regular Christmas trips to see relatives who stayed in Henderson. See Twelfth Census of the United States, 1900: Middlesex County, Mass., Population Schedule, National Archives, Washington, D.C., and Pleck, *Black Migration,* 50—55.

24. Jenkins, "Early Life," 5, 8—9; Brown, "Where We Are in Race Relations"; Brown, "Biography," 13.

25. Brown, "Biography," 1, 12.

26. *Cambridge (Mass.) Chronicle,* July 11, 1885, 1, retyped by Cambridge Historical Commission; Jenkins, "Early Life," 9—10. Many southern blacks in Boston created churches separate from white and, in large part, northern black churches. Kin and community also supported transplanted southerners. See Pleck, *Black Migration,* 77, 85, 187—88.

27. Twelfth Census of the United States, 1900: Middlesex County, Mass., Population Schedule, National Archives, Washington, D.C.; Addie Willis, interview by

Marie Hart, Boston, Mass., February 28, 1981; Jenkins, "Early Life," 16–17; Brown, "Biography," 14.

28. Sarah J. Zimmerman to Richard F. Knapp, March 26, 1987, Brown Collection; Twelfth Census of the United States, 1900: Middlesex County, Mass., Population Schedule, National Archives, Washington, D.C.; *Cambridge City Directory* ([1899]), 262, copy with Sarah J. Zimmerman to Richard F. Knapp, March 26, 1987, Brown Collection; Tenth Census of the United States, 1880: Granville County, N.C., Population Schedule, National Archives, Washington, D.C.

29. Twelfth Census of the United States, 1900: Middlesex County, Mass., Population Schedule, National Archives, Washington, D.C.; Sarah J. Zimmerman to Richard F. Knapp, March 26, 1987, Brown Collection; Jenkins, "Early Life," 15–17; Cott, "South and the Nation," 23. African Americans found it difficult to establish businesses in Boston around 1900. Only 13 percent of southern-born blacks did so, compared with 45 percent of Jews. Several studies erroneously have placed the Willises at 69 Dana Street around 1900. They lived at 51 Essex Street from 1901 until at least 1912. By 1919, they owned the Dana Street house.

30. Marteena, *Lengthening Shadow*, 17; Jenkins, "Early Life," 11.

31. Brown, "Biography," 12; Jenkins, "Early Life," 11–12.

32. Cambridge School Committee, *Annual Report of the School Committee*, 8–11.

33. Brown, "Biography," 13. Around 1900, almost all Boston teachers were white, and most black students went to two West End schools because of housing segregation. See Pleck, *Black Migration*, 34.

34. Brown, "Biography," 13; Jenkins, "Early Life," 12–13; Thernstrom, *Other Bostonians*, 205.

35. Derry, "History of the Cambridge High and Latin School," 95–96. See also Cambridge School Committee, *Annual Report of the School Committee*, 34.

36. Derry, "History of the Cambridge High and Latin School," 96, 105–7; Cambridge School Committee, *Annual Report of the School Committee*, 11, 15, 33. Brown was the speaker at the fiftieth reunion of the class of 1900. Textile magnate J. Spencer Love, a later graduate of the merged Cambridge High and Latin School and founder of Burlington Industries, provided financial and administrative support to Palmer for several years. Huling, Close, and several alumni of the Cambridge school actively supported Brown's school in North Carolina. In 1904, for instance, Huling was one of three members of an early board of friends for Palmer. See Brown to Wallace Buttrick, October 22, 1904, GEB Papers.

37. Brown, "Biography," 13–14; Jenkins, "Early Life," 14. Drawing and choral singing were weekly requirements for freshmen; art was optional in later grades. See Cambridge School Committee, *Annual Report of the School Committee*, 34.

38. Brown, "Biography," 15–16; Jenkins, "Early Life," 17–19; Willis interview. In 1900, this was a high wage for a young girl, more per hour than most manufacturing workers earned.

39. Brown, "Biography," 16; Jenkins, "Early Life," 19; Marteena, *Lengthening Shadow*, 20.

40. Marteena, *Lengthening Shadow*, 21, 51; Tera Hunter, "Biographical Study of Charlotte Hawkins Brown," 11.

41. Low and Clift, *Encyclopedia*, 839; Lewis, *W. E. B. Du Bois*, 174–75.

42. Low and Clift, *Encyclopedia*, 842.

43. Ibid.; Tera Hunter, "Biographical Study of Charlotte Hawkins Brown," 11. On industrial education, see Franklin and Moss, *From Slavery to Freedom*, 246–48; on Washington, see Harlan, *Making of a Black Leader, 1856–1901* and *Wizard of Tuskegee, 1901–1915*. Outside the public eye, Washington did offer some support to those more active than he in seeking immediate changes in Jim Crow society.

44. Low and Clift, *Encyclopedia*, 326–27. See David L. Lewis, *W. E. B. Du Bois*, and Lacy, *Cheer the Lonesome Traveler*. On the "talented tenth," see Du Bois, *Souls of Black Folk, Dusk of Dawn*, and *Autobiography*.

45. Daniels, *Freedom's Birthplace*, 188–89, 194; Jenkins, "Early Life," 29; Marteena, *Lengthening Shadow*, 22.

46. Brown, "Some Incidents," 9.

47. Laney also influenced other African American educators of Brown's generation, such as Mary McLeod Bethune and Nannie Helen Burroughs, who became very close to Brown. See McCluskey, "'We Specialize in the Wholly Impossible,'" 403–8, and Neverdon-Morton, *Afro-American Women*, 5, 41.

48. Brown, "Some Incidents," 3–4.

49. Ibid., 4.

50. Ibid. Brown said the party, at Harvard Square Hall, attracted nearly 200 couples.

51. Jenkins, "Early Life," 21–22; Brown, "Biography," 16–17.

52. Brown, "Biography," 22–23.

53. *Dictionary of American Biography*, s.v. "Palmer, Alice F."

54. Ibid.; Jenkins, "Early Life," 17. Palmer helped many young women apply for financial aid for higher education. Her tenure as president ended in 1887. See Palmer, *Alice Freeman Palmer*, and Leslie, "Alice Freeman Palmer."

55. Brown, "Biography," 17–18; Jenkins, "Early Life," 20, 23–24. In 1900, out of 27,410 students who graduated from American colleges, only 5,237 were women. Four percent of citizens aged eighteen to twenty-one were enrolled in institutions of higher education. See Bureau of the Census, *Historical Statistics*, 211–12.

56. Jenkins, "Early Life," 25–28; Brown, "Biography," 18.

57. Jenkins, "Early Life," 29–30; Francis Wilson, "Pioneer," 1.

58. Jenkins, "Early Life," 28–30, 32; Francis Wilson, "Pioneer," 2.

59. Jenkins, "Early Life," 31–33; Francis Wilson, "Pioneer," 2.

60. Jenkins, "Early Life," 33–34.

61. Webb, *Bethany United Church of Christ*, 2. A post office existed at "Allemance" as early as 1828. Later AMA records indicated that the place of Douglass's work was McLeanville, several miles to the west in Guilford County. The current name of the area, Sedalia, did not appear until after 1901.

62. Letter from John Scott, May 23, [1873], *American Missionary* 17 (April 1873): 83; (July 1873): 150, AMA Papers. Scott served several local AMA churches.

63. John Scott, "Swords into Plowshares," *American Missionary* 17 (September 1873): 210, AMA Papers.

64. *American Missionary* 17 (November 1873): 246; 18 (January 1874): 8, AMA Pa-

pers; Webb, *Bethany United Church of Christ,* 2. Allemance, Alamance, McLean, Mc-Leanville, and McLeansville are all names for the same place. The gun factory was located about a half a mile east of Bethany Church. The racial amity in the area actually predated Douglass. John McLean taught Freedmen's Bureau schools there in 1868 and two years later sold the Bethany site to the AMA.

65. *American Missionary* 18 (August 1874): 175, AMA Papers; Webb, *Bethany United Church of Christ,* 2; *American Missionary* 32 (September 1878): 11, AMA Papers.

66. *American Missionary* 32 (October 1878): 287; (February 1879): 46, 49, AMA Papers. By 1884, Douglass reappeared at an AMA school in nearby Oaks, Guilford County.

67. Ibid. 34 (March 1880): 75–76; (April 1880): 107.

68. Ibid. 34 (March 1880): 76.

69. Ibid. 34 (April 1880): 107–9; 35 (November 1881): 330. Alamance County, east of Guilford, had been a hotbed of Klan terrorism from 1868 to 1870, but the Klan was virtually defunct in the state by 1872. See Powell, *North Carolina,* 398–403.

70. *American Missionary* 35 (November 1881): 332, AMA Papers. At that time, the state was just beginning to experiment, with mixed results, with teacher training in normal schools and summer institutes. See Leloudis, *Schooling the New South,* 74–75.

71. Alfred Connet to M. E. Strieby, December 15, 1881, AMA Papers, subseries North Carolina. On the AMA's original mission at McLeansville, see Mable Cook Pattishaul, interview by C. W. Wadelington, Sedalia, N.C., March 31, 1988.

72. *American Missionary* 40 (January 1886): 37; 42 (February 1888): 35, AMA Papers; *AMA Annual Report* 46 (1892): 58, 64; Webb, *Bethany United Church of Christ,* 3; *AMA Annual Report* 47 (1893): 53, 56.

73. *AMA Annual Report* 48 (1894): 57; 49 (1895): 55, 62.

74. Ibid. 50 (1896): 52; 51 (1897): 62; 53 (1899): 60–61, 68–69; Webb, *Bethany United Church of Christ,* 2; *American Missionary* 51 (February 1897): 40–42; 52 (March 1898): 13, AMA Papers; *AMA Annual Report* 54 (1900): 68.

75. *AMA Annual Report* 55 (1901): 60–61; 56 (1902): 50–52. In 1900–1901, seventy-three students were enrolled at Bethany, and in 1901–2, ninety students were enrolled.

76. Jenkins, "Early Life," 34–35. Apparently no uniform Jim Crow system of travel existed on North Carolina railroads in 1901. White and black passengers sometimes rode in the same cars. But all southern states, including North Carolina by 1899, passed Jim Crow laws to segregate white and black passengers. See Woodward, *Strange Career of Jim Crow,* 97.

77. Jenkins, "Early Life," 35–37.

78. Ibid., 38–39, 55.

79. Ibid., 39–40; Twelfth Census of the United States, 1900: Guilford County, N.C., Population Schedule, National Archives, Washington, D.C.; Francis Wilson, "Pioneer," 2.

80. Jenkins, "Early Life," 41–42.

81. "Quarter Century of Progress," 1–2; Jenkins, "Early Life," 42. According to Brown, fifteen girls boarded at the school at the time.

82. Jenkins, "Early Life," 43–45. For a dramatization of Brown's initial encoun-

ters with Palmer and Baldwin and her first days as a teacher at Bethany, see "The Will and the Way: Palmer Memorial Institute, April 1927." This nine-scene pageant provides an excellent account of the struggles and triumphs Brown faced from her high school years to her first experiences as an administrator.

83. Jenkins, "Early Life," 45–48.

84. "Quarter Century of Progress," 2; Jenkins, "Early Life," 47–48.

85. Jenkins, "Early Life," 48–50.

86. Ibid., 55–56.

87. Hornsby, *Black Almanac*, 41; Harlan, *Making of a Black Leader, 1856–1901*, 230. On the Atlanta Compromise, see Franklin and Moss, *From Slavery to Freedom*, 244–51.

CHAPTER TWO

1. Brown, "Teacher's First Grade Certificate"; Jenkins, "Early Life," 50.

2. Jenkins, "Early Life," 51–52; "Address of Mrs. Alice Freeman Palmer," *American Missionary* 51 (January 1897): 19–21, AMA Papers; Helen F. Kimball to Brown, March [27], 1902. Personal appeals and so-called begging letters were a common tactic of nineteenth-century fund-raisers. See Cutlip, *Fundraising*, xii, 7, 39–47.

3. Brown to Wallace Buttrick, August 31, 1904, December 19, 1912, GEB Papers; Frances Coble, interview by C. W. Wadelington, Winston-Salem, N.C., October 29, 1986; Holloway, "Palmer Institute," 3, 32–33; Jenkins, "Early Life," 53–54. Grace L. Deering, Maria L. Baldwin, Caroline Close, and Helen F. Kimball were interested in Brown personally. Other northern supporters who were also intimate friends were Daisy S. Bright, Mary R. Grinnell, and Frances A. Guthrie.

4. Johnson, Williamson, and Hotchkiss, *Our American Missionary Association Heritage*, 37, 60–63. The AMA in some cases turned its schools over to public control without charge. The South was slow to accept public responsibility for education of African Americans; in 1946, the AMA still supported seven secondary schools in the region.

5. Brown to Wallace Buttrick, August 31, 1904, GEB Papers; Jenkins, "Early Life," 57; Francis Wilson, "Pioneer," 3.

6. Francis Wilson, "Pioneer," 3–5; Whitney, *Little Story of Achievement*, 2–4. Whitney described Brown as "throbbing with the spirit of Uplift."

7. Jenkins, "Early Life," 58.

8. *AMA Annual Report* 57 (1903): 66; 58 (1904): 49; 59 (1905): 51–52. See also *AMA Annual Reports*, 1906–19. Baldwin served AMA missions in piedmont and coastal North Carolina after leaving Bethany: in Burlington in 1906, Greensboro in 1906–9, Wilmington in 1910–12, and Dudley in 1912–18. See Ada Hooker, interview by C. W. Wadelington, Burlington, N.C., June 25, 1986; *Palmer Memorial Institute*, brochure, [1910], GEB Papers; Charles Fry to Booker T. Washington, December 24, 1903, McIver Papers; and Brown to Trevor Arnett, August 16, 1930, GEB Papers.

9. *Dictionary of North Carolina Biography*, s.v. "McIver, Charles Duncan"; ibid., "McIver, Lula Verlinda Martin"; *Palmer Memorial Institute*, brochure, [1910], GEB Papers. Lula McIver was an influential educational leader in North Carolina. She be-

came a trustee of what she referred to as Brown's "air castle" and followed the work, helping "to bring it to ground," for more than four decades.

10. Helen F. Kimball to Brown, March 27, 1902. This is the earliest record of Kimball's interest in Brown's school. Other classmates, family members of classmates, and teachers from Cambridge were among Brown's early supporters.

11. *Dictionary of American Biography,* s.v. "Palmer, Alice Freeman"; [Palmer Memorial Institute], brochure, [1941]; Marteena, *Lengthening Shadow,* 36; "Dedicatory Exercises of the Alice Freeman Palmer Building, Palmer Memorial Institute, Friday, April 7, 1922," program, 4.

12. Marteena, *Lengthening Shadow,* 37; Webb, "Dr. Brown," 8; Vina Wadlington Webb, interview by C. W. Wadelington, High Point, N.C., December 6, 1983.

13. "A Service of Memory for Vina Wadlington Webb, 1890–1986," program, June 11, 1986, Brown Collection; Webb, "Dr. Brown," 5; *Greensboro Daily News,* June 11, 1986.

14. Webb, "Dr. Brown," 5. Brown's collapse from overwork caused one Palmer supporter to comment: "It is hard for me to think of you as suffering both in body and mind. Like a tired child you are accepting a much needed rest, for it was inevitable that you should break down, and you yourself perhaps least understand it." See Mary R. Grinnell to Brown, February 23, 1904.

15. Manuel L. Baldwin to Palmer trustees, April 9, 1904, Book 161, p. 278, Guilford County deeds; Webb, "Dr. Brown," 9–10; Webb, *Bethany United Church of Christ,* 1–3; Baldwin to John H. Smith et al., March 27, 1905, Book 176, p. 128, Guilford County deeds; Brown to Charles D. McIver, October 13, 1904.

16. *Greensboro Daily News,* January 7, 1918. Brown stated that "one would have to be black to know what courage it took to walk into his [Guthrie's] hotel on such a mission." See Holloway, "Palmer Institute," and DeBerry, "Palmer Memorial Institute."

17. "Quarter Century of Progress," 1. This source says the building was completed in 1906, but that date is likely an error since it contradicts other primary sources.

18. Mable Cook Pattishaul, interview by C. W. Wadelington, Sedalia, N.C., June 12, 1991; W. T. B. Williams, report on Palmer Memorial Institute to trustees of the John F. Slater Fund, February 15, 1908, GEB Papers; Marteena, *Lengthening Shadow,* 38–40; Brown, "The Will and the Way," scene 4, lines 3–4; *AMA Annual Report* 62 (1908): 52. Zula and other members of her class had to repeat the tenth, eleventh, and twelfth grades before graduating. Brown added the twelfth year to allow extra remedial time and to conform to the curriculum of the Cambridge English High School. Local postmaster R. B. Andrew named the community Sedalia about this time.

19. Brown, "Teacher's First Grade Certificate." Brown was certified to teach all of the courses.

20. Cambridge School Committee, *Rules of the School Committee,* 38–41.

21. Ibid.

22. Otis N. Pierce to Brown, February 15, 1906; Caroline Close to Brown, April 20, 1908; Helen F. Kimball to Brown, August 17, 1907.

23. Frances A. Guthrie to Brown, [1906–8].

24. Ibid.

25. Helen F. Kimball to Brown, March 27, 1902; Daisy S. Bright to Brown, August 8, 1904; Grace L. Deering to Brown, Easter Day, 1906; David Kimball to Brown, December 1, 1906; R. B. Andrew to Brown, September 16, 1907; Frances A. Guthrie to Brown, April 4, 1908; Caroline Close to Brown, August 27, 1908; Una S. Connfelt to Brown, April 29, 1910; Charles Fry to Brown, June 12, 1910; Fry to Booker T. Washington, December 24, 1903, and graduation invitation, "PMI, Normal Class of 1905," both in McIver Papers.

26. *Dictionary of North Carolina Biography,* s.v. "McIver, Charles D."; Brown to Charles D. McIver, May 21, 1904, McIver Papers.

27. Brown to Charles D. McIver, May 21, 1904, and Charles Fry to Booker T. Washington, December 24, 1903, both in McIver Papers; Brown to Wallace Buttrick, October 22, 1904, GEB Papers.

28. Brown to Charles D. McIver, October 13, 1904, March 25, April 13, 1905, McIver Papers; McIver to whom it may concern, June 5, 1905. Brown noted in the 1904 letter that Palmer had fifteen acres of land, a girls' dormitory valued at $400, furnishings valued at $800, a library containing 1,000 volumes, and a half-complete school building that would be valued at $2,000 when finished. Palmer needed $1,000 to complete Memorial Hall and purchase fifty student desks.

29. The GEB had received $129 million from the Rockefellers by 1932 and existed until 1964. Over the years, about 20 percent of GEB gifts went to African American schools, especially private colleges such as Fisk and Atlanta Universities. See Dabney, *Universal Education,* 2:123–24, 451, and *Encyclopedia of Southern Culture,* s.v. "General Education Board." The GEB Papers contain three large folders of materials that document Brown's efforts. See Brown to Wallace Buttrick, August 31, October 22, 1904, January 4, 1906, September 4, 1907; John D. Rockefeller Jr. to Buttrick, April 1, 1909; Rockefeller to Daisy S. Bright, October 20, 1911; and Buttrick to Brown, October 31, 1907, all in GEB Papers.

30. Brown to Charles D. McIver, May 21, 1904, McIver Papers; Webb and Hooker interviews; W. T. B. Williams, report on Palmer Memorial Institute to trustees of the John F. Slater Fund, February 15, 1908, and Brown to Wallace Buttrick, October 15, 1907, both in GEB Papers; *Palmer Memorial Institute: C. E. Hawkins, Principal,* brochure [Greensboro, N.C., 1907]. Brown offered special literacy classes and private tutoring for uneducated young men. On Harkness, see *Who Was Who in America* (Chicago: A. N. Marquis Company, 1943), 1:520.

31. Hooker interview.

32. Grace L. Deering to Brown, November 14, 1907; W. T. B. Williams, report on Palmer Memorial Institute to trustees of the John F. Slater Fund, February 15, 1908, GEB Papers; Marteena, *Lengthening Shadow,* 42.

33. Brown to Frederic T. Gates, November 26, 1907; *Palmer Memorial Institute,* brochure, [1910]; and Brown to Wallace Buttrick, August 4, 1904, all in GEB Papers. Brown reported that local whites treated her with "utmost respect" and helped with some projects at Palmer. See Brown to Charles D. McIver, May 21, 1904. Washington was the only African American listed on the letterhead.

34. Palmer Memorial Institute Charter of Incorporation, November 23, 1907.

CHAPTER THREE

1. Constitution and bylaws, Palmer Memorial Institute, April 19, 1908; Janette L. Smith et al. to Helen F. Kimball, November 23, 1906, Book 186, p. 576, Guilford County deeds; David Kimball to Brown, December 1, 1906.

2. Helen F. Kimball to Brown, July 25, August 10, 1907. Kimball chastised Brown for presuming to speak for her concerning land sales.

3. Helen F. Kimball to Brown, August 10, 1907. Hobgood did most of Palmer's legal work without charge for decades. See Brown to Board, 1942–43. Other supporters for half a century, Daisy Bright and Lula McIver, also were firmly in place by this time.

4. Helen F. Kimball to Brown, August 17, 1907, April 9, 1908. Kimball also supported other African American schools. The Calhoun school was one of her favorites. See Dabney, *Universal Education,* 1:480, 486–88.

5. Helen F. Kimball to Brown, April 9, 1908; Dabney, *Universal Education,* 1:486 (see also 476–82); Neverdon-Morton, *Afro-American Women,* 99–100. Thorn and Mabel W. Dillingham cofounded the school after gaining teaching experience at Hampton. Kimball often referred to the Calhoun school as a model for Palmer.

6. Helen F. Kimball to Brown, August 10, 17, 1907; Neverdon-Morton, *Afro-American Women,* 100; Grace L. Deering to Brown, July 8, 1908; Marteena, *Lengthening Shadow,* 57. On Brown's visit to Hampton, see Deering to Brown, August 29, 1907. Brown later visited Hampton to conduct research on "Negro school development." When she arrived at Sedalia, only two families owned their farms. Three decades later, most of the residents were property owners. See James Mitchell, interview by C. W. Wadelington, Sedalia, N.C., September 18, 1997; Brown to Wallace Buttrick, September 4, 1907, GEB Papers.

7. Helen F. Kimball to Thomas Foust, February 22, 1908, Book 200, p. 468, Guilford County deeds; Kimball to Brown, March 8, 1908. It is not known whether Kimball was aware that the sixty acres were sold to a white man.

8. T. L. Dick et al. to Brown, March 14, 1908, Book 202, p. 154; Dick et al. to Jacob Smith, April 18, 1910, Book 230, p. 140; and Brown et al. to Brown, December 22, 1910, Book 224, p. 428, all in Guilford County deeds. To purchase the land, Brown made out a deed of trust to Dick in the amount of $600 in addition to paying $300 in cash. The remainder was to be paid by March 29, 1910.

9. Frances A. Guthrie to Brown, March 4, [1907/8]. Guthrie was not fully aware that Brown was an agent selling land on behalf of Kimball.

10. Guilford County Board of Education Minutes, January 2, 1904, January 2, 1905, January 1, February 6, 1910; Batchelor, *Guilford County Schools,* 53–55; Brown to Wallace Buttrick, August 31, 1904, July 24, 1909; Buttrick to John D. Rockefeller Jr., March 30, 1909; Thomas Foust to Buttrick, June 8, 1909; and Buttrick to Foust, June 14, 1909, all in GEB Papers. In 1911, for instance, Brown had Bright approach John D. Rockefeller Jr. about funding Palmer's conversion to a public high school. Then in early 1915, Brown sought $1,500 annually from the GEB to make her acad-

emy a county training school. The GEB rejected both ideas. See Daisy S. Bright to Rockefeller, July 1, 1911; Rockefeller to Bright, July 2, 1911; and Brown to Buttrick, January 22, 1915, all in GEB Papers. Foust set up several so-called farm-life programs to teach rural whites agriculture and domestic science that flourished for a number of years. He found it hard to provide new programs for blacks, partly because of demographics; the number of rural African American children actually decreased in Guilford County from 1905 to 1945, whereas the white population grew. See Batchelor, *Guilford County Schools,* 56–61, 86–87.

11. Helen F. Kimball to Brown, August 30, 1908. The new structure was Grinnell Cottage. Kimball addressed the letter to "my dear Miss Hawkins," a salutation she used when she was upset with Brown's actions. Almost as if she had forgotten her harsh words, Kimball closed her letter by asking to whom she should send her contributions.

12. Mary R. Grinnell to Brown, March 7, August 13, 1908, January 22, May 29, 1909. For several years, Grinnell donated far more than $200 a year.

13. Mary R. Grinnell to Brown, June 20, July 21, October 11, 31, 1909; *Palmer Memorial Institute,* brochure, [1910], GEB Papers.

14. Clifton Conference Committee, *Era of Progress,* 362; Marteena, *Lengthening Shadow,* 41; *Palmer Memorial Institute Catalog,* 1968–69, Brown Collection; Batchelor, *Guilford County Schools,* 49, 56, 64, 68–69, 82, 84. In 1908, Palmer had two buildings and eighty acres valued at $15,000. On Wharton and Ireland, see ibid., 48–95. Cyrus A. Wharton was the father of Cyrus R. Wharton and grandfather of Richard L. Wharton, both future chairmen of Palmer's board. Edward Wharton was also related. See Richard L. Wharton, interview by C. W. Wadelington, Greensboro, N.C., May 23, 1984, and Brown to Wallace Buttrick, May 31, 1910, GEB Papers.

15. Marteena, *Lengthening Shadow,* 77, 82–83; *Dictionary of North Carolina Biography,* s.v. "Brown, Charlotte Hawkins"; Gilmore, *Gender and Jim Crow,* 156, 178–79, 190–91. Brown had attended a conference of women's clubs in Atlanta as early as 1902.

16. Marteena, *Lengthening Shadow,* 42; Virginia B. Randolph to Brown, July 27, 1909. Both Randolph and Brown worked with Jeanes teachers, instructors in the rural South paid jointly by the GEB and the counties. The black Jeanes teachers did social work and taught industrial education at African American public schools. North Carolina had twenty-two Jeanes teachers by 1914. See Gilmore, *Gender and Jim Crow,* 161–65. Brown introduced Jeanes work to Guilford County and supervised Jeanes teachers there for several years. See Brown to N. C. Newbold, January 22, 1914, NE Papers.

17. Totton family, interviews by C. W. Wadelington, Sedalia, N.C., June 17–18, 1987; Mildred Burris Dudley, interview by C. W. Wadelington, Philadelphia, Pa., February 23, 1987; Frances Coble, interview by C. W. Wadelington, Winston-Salem, N.C., October 29, 1986; Holloway, "Palmer Institute," 26, 34. Henry Sutton was the agricultural supervisor at this time. See Palmer Memorial Institute budget, 1922, GEB Papers.

18. "PMI Report to the President, 1934–35," 14, 30; Palmer Memorial Institute budget, 1922; Brown to Trevor Arnett, June 21, 1933, GEB Papers; Holloway,

"Palmer Institute," 24, 31–33, 36–37; Totton family interviews; DeBerry, "Palmer Memorial Institute," 28, 40; *Palmer Memorial Institute: The Mission ;* Marteena, *Lengthening Shadow,* 55–57.

19. Franklin and Moss, *From Slavery to Freedom,* 286–88.

20. Ibid., 288–89. Many Palmer supporters were members of the National Urban League. Brown played a limited role in the organization until after the 1940s.

21. Brown later became the first African American on the national YWCA board, but the board generally ignored her for several years. See Franklin and Moss, *From Slavery to Freedom,* 289–90; Gilmore, *Gender and Jim Crow,* 194–95; and Mae D. Holmes, interview by C. W. Wadelington, Kinston, N.C., August 24, 1984.

22. Caroline Close to Brown, April 20, 1908. One of the teachers who planned to marry soon was Lelia Ireland, who joined Palmer in 1903.

23. Mary R. Grinnell to Brown, July 28, 1909.

24. Marteena, *Lengthening Shadow,* 43; Warmoth T. Gibbs, interviews by L. Annette Gibbs and C. W. Wadelington, Greensboro, N.C., June 4–6, 1985, and interview by C. W. Wadelington and Flora Hatley, Greensboro, N.C., December 6, 1983. Gibbs, former president of North Carolina Agricultural and Technical College, was a student of Edward Brown's at Gilbert Academy. During his Harvard years, Gibbs also rented a room from the Willis family. See Warmoth T. Gibbs interview by Marie Hart, Greensboro, N.C., March 8, 1981. Although Edward Brown was a hard worker, he withdrew from Harvard in 1909 without receiving a degree. See Dannielle Green, telephone interview by Richard F. Knapp, April 7, 1995, and Edward S. Brown, quinquennial alumni card, Harvard University Archives, Cambridge, Mass.

25. Marteena, *Lengthening Shadow,* 43–44; Green interview.

26. Grace L. Deering to Brown, October 4, 1910. Deering hoped that marriage would make Brown take better care of herself.

27. Mary R. Grinnell to Brown, February 8, 1911; Helen F. Kimball to Brown, March 5, 1911; Daisy S. Bright to Brown, May 2, 1911; Maria Baldwin to Brown, June 11, 1911.

28. Marteena, *Lengthening Shadow,* 44. See also Brown's wedding invitation; Helen F. Kimball to Brown, June 12, 1911; Mary R. Grinnell to Brown, July 12, 1911; and Frances A. Guthrie to Brown, July 13, 1911.

29. Mary R. Grinnell to Brown, July 12, 1911; Vina Wadlington Webb, interview by C. W. Wadelington, High Point, N.C., December 6, 1983; Rebecca Fuller, interview by C. W. Wadelington, Sedalia, N.C., May 22, 1986; Marteena, *Lengthening Shadow,* 44. On Brown's separation from Edward, see Mary R. Grinnell to Brown, September 6, 1912.

30. Mary R. Grinnell to Brown, September 6, 1912. The Browns apparently both wanted to separate.

31. Ibid.

32. Ibid., February 17, 1913; Marteena, *Lengthening Shadow,* 44. After leaving Charlotte and Palmer Memorial Institute, Edward Brown continued to teach and preach, primarily in northeastern Georgia. He married again, had a child, and owned several pieces of real estate. He died in Indianapolis in 1961. See Edward S. Brown,

quinquennial alumni card, and alumni directories, 1929, 1934, 1940, 1948, Harvard University Archives, Cambridge, Mass.

33. Daisy S. Bright to Brown, May 2, 1911; Brown to Jacob Smith, March 31, 1911, Book 228, p. 228, and Brown to Palmer Memorial Institute, May 22, 1911, Book 230, p. 96, both in Guilford County deeds. See also a deed for registration of land dated June 3, 1911, which was first filed on April 18, 1910, Book 230, p. 140, Guilford County deeds.

34. Walter H. and Eugenia McLean to Palmer Memorial Institute, February 13, 1911, Book 226, p. 519, Guilford County deeds; Marteena, *Lengthening Shadow,* 41–42; *Palmer Memorial Institute: A Brief History,* brochure, [1919]; Robert Hughes to Brown, January 1, 1916, Book 283, p. 52, Guilford County deeds. No property transactions were made in Brown's name between 1911 and 1916.

35. Monroe Work to Brown, May 22, 1911. Work was director of research and records at Tuskegee.

36. Ibid.; Mary R. Grinnell to Brown, July 12, 1911; Frances A. Guthrie, undated letters, [1908–21]; *Palmer Memorial Institute: A Brief History,* brochure, [1919]. In 1910, property at Palmer was valued at $10,000.

CHAPTER FOUR

1. *Annual Report for Palmer Memorial Institute, 1914–1915,* 8, C. W. Eliot Papers; *Palmer Memorial Institute: A Brief History,* brochure, [1919]; Brown to Wallace Buttrick, December 19, 1912, GEB Papers.

2. Palmer Memorial Institute letterhead, [1912]; Clarence C. Cone to Brown, May 27, 1914.

3. *Appleton's Cyclopedia of American Biography,* s.v. "Stone, Galen Luther." See also *National Cyclopedia of American Biography,* s.v. "Stone, Galen Luther."

4. *National Cyclopedia of American Biography,* s.v. "Stone, Galen Luther." Stone was one of the richest men in New England.

5. "Memorial Service in Honor of Mr. Galen L. Stone Held at Palmer Memorial Institute," program, 1926.

6. Daisy S. Bright to Brown, September 8, [1914]; Brown to G. Stone, [1917], fragment, 2.

7. Booker T. Washington to Brown, March 27, 1915; Grace L. Deering to Brown, April 4, 1907; Whitney, *Little Story of Achievement.*

8. Brown, "Washington's Philosophy," 1–5. See also Brown, "Eulogy to Dr. Booker T. Washington," August 1920.

9. Brown, "Washington's Philosophy," 10–12.

10. Seth Low to Charles W. Eliot, September 11, 1916.

11. *Dictionary of American Biography,* s.v. "Eliot, Charles William."

12. Charles W. Eliot to Brown, June 24, 1916, and Brown to Eliot, August 28, 1916, both in C. W. Eliot Papers.

13. Brown to Charles W. Eliot, August 28, 1916, and Eliot to Brown, August 31, 1916, both in C. W. Eliot Papers; Brown to E. C. Sage, August 30, 1916, GEB Papers.

14. Brown to Charles W. Eliot, November 4, 1916; Seth Low to Eliot, September 11, 1916; and Eliot to Low, September 14, 1916, all in C. W. Eliot Papers.

15. Mary R. Grinnell to Brown, January 20, November 7, 22, 1913. See also Grinnell to Brown, May 23, 1913.

16. George H. Palmer to Brown, July 17, 1913.

17. Clarence C. Cone to Brown, May 22, 1914.

18. Palmer Memorial Institute scrapbook, 1916–24; "The Sedalia Quartette from Palmer Memorial Institute, Cambridge, Massachusetts, Jordan Hall, Thursday Evening, April 24, 1919," program; "Negro Folk Song, for the Benefit of Palmer Memorial Institute, by the Faculty, Students and the Sedalia Quartette, Greensboro, Municipal Theater, April 15, 1920," program. See also Alex M. Rivera, interview by C. W. Wadelington, Durham, N.C., March 15, 1988, and Ada Hooker, interview by C. W. Wadelington, Burlington, N.C., June 25, 1986.

19. Debts, mainly mortgages on land, rose to about $6,000 in early 1915, including nearly $2,000 in unpaid salary due to Brown. See Una S. Connfelt to Brown, June 15, 1914; C. A. Bray to E. L. Smith, May 23, 1915; and Brown to E. C. Sage, March 14, 1916, and Brown to Abraham Flexnor, February 28, 1916, both in GEB Papers. Copies of Brown's appeals in the GEB Papers include Sage to Brown, January 2, 1913; Brown to Wallace Buttrick, January 8, 1913; Brown to Sage, December 15, 1916, July 11, 1917; and Jackson Davis, report of visit to Palmer, February 13, 1917.

20. L. L. Carlisle to Brown, February 27, [1916]; James H. Dillard to Brown, June 27, 1917; Brown to Daisy S. Bright, August 29, 1917; Brown to Charles W. Eliot, October 15, 1917; *Greensboro Daily News*, December 31, 1917. George Palmer asked Eliot as a "personal favor" to endorse Brown's work.

21. Laura I. Heathfield to Brown, June 23, 1921; Sedalia Club, "The Cotter's Saturday Night," program, October 25, 1921; Annie Howe to Brown, Easter Sunday, [1914]; Palmer Memorial Institute scrapbook, 1916–24; Elizabeth W. MacMahon to Brown, October 1, 1915. The club's directors included Kimball, honorary president; Louise Winsor Brooks, president; Mrs. Frank K. Nash and Mrs. J. E. Williams, vice presidents; Laura I. Heathfield, secretary; Agnes Plimpton, assistant secretary; Elizabeth W. MacMahon, treasurer; and Mrs. B. M. Sherrill, assistant treasurer. Other members of the board included the wives of J. B. Goddard, D. S. Knowlton, J. K. Marshall, G. W. May, G. W. Nowell, J. St. P. Ruffin, and H. F. Vickery.

22. William G. Wilcox to Brown, October 21, 1916; Mary R. Grinnell to Brown, November 6, 1916; William Graves to Brown, December 21, 1916; William Rich to Brown, December 23, 1916; Graves to Brown, February 27, 1917. Graves was Rosenwald's personal secretary. Scott had been Washington's secretary for eighteen years. The official biography by Emmett J. Scott and Lyman Beecher Stowe was *Booker T. Washington: Builder of a Civilization* (New York: Doubleday, Page, 1916).

23. Brown to Julius Rosenwald, April 7, 1917.

24. Brown to N. C. Newbold, January 22, 1914, NE Papers; *Annual Report for Palmer Memorial Institute, 1914–1915,* 13, C. W. Eliot Papers; Thomas Foust to Brown,

January 24, 1914; Newbold to Foust, February 3, 1914; Newbold to Brown, February 4, 1914; Brown to Newbold, April 28, 1914; Newbold to Brown, April 30, 1914; and Brown to Newbold, May 4, 1914, all in NE Papers; Newbold to E. C. Sage, December 20, 1916, GEB Papers. Palmer had received a per student allotment from the county since 1905; by 1911, the county provided additional funds to train more teachers.

25. Clifton Conference Committee, *Era of Progress,* 370–71; Guilford County Board of Education Minutes, January 3, 1910, February 6, 13, 1915; Brown to E. C. Sage, June 17, 1916, GEB Papers.

26. Brown to N. C. Newbold, February 8, 1915, NE Papers; Lefler and Newsome, *North Carolina,* 580; Brown to G. Stone, June 19, 1920. See also Guilford County Board of Education Minutes, January 13, 1910; Palmer Board Minutes, January 13, 1910, June 23, 1921; and Gatewood, "Eugene Clyde Brooks," 325.

27. Mary R. Grinnell to Brown, May 23, 1913. Sex education then concentrated more on morality and less on biology than similar efforts later in the century. Premarital abstinence was the norm.

28. *Annual Report for Palmer Memorial Institute, 1914–1915,* 4–5, C. W. Eliot Papers. A number of southern schools sent students north during the summer to work as domestics. See Jackson Davis, report of visit to Palmer, February 13, 1917, GEB Papers.

29. *Annual Report for Palmer Memorial Institute, 1914–1915,* 4–7, C. W. Eliot Papers; "Report of Graduates of Palmer Institute," February 20, 1917; Brown to Jackson Davis, April 18, 1921; E. P. Wharton to Davis, March 4, 1912; and John Price Jones survey, [1923], all in GEB Papers; Holloway, "Palmer Institute," 25–26; Totton family, interviews by C. W. Wadelington, Sedalia, N.C., June 17–18, 1987; James Rudd, interview by C. W. Wadelington, Sedalia, N.C., September 30, 1986. By about 1950, farm production had dwindled to basically tobacco and sweet potatoes.

30. Francis Wilson, "Pioneer," 1; "Private and Higher Schools in North Carolina, 1916," NE Papers. Various localities also had public schools for African Americans in 1916. After the introduction of public high schools around 1937, Palmer's distinctiveness as an independent school increased. See *Greensboro Daily News,* December 31, 1917, and "Ladies at Sedalia," April 29, 1916.

31. C. J. Walker to Brown, October 17, 1916; Brown to Mrs. Booker T. Washington, September 27, 1916; Grace L. Deering to Brown, October 1, 1916; Annie L. Vickery to Brown, October 9, 1916; Helen F. Kimball to Brown, November 6, 1916; Caroline Close, Deering, and Ray G. Huling to Brown, November 7, 1916.

32. Louise W. Rodgers to Brown, March 31, 1917; Grace Park to Brown, April 15, 1917. The structure was subsequently named the Alice Freeman Palmer Building.

33. Palmer Board Minutes, September 27, 1917; Richard L. Wharton, interview by C. W. Wadelington, Greensboro, N.C., May 23, 1984; Batchelor, *Guilford County Schools,* 49–51; E. P. Wharton to Brown, January 12, [1918]. Cyrus A. Wharton had been a member of the board as early as 1910. When his relative Edward P. Wharton joined the board, there were two Whartons on that body. Vick Chemical Company of Greensboro was a world-famous drug company and maker of such prod-

ucts as Vick's Vapo-Rub. Grimsley had been Greensboro school superintendent before entering the life insurance business. He was a founder and president of Jefferson Standard Life Insurance Company.

34. E. P. Wharton to Brown, January 12, [1918]; address by R. R. Moton to Palmer supporters in Greensboro, March 31, 1919. See Charles W. Eliot to Brown, June 1916, C. W. Eliot Papers, and Whitney, *Little Story of Achievement.* For more on race relations in Sedalia, see Holloway, "Palmer Institute," 3–4, 38, and Elsie A. Paisley, interview by C. W. Wadelington, Sedalia, N.C., August 25, 1984.

CHAPTER FIVE

1. *Greensboro Daily News,* December 31, 1917, January 1, 1918.

2. Ibid., January 1, 1918. Brown was about to go north for aid, but Wharton convinced her to try Greensboro first. See Holloway, "Palmer Institute," 11.

3. *Greensboro Daily News,* January 2, 1918.

4. Mary R. Grinnell to Brown, January 4, 1918; Grace L. Deering to Brown, January 6, 1918; C. J. Walker to Brown, January 9, 1918; William Graves to C. A. Bray, February 14, 1918.

5. George Palmer to Brown, March 1, 1918; "Quarter Century of Progress"; Brown to G. Stone, January 13, 1918.

6. *Dictionary of North Carolina Biography,* s.v. "Dudley, James B."; Brown to Wallace Buttrick, December 19, 1912, and Brown to F. C. Sage, August 2, 1917, both in GEB Papers.

7. Franklin and Moss, *From Slavery to Freedom,* 360–68; James B. Dudley to Brown, January 2, 1918; *Greensboro Daily News,* January 4, 1918.

8. *Greensboro Daily News,* January 4, 1918; *Educational Rally.* The upper floor of the theater was reserved for African Americans. The black community launched a campaign to raise $1,000 to replace the destroyed food. Area churches leading this drive were Bethany, Clapps Chapel, Wadsworth, and Saint James.

9. *Greensboro Daily News,* January 1–7, 1918; C. H. Ireland to E. C. Sage, February 9, 1918, GEB Papers. White citizens of Greensboro provided trucks to carry singers and other students to the concert. For a decade to come, Greensboro concerts yielded $1,000 annually for Palmer. See *Ebony,* questionnaire, 1947.

10. Brown to G. Stone, February 21, 1918; Palmer Board Minutes, May 5, 1917. In 1912, the board approved a $2,500 life insurance policy for Brown. The board also established a fifty-acre homestead to compensate her for her years of service. At that meeting, the charter was amended to allow Brown to serve as principal for life, subject to removal only if disabled by "health or character." See ibid., September 27, November 27, 1917.

11. *Educational Rally;* Brown to G. Stone, May 4, 1918.

12. *The Palmer Memorial Institute,* brochure, [1920], C. W. Eliot Papers.

13. Franklin and Moss, *From Slavery to Freedom,* 308–14. The Klan opposed African Americans, Asian Americans, Catholics, Jews, and all foreign-born persons.

14. Frances A. Guthrie to Brown, [1919]. See also Mary R. Grinnell to Brown, August 15, 1918.

15. Palmer Memorial Institute scrapbook, 1916–24, clipping from unidentified Boston newspaper; Brown, *Mammy,* viii, 1, 4, 5. A mammy is defined as an African American woman serving as a nurse to white children, especially in the South.

16. Brown, *Mammy,* 14–17.

17. Frances A. Guthrie to Brown, [1919], [1920]; C. Stone to Brown, [1919]; Lula McIver to Brown, April 6, 1920; Brown, *Mammy,* vii. The book was well received by southern women of means, many of whom still maintained large households run by African Americans. Copies of *Mammy* sold as fast as distributors could get them. See also Louise W. Brooks to Brown, May 13, 20, 1920; Carolyn C. Denard's introduction to *Mammy* in Gates, *African-American Women Writers;* and Gilmore, *Gender and Jim Crow,* 189–90.

18. Brown, "Some Incidents," 6–7; Gilmore, *Gender and Jim Crow,* 200–201, 213–18.

19. Frank P. Hobgood Jr. to Brown, October 4, 1921; Brown to Hobgood, October 19, 1921.

20. Brown to Frank P. Hobgood Jr., October 19, 1921; *Greensboro Daily News,* March 21, 1921; Brown to B. Holt, April 12, 1921. See also Bland, review of *Lugenia Burns Hope.*

21. Brown, "Where We Are in Race Relations," 3–7.

22. *The Palmer Memorial Institute,* brochure, November 3, 1920; Brown to G. Stone, March 4, 1918; Stone to Brown, March 7, 1918.

23. Brown to G. Stone, May 4, 1918; Annie L. Vickery to Brown, July 13, 1917; Stone to Brown, April 10, 1918. Physical culture and music later became primary courses at Palmer.

24. Brown to G. and C. Stone, February 12, 1918; G. Stone to Brown, February 23, April 10, 1918.

25. Brown to G. Stone, May 4, 1918; Stone to Brown, May 24, 1918; *Educational Rally;* "Ladies at Sedalia," April 29, 1916. By 1922, Palmer's student population reached approximately 250 pupils. Brown admitted to one teacher that she raised money mainly by wearing donors down. See Mary Jane Brown Sitzer, interview by C. W. Wadelington, Greensboro, N.C., March 28, 1987.

26. Palmer Board Minutes, May 30, 1918; Brown to Ola Glover, February 3, 1920; Glover to Brown, January 19, 10, 1920; Brown to Glover, April 19, 1920; Marteena, *Lengthening Shadow,* 68–69; Brown to Glover, February 21, 1920; Glover to Brown, February 29, 1920.

27. Palmer Board Minutes, February 21, 1922; Report of Principal to the Board of Trustees with General Summary of the Work, October 11, 1922; High School Reports, 1922–31, NE Papers; "PMI Report to the President, 1934–35." Scott was made business manager in 1922.

28. Brown to Board, October 1922; Mildred Burris Dudley, interview by C. W. Wadelington, Philadelphia, Pa., February 23, 1987; Ezra Totton, interview by C. W. Wadelington, Durham, N.C., June 24, 1987; Totton family, interviews by C. W. Wadelington, Sedalia, N.C., June 17–18, 1987; Frances Coble, interview by C. W. Wadelington, Winston-Salem, N.C., October 29, 1986; *Palmer Memorial Institute: The Mission.*

29. Marteena, *Lengthening Shadow,* 44, 55–56, 96; Brown to Board, October 11, 1922.

30. *Annual Report for Palmer Memorial Institute, 1914–1915,* C. W. Eliot Papers; Palmer Board Minutes, February 21, 1922; McCusker, "How Much Is That in Real Money?," 330; Brown to E. C. Sage, April 12, August 22, 1917, and Palmer Institute, "Financial Condition," January 2, 1922, all in GEB Papers; Palmer Board Minutes, October 25, 1921. Use of in-kind items offset some inflation.

31. Brown to G. Stone, June 19, 1920; Sarah H. Blanchard to E. P. Wharton, November 15, 1920.

32. Palmer Board Minutes, November 11, 1918, January 4, 1919; E. P. Wharton to Jackson Davis, September 2, 1918, GEB Papers. Born and educated in Philadelphia, Harry Barton (1876–1936) studied architecture at Washington University in St. Louis. He pursued a career in Greensboro, where he designed the Jefferson Standard Building, the Guilford County Courthouse, the city hall, and buildings at the State College for Women. He also designed other courthouses in the state. See *Biographical Dictionary of American Architects (Deceased),* s.v. "Barton, Harry."

33. Harry Barton to Brown, January 11, 1919. Much of the manual labor was done by Palmer students and workers. See Brown to C. Stone, September 1, 1918; Stone to Brown, September 19, 1918. Carrie Stone pledged $1,000 to Palmer's water and physical plant fund without her husband's approval. She stated that Brown's courage was so great and her "trust in God so grand" that efforts to better her race "do appeal to me." The Delco electric plant was built in 1921. See Bell, "Charlotte Hawkins Brown," 18; Palmer Institute, "Financial Condition," January 1, 1922, GEB Papers; and Ezra Totton interview.

34. McCusker, "How Much Is That in Real Money?," 331; Palmer Board Minutes, February 16, 1919.

35. Louise W. Brooks to Charles W. Eliot, August 2, 1919; Brown to Eliot, August 29, September 5, 1919; and Eliot to Brown, September 12, 1919, October 19, 1917, all in C. W. Eliot Papers; "Quarter Century of Progress." It is likely that Eliot made small contributions to Palmer as early as 1904.

36. Palmer Board Minutes, October 25, 1921.

37. Brown to G. Stone, June 19, 1920; Brown to C. Stone, March 10, 1921. The other two large contributors were S. H. Tingley of Providence and Clara P. Hemmenway of Boston. Both died without placing Palmer in their wills. By that time, Palmer's debt to Brown for unpaid salary for various months over four or five years had reached $2,200. See Palmer Memorial Institute budget, 1920, 14, GEB Papers.

38. G. Stone to Brown, March 7, 1921; Brown to C. Stone, March 10, 1921; Palmer Board Minutes, October 25, 1921. See also Carl A. de Gersdorff to Brown, February 19, 1921. De Gersdorff was the person to whom Bright wanted to sell her shooting club. He was a Palmer trustee and contributed $250 a year to the school.

39. Brown to C. Stone, March 10, 1921; *Greensboro Daily News,* March 3, 1921.

40. C. Stone to Brown, March 7, 1921; Brown to C. Stone, March 10, 1921; Brown to Louise W. Brooks, March 10, 1921.

41. E. P. Wharton to Brown, July 28, 1921; G. Stone to Brown, August 8, 12, 1921. See also Palmer Board Minutes, October 25, 1921, February 21, 1922.

42. Laura Heathfield to Brown, September 16, 1921; Brown to C. C. MacMahon, October 14, 1921; Palmer Board Minutes, October 25, 1921; Brown to Palmer students, November 24, 1921. Brown had a similar sickness in 1905. See Palmer Memorial Institute budget, 1921, GEB Papers.

43. L. Wheeler to C. Stone, December 1, 1921; G. Stone to Brown, January 8, 1921. In addition to Stone, other friends were sending larger-than-usual contributions. See Annie L. Vickery to Brown, January 16, 1921; Henry W. Farman to Brown, January 19, 1921; Charles A. Munn to Brown, February 8, 1921; Elizabeth M. Richardson to Brown, February 8, 1921; G. Stone to Brown, March 7, 1921; and Brown to C. Stone, March 10, 1921. On Palmer's annual budget, see Brown to Louise W. Brooks, April 7, 1921, and Brown to G. Stone, March 17, 1921.

44. G. Stone to Brown, April 20, 25, 1921; Brown to Stone, June 17, 1921; Stone to Brown, May 9, 1921.

45. Mary R. Grinnell to Brown, June 16, 1921; Brown to G. Stone, June 17, 1921; G. Stone to Brown, June 21, 1921; Betty L. Stone to Brown, January 19, [1921]; K. H. Stone to Brown, February 17, 1921. Betty Stone was the wife of Robert Gregg Stone, the son of Galen Stone.

46. *National Cyclopedia of American Biography,* s.v. "Stone, Galen Luther." In 1948, a teachers' cottage was built and dedicated to Carrie Morton Stone.

47. K. H. Stone to Brown, February 17, 1921; Betty L. Stone to Brown, January 19, [1921]; C. Stone to Brown, March 7, 1921. On the personal relationship between Carrie Stone and Brown, see C. Stone to Brown, [1919], June 14, 1919, December 21, [1919], February 9, [1920], [June 12, 1920], July 2, 1920, December 26, [1920]. Carrie Stone had a habit of omitting the year when dating her letters. Years were determined by the use of a perpetual calendar.

48. G. Stone to Brown, March 21, 1919; Norton et al., *A People and a Nation,* 681. Recovery from the depression began in 1922.

49. Brown to G. Stone, June 19, 1920; Ada C. Gates to Brown, July 15, 1920; M. L. Schieffelin to Brown, August 16, 1920; Robert B. Osgood to E. P. Wharton, November 24, 1920; Edward Brewer to Wharton, December 3, 1920.

50. G. Stone to Brown, November 6, 1920; Caroline Caswell to Brown, February 17, 1921. Settlement houses were attempts by young, educated men and women to bridge the gap between classes by living in slum communities. See Norton et al., *A People and a Nation,* 529—30.

51. Louise W. Brooks to Charles W. Eliot, August 2, 1919, C. W. Eliot Papers.

52. Annie L. Vickery to Brown, January 10, 1920; Laura Heathfield to Brown, February 3, 1920; Harry W. Merrill to Brown, February 28, 1920.

53. Louise W. Brooks to A. H. Alderman, May 17, 1920. Alderman wrote "$40,000" beside the question, "How much is it yet necessary to raise to complete the new building?" This increased the cost of the building to more than $100,000.

54. Louise W. Brooks to Brown, May 17, 1920; Brown to Brooks, May 22, 1920, March 10, April 7, 1921. Stone was being approached by the club and Brown for donations. The club soon decided to let Merrill go to save money.

55. Brown to C. Stone, April 7, 1921; Brown to Louise W. Brooks, April 7, 1921;

C. Stone to Brown, April 19, 1921; G. Stone to Brown, April 20, 1921; Helen F. Kimball to Brown, April 23, 1921; Annie L. Vickery to Brown, April 26, 1921.

56. Annie L. Vickery to Brown, April 26, 1921; G. Stone to Brown, May 9, 1921; Brown to Louise W. Brooks, May 18, 1921.

57. G. Stone to Brown, July 9, 1921; Louise W. Brooks to Brown, July 15, 1921; Laura Heathfield to Brown, September 16, 1921.

58. Brown to Elizabeth W. MacMahon, October 14, 1921.

59. Brown to Elizabeth W. MacMahon, October 14, 1921; Brown to C. Stone, October 18, 1921; L. Wheeler to C. Stone, December 1, 1921; E. H. MacFadden to Brown, December 17, 1921. In 1927, the Sedalia Club disbanded after Palmer came under AMA control. See Palmer Board Minutes, May 13, 1927. On MacFadden's role, see MacFadden to Charles W. Eliot, December 25, 1920, and Eliot to MacFadden, December 27, 1920, both in C. W. Eliot Papers; Brown to C. Stone, March 10, 1921; Brown to Louise W. Brooks, April 7, 1921; G. Stone to Brown, April 8, 1921; and Palmer Memorial Institute budget, 1921, and MacFadden to Wallace Buttrick, February 7, 25, 1922, all in GEB Papers. MacFadden was particularly irked by Brown's irregular methods of prioritizing bills and expenses. She questioned Brown's spending $3,000 on auto expenses when coal bills were unpaid and some students lacked desks. See MacFadden to Buttrick, April 20, 1922, GEB Papers.

60. Charles W. Eliot to E. H. MacFadden, December 27, 1920, C. W. Eliot Papers; Brown to Mr. Piper, April 1, 1920; E. J. Davis to Brown, January 20, 1921; J. Norman Willis to Brown, January 20, 1921; *Greensboro Daily News,* March 2, 1921; E. P. Wharton to Jackson Davis, March 4, 1921, GEB Papers.

61. Howard M. Briggs to Brown, January 4, 1921; Mary McLeod Bethune to Brown, January 8, 1921; Low and Clift, *Encyclopedia,* 806; C. C. Spaulding to Brown, February 14, 1921. See also Asa T. Spaulding in Low and Clift, *Encyclopedia,* 806.

62. Palmer Board Minutes, February 21, 1922; Brown to Charles W. Eliot, August 29, 1919, C. W. Eliot Papers; Brown to G. Stone, June 19, 1920; Frederick Archer to Brown, March 7, 1921; Carl A. de Gersdorff to Brown, February 25, 1921; Stone to Brown, February 26, 1921; Stone to Wallace Buttrick, February 28, 1921; Brown to Eliot, February 24, 1921. On efforts by Brown to obtain support from Rosenwald, see Frank Trumbull to Brown, March 12, April 11, 1918; Stone to Brown, April 10, 1918; C. H. Ireland to Brown, April 13, 1918; and Brown to Stone, June 19, 1920. Rosenwald had contributed $2,000 to Palmer's building fund. On the John F. Slater Fund, see James H. Dillard to Brown, May 12, 1920, May 6, 1921. Dillard, as president of the Slater Fund, appropriated $500 for Palmer's 1920–21 and 1921–22 terms. The GEB previously had provided equipment for Palmer's domestic service department.

63. Carl A. de Gersdorff to Brown, February 25, 1921. See also Wallace Buttrick to E. H. MacFadden, January 6, 1922, and Jackson Davis to Buttrick, March 9, 1921, both in GEB Papers. The GEB consistently gave a negative response to the various emissaries sent by Brown.

64. Brown to G. Stone, June 19, 1920; Palmer Board Minutes, October 25, 1921, February 21, 1922; Jackson Davis, memo, April 12, 1921, GEB Papers. County fund-

ing of the six teachers continued into the 1930s. See Brown to Trevor Arnett, June 21, 1933, GEB Papers.

65. Brown to G. Stone, June 19, 1921; "Quarter Century of Progress."

66. E. H. MacFadden to Brown, December 17, 1921; *Greensboro Daily News,* April 8, 1922. On Morrison, see Crabtree, *North Carolina Governors,* 120–21, and *Dictionary of North Carolina Biography,* s.v. "Morrison, Cameron." Cameron Morrison (1869–1953) gained statewide attention as a notorious white supremacist in 1898 and 1900 but later attempted to improve race relations. As governor in 1921, he summoned a conference of prominent citizens, including Brown, out of which evolved the North Carolina Commission on Interracial Cooperation. Morrison openly opposed lynching, and no lynchings occurred in North Carolina during the last three and a half years of his term.

67. "Dedicatory Exercises of the Alice Freeman Palmer Building, Palmer Memorial Institute, Friday, April 7, 1922," program, 22–28. The $14,000 was equivalent to about $135,000 in 1999 dollars.

68. High School Report, 1922–23, NE Papers; Sitzer and Totton family interviews. The building was about 115 feet wide and 65 feet deep.

69. Brown to Board, April 20, October 11, 1922.

70. Ibid., October 11, 1922; Daisy S. Bright to Brown, April 22, [1922]; High School Report, 1923–24, NE Papers. Graduation took place on May 15, 1922. During the 1920s, more black public high schools were accredited; the total reached fifty-six by 1928. See Link, *Paradox of Southern Progressivism,* 245.

CHAPTER SIX

1. H. Smith Richardson to Brown, December 8, 1920; Frances A. Guthrie to Brown, February 5, [1921]; *Greensboro Daily News,* March 2, 1921. Richardson was president of Greensboro's Vick Chemical Company. See Brown to Mr. Piper, April 1, 1920. The "great question" was whether African Americans were innately inferior. See Noble, *Public Schools,* 273, and Dabney, *Universal Education,* 1:450–56.

2. High School Reports, 1922–24, NE Papers; Brown to Board, October 11, 1922; Holloway, "Palmer Institute," 22; John Price Jones survey, [1923], GEB Papers.

3. Palmer Board Minutes, October 25, 1921, February 21, 1922. On curriculum improvements, see ibid., April 8, 1922, and Brown to Board, October 11, 1922. On accreditation, see Palmer Board Minutes, February 21, 1922; High School Report, 1922–23, and Ferguson, "Some Facts about the Education of Negroes in North Carolina, 1921–1960," 4, 7–8, both in NE Papers. See also *The Alice Freeman Palmer Memorial,* brochure, [1924].

4. Brown to Board, October 11, 1922.

5. Ibid.; North Carolina Superintendent, *Biennial Report,* 1940–42, 5. Most other states had twelve-year programs by that time.

6. Brown to G. Stone, June 17, 1921; Stone to Brown, June 21, 1921. Stone had warned Brown three months earlier not to depend solely on his increasing generosity. See Brown to Wallace Buttrick, October 8, 1923, GEB Papers.

7. Palmer Board Minutes, June 23, 1921; E. H. MacFadden to Wallace Buttrick, February 7, 1922, GEB Papers. The board made its formal offer to the AMA in October 1922.

8. Palmer Board Minutes, February 22, November 15, 1923. On AMA requirements, see Smith and West, "Charlotte Hawkins Brown," 195–96; Tera Hunter, "Biographical Study of Charlotte Hawkins Brown," 64; Brown to Frank Porter Graham, October 16, 1933.

9. Palmer Board Minutes, November 15, 1923; John Price Jones survey, [1923], GEB Papers. Jones began as a fund-raiser for Liberty Loans during World War I. He was so successful that his firm became the major company of its type in the nation. See George Brakeley, telephone conversation with Richard F. Knapp, June 6, 1991. The John Price Jones Corporation Papers at Baker Library, Harvard Business School, Harvard University, Cambridge, Mass., do not contain a file on Palmer so the extent of further relations, if any, between Palmer and Jones is unknown.

10. License of marriage of Charlotte H. Brown to John W. Moses, October 1, 1923, Guilford County Marriage Books, p. 1025, NCDAH; High School Reports, 1922–24, NE Papers; Brown to Charles W. Eliot, February 28, 1923, C. W. Eliot Papers; John W. Moses, Tuskegee University registration and student record, enclosed with Elva E. Bradley to Richard F. Knapp, September 23, 1992, Brown Collection. Information on Moses has been obtained from the marriage license, the NE Papers, data from Tuskegee University, and Mildred Burris Dudley, interview by C. W. Wadelington, Philadelphia, Pa., February 23, 1987.

11. Brown to Charles W. Eliot, February 28, 1924; Dudley interview.

12. License of marriage of Charlotte H. Brown to John W. Moses, October 1, 1923, Guilford County Marriage Books, p. 1025, NCDAH; Dudley interview. Moses' last known address, in 1932, was in New York.

13. Brown to Charles W. Eliot, March 13, 1924, C. W. Eliot Papers.

14. Palmer Board Minutes, December 13, 1924; *Greensboro Daily News,* December 13, 1924.

15. Palmer Board Minutes, December 13, 1924. Only one of the campus's original wooden buildings, Grinnell Cottage, remained; it also became a boys' dormitory after the fire.

16. Brown to Charles W. Eliot, March 13, 1924, C. W. Eliot Papers. See also Brown to Eliot, February 28, 1924, and Eliot to Brown, March 1, 1924, both in C. W. Eliot Papers. The last time Brown was known to use the surname Brown-Moses was in the March 13, 1924, letter to Eliot.

17. John Price Jones survey, [1923], GEB Papers; Charles W. Eliot to Brown, November 10, 1924, C. W. Eliot Papers. Eliot sent a $30 contribution. Others signing the letter of support were Galen Stone, Edward Wharton, George Palmer, William Schieffelin, and Charles Ireland.

18. G. Stone to Brown, January 2, 1925, telegram, GEB Papers; Holloway, "Palmer Institute," 14–15; Elizabeth Dean, "Development of Palmer Memorial Institute," student paper, 1932; Ferguson, "Some Facts about the Education of Negroes in North Carolina, 1921–1960," NE Papers; AMA Executive Committee Minutes, Feb-

ruary 9, 1926; Palmer Board Minutes, October 27, 1925; Joint Meeting of Trustees of Palmer Memorial Institute and Representatives of the AMA Minutes, November 9, 1925.

19. Brown to Charles W. Eliot, March 14, 1925, and Eliot to Brown, March 23, 1925, both in C. W. Eliot Papers. Rockefeller turned down Eliot's request.

20. Palmer Board Minutes, October 27, November 9, 1925, April 14, 1926.

21. Ibid., January 5, April 14, 1926; Una S. Connfelt to Brown, May 8, 1926; Norton et al., *A People and a Nation,* 490, 685–86.

22. Palmer Board Minutes, January 5, 1926.

23. Ibid., March 12, 1926; AMA Executive Committee Minutes, April 13, 1926; Palmer Board Minutes, April 14, 1926.

24. Palmer Board Minutes, April 14, 1926. Palmer did not officially acquire Canary Cottage until the 1960s. Brownlee, a believer in social uplift, was an alumnus of Union Theological Seminary and had done graduate work at Columbia University's Teachers College. Like Brown, he proved to be very strong willed. See *New York Times,* November 12, 1962. Five-year pledges being paid in advance went directly to the AMA. The sole exception was "$6,000 given by Mr. Duke" (Benjamin Duke), which "was placed in the Greensboro bank." Benjamin Duke was the brother of James B. Duke and chief philanthropic agent for the wealthy tobacco family. During the 1920s, he gave huge amounts of money to African American educational institutions such as Kittrell College. In 1925, he gave $203,000 to that institution. See Durden, *Dukes of Durham,* 248–50.

25. Palmer Board Minutes, April 14, 1926. After Frances Guthrie resigned from the board and Frank Hobgood gave up his seat at the end of the term, Brownlee was elected to take Hobgood's place, and a Mrs. Lawrence of Cambridge was elected to complete Guthrie's unexpired term. Both Guthrie and Hobgood left the board because of failing health.

26. AMA Executive Committee Minutes, May 11, 1926.

27. Palmer to AMA, June 2, 1926, Book 535, p. 274, Guilford County deeds; AMA Executive Committee Minutes, April 19, 1927. Other Guilford County deeds of interest are Ola Glover to AMA, January 9, 1926, Book 535, p. 273; Brown to Palmer, March 10, 1926, Book 516, p. 511; J. C. McLean and wife to AMA, July 24, 1926, Book 565, p. 450; and Palmer to Brown, September 23, 1942, Book 997, p. 241.

28. Stanley, *The Children Is Crying,* 43. Among the distinguished AMA institutions that began under the primary plan were Howard University in Washington, D.C.; Hampton Institute in Virginia; Avery Institute in South Carolina; Atlanta University in Georgia; Talladega College in Alabama; Berea College in Kentucky; LeMoyne-Owen College and Fisk University in Tennessee; Tougaloo University in Mississippi; and Straight University in Louisiana. North Carolina schools included Gregory Normal in Wilmington, Brick Junior College in Brick, Peabody Academy in Troy, Lincoln Academy in Kings Mountain, and Washburn Seminary in Beaufort.

29. Du Bois, *Souls of Black Folk,* 100, quoted in Stanley, *The Children Is Crying,* 47–48.

30. Palmer Board Minutes, January 2, 1925.

31. Ibid., October 27, 1925, January 5, April 14, 1926. In 1942, the Palmer board

transferred Canary Cottage to Brown. See Palmer to Brown, September 23, 1942, Book 997, p. 241, Guilford County deeds.

32. Laura Phillips, National Register of Historic Places, 1988, Brown Collection; Totton family, interviews by C. W. Wadelington, Sedalia, N.C., June 17–18, 1987; Ada Hooker, interview by C. W. Wadelington, Burlington, N.C., June 25, 1986; Frances Coble, interview by C. W. Wadelington, Winston-Salem, N.C., October 29, 1986; Elsie A. Paisley, interview by C. W. Wadelington, Sedalia, N.C., August 25, 1984.

33. *AMA Annual Report* 80 (1926): 21–22, 86; Palmer Board Minutes, April 14, 1926, January 13, 1927. On the naming of the buildings, see Una S. Connfelt to Brown, May 12, [1926], and C. Stone to Brown, May 17, [1926], May 28, 1927.

34. C. Stone to Brown, May 7, [1927]. See Brown's "On the Passing of Mr. Galen L. Stone," [1926]. Galen Stone disliked his middle name, Luther.

35. Palmer Board Minutes, January 13, 1927; AMA Executive Committee Minutes, April 19, 1927.

36. Palmer Board Minutes, May 13, 1927; Laura Phillips, National Register of Historic Places, 1988, Brown Collection; McCracken and Associates, "Appraisal Report of 40.057 Acre Tract," 22–23.

37. Palmer Board Minutes, May 13, 1927; *AMA Annual Report* 81 (1927): 23. The AMA takeover made the Sedalia Club obsolete. The faculty home is located at the west end of the campus, across from Bethany Church. It was constructed at approximately the same time as Canary Cottage. See Marteena, *Lengthening Shadow*, 45–46.

38. *AMA Annual Report* 81 (1927): 23, 52; High School Report, 1927–28, NE Papers.

39. "Certificates, Awards, Honorary Degrees," 1900, 1921–45; Marteena, *Lengthening Shadow*, 50.

CHAPTER SEVEN

1. Palmer Board Minutes, May 13, 1927.

2. C. Stone to Ethel L. Williams, [1927].

3. C. Stone to Brown, May 28, [1927].

4. Elaine M. Smith, "Bethune," 86–87. Bethune's father, Sam McLeod, was of African and Native American descent, but her mother Patsy was pure African.

5. Ibid., 87–88; Mary McLeod Bethune to Brown, October 29, 1927; McCluskey, "'We Specialize in the Wholly Impossible,'" 409. Brown's wording of her triangle of achievement concept varied over the years, but the themes of education, culture, and religion were constant.

6. *Encyclopedia of African-American Education,* s.v. "Burroughs, Nannie Helen"; *Black Women in America,* s.v. "Burroughs, Nannie Helen"; Casper LeRoy Jordan, "Nannie Helen Burroughs," in *Notable Black American Women,* 137–38.

7. McCluskey, "'We Specialize in the Wholly Impossible,'" 403, 406, 413–19.

8. Mary McLeod Bethune to Brown, October 29, 1927; Frances A. Guthrie to Brown, December 12, 1927; "Quarter Century of Progress"; Cecie Jenkins, "Welles-

ley," handwritten draft, [1946], 1–2. See also Mary R. Grinnell to Brown, January 5, 1928, and Samuel Eliot to Brown, January 25, 1928.

9. Cecie Jenkins, "Wellesley," handwritten draft, [1946], 2; Mary McLeod Bethune to Brown, October 29, 1927; Elaine M. Smith, "Bethune," 89. She might have visited several preparatory schools in Massachusetts, such as Dana Hall, a school for girls in Wellesley.

10. Mary McLeod Bethune to Brown, October 29, 1927.

11. Jenkins, "Life and Story," 1; "Quarter Century of Progress"; Slattery, *Carolina Moon,* 1–12; Jenkins, "Dr. Charlotte Hawkins Brown" [1933]; Mildred Burris Dudley, interview by C. W. Wadelington, Philadelphia, Pa., February 23, 1987; Marie Gibbs, interview by Marie Hart, Greensboro, N.C., March 3, 1981, and interview by C. W. Wadelington, Greensboro, N.C., November 8, 1984; Lacy, *Rise and Fall,* 48–49.

12. Brown, "What the Negro Woman Asks." See also Brown, "Where We Are in Race Relations."

13. Brown, "Quest of Culture."

14. Ibid.

15. Ibid. Brown did not mean that blacks should learn white culture and abandon their own. She felt that blacks should acquire knowledge of the world's best cultures.

16. Brown, "Quest of Culture"; Dudley interview; Elsie A. Paisley, interview by C. W. Wadelington, Sedalia, N.C., August 25, 1984; Ezra Totton, interview by C. W. Wadelington, Durham, N.C., June 24, 1987; Totton family, interviews by C. W. Wadelington, Sedalia, N.C., June 17–18, 1987.

17. Brown, "Some Incidents," 7–11. Brown experienced racism in hotels, theaters, buses, and schools. See Slattery, *Carolina Moon,* 6–8.

18. Brown, "Some Incidents," 11.

19. Brown, "What to Teach." Brown hoped to impart to the audience the "oneness of a cry for knowledge" from the youth of both races.

20. Ibid. Carter G. Woodson (1875–1950) founded the Association for the Study of Negro Life and History in 1915. See Adams, *Great Negroes,* 142. On inequities in 1927, see Leloudis, *Schooling the New South,* 226.

21. Frances Coble, interview by C. W. Wadelington, Winston-Salem, N.C., October 29, 1986; Dudley and Paisley interviews; Mary Jane Brown Sitzer, interview by C. W. Wadelington, Greensboro, N.C., March 28, 1987; Ezra Totton and Totton family interviews; Lacy, *Rise and Fall,* 48; Griffith Davis, "Finishing School," 22–27; H. M. Michaux Jr., quoted in *Palmer Memorial Institute: The Mission.*

22. Brown to Frank Porter Graham, March 5, 1934. See also Sedalia Singers scrapbook, 1916–24; Laura Heathfield to Brown, January 21, 1920; and W. C. Jackson to Brown, May 5, 1921.

23. Palmer Board Minutes, May 13, 1927; Paisley interview; Marteena, *Lengthening Shadow,* 64–65; DeBerry, "Palmer Memorial Institute," 26; Holloway, "Palmer Institute," 16–17, 23. See also Roland W. Hayes to Brown, December 21, 1931; Brown to Samuel Eliot, October 30, 1933; and *Time,* December 18, 1933, 7. The last major performance by the group occurred at Symphony Hall on April 11, 1948. See

Ruth Totton, interview by C. W. Wadelington, Sedalia, N.C., November 16, 1992; Brown to Board, [late 1922]; *Ebony,* questionnaire, 1947; and Ezra Totton interview.

24. Daniel, *Women Builders,* 161–62; L. R. Reynolds to Frank Porter Graham, July 3, 1933, and "N.C. Summer School Plans," [July 3, 1933], both in Graham Papers; J. C. B. Ehringhaus to Brown, July 5, 1934; Brown to Graham, December 16, 1935, and Graham to Brown, December 17, 1935, both in Graham Papers; Holloway, "Palmer Institute," 47. On Brown's role in the home in Efland, see Mae D. Holmes, interview by C. W. Wadelington, Clinton, N.C., August 24, 1984.

25. Daniel, *Women Builders,* 162–63; Holloway, "Palmer Institute," 1–2; Marteena, *Lengthening Shadow,* 50. See also Samuel Eliot to Brown, December 28, 1927.

26. Johnson, Williamson, and Hotchkiss, *Our American Missionary Association Heritage,* 44–47; James H. Dillard to Brown, May 2, 1928. On Brown's obsession with starting a junior college, see Mary McLeod Bethune to Brown, October 29, 1927. Burroughs's school also became a junior college in 1929. See McCluskey, "'We Specialize in the Wholly Impossible,'" 420.

27. AMA Executive Committee Minutes, May 28, 1928.

28. Ibid., June 12, 1928; *AMA Annual Report* 83 (1929): 37.

29. *AMA Annual Report* 84 (1929–30): 41. Palmer had 258 students, 25 of whom were in the college department. The junior college instructors included people with training at Boston and Emerson Colleges as well as Harvard University. See Holloway, "Palmer Institute," 21.

30. Fred L. Brownlee to Brown, April 14, 1930; AMA Executive Committee Minutes, May 23, 1930; Palmer Board Minutes, February 10, 1931.

31. *AMA Annual Report* 85 (1931): 35; DeBerry, "Palmer Memorial Institute," 23–25; Brown to Board, April 28, 1928; Holloway, "Palmer Institute," 23; Tera Hunter, "Biographical Study of Charlotte Hawkins Brown," 21–23.

32. Brown, "Pronouncements of the Ideals for the New Palmer," speech, [1930]. Brown believed that Palmer graduates would carry culture back to their communities.

33. Ibid. See also *Palmer Memorial Institute Bulletin,* 1931–32. In 1928, Du Bois visited Palmer and gave a speech entitled "The Negro in Literature and Art." See Brown to Marvel Jackson, October 30, 1928; W. E. B. Du Bois to Brown, November 1, 1928; and Brown to Du Bois, November 7, 1928, all in W. E. B. Du Bois Papers, University of Massachusetts, Amherst, Mass.

34. Franklin and Moss, *From Slavery to Freedom,* 362–63; Brown to Trevor Arnett, June 21, 1933, and Brown to Jackson Davis, March 27, 1940, both in GEB Papers. Brown used 100 acres of school land as collateral; the debt remained until sometime after 1943. See Brown to Board, 1942–43.

35. AMA Executive Committee Minutes, May 8, 1928; McCracken and Associates, "Appraisal Report of 40.057 Acre Tract," 34–35. On how funds were obtained, see AMA Executive Committee Minutes, September 11, October 9, 1928. See also *AMA Annual Report* 82 (1928): 13.

36. Mrs. Richard C. Cabot to Brown, June 28, 1933, S. Eliot Papers.

37. Samuel Eliot to Brown, November 4, 18, 1927; Brown to Eliot, April 30, 1928, and sample appeal letter, December 20, 1929, both in S. Eliot Papers.

38. *AMA Annual Report* 83 (1929): 37, 67; 84 (1930): 41, 71, 74; 85 (1931): 58, 69; 86 (1932): 72; 87 (1933): 88.

39. *Greensboro Daily News,* February 5, 1931; Brown to Samuel Eliot, [summer 1933], S. Eliot Papers. See also Elizabeth W. MacMahon to Eliot, July 18, August 28, 1932, and Eliot to Brown, October 19, 1933, all in S. Eliot Papers.

40. Palmer Board Minutes, December 13, 1924; "Facts about the Fire."

41. "Facts about the Fire"; *Greensboro Daily News,* November 1, 1932; *AMA Annual Report* 87 (1933): 48; AMA Executive Committee Minutes, December 13, 1932. A water system project began in 1931, using $25,000 approved by the AMA.

42. "Facts about the Fire."

43. Brown to Samuel Eliot, [summer 1933], S. Eliot Papers.

44. Ibid. Brown also asked the General Education Board several times for funds to build Eliot Hall. See Brown to Trevor Arnett, August 16, 1930, and Brown to Jackson Davis, February 23, March 14, 1933, all in GEB Papers.

45. Brown to Samuel Eliot, [summer 1933], S. Eliot Papers; Brown to Frank Porter Graham, December 12, 1933, February 9, 1934, Graham Papers; Mary White Ovington to Brown, March 19, 1934; Brown to Jessie Laird, April 10, 1934.

46. Scrapbook of Palmer's thirty-third anniversary, 1934. Frank Porter Graham (1886−1972) later served as U.S. senator and United Nations mediator. A member of the President's Committee on Civil Rights, he was committed to human rights. See *Dictionary of North Carolina Biography,* s.v. "Graham, Frank Porter."

47. C. Stone to Samuel Eliot, November 1, 1933, S. Eliot Papers. Clifton Johnson, a leading scholar of AMA history, revealed that Brownlee informed him that Brown was the most frustrating person with whom he had ever worked. See Clifton Johnson, interview by C. W. Wadelington, Durham, N.C., January 22, 1993.

48. AMA Executive Committee Minutes, February 14, 1933; "AMA Action," April 25, 1933; AMA Executive Committee Minutes, December 13, 1932; Fred L. Brownlee to Brown, May 1, 1933.

49. Fred L. Brownlee to Brown, May 1, 1933; "AMA Action," June 13, 1933; AMA Executive Committee Minutes, June 13, 1933.

50. "AMA Action," June 13, 1933.

51. AMA Executive Committee Minutes, June 13, 1933.

52. Ibid., June 13, September 12, 1933. Members of the AMA special subcommittee on Palmer were Robert Coe, George E. Haynes, Mrs. Leslie R. Rounds, and Frederic Q. Blanchard. Coe, Rounds, and Blanchard later became Palmer trustees.

53. Brown to Frank P. Hobgood Jr., September 27, 1933; Brown to Frank Porter Graham, October 16, 1933. Graham became an important supporter of Palmer.

54. William Horace Day to Samuel Eliot, December 4, 1933, and Brown to Eliot, December 7, 1933, both in S. Eliot Papers.

55. Brown to Frank P. Hobgood Jr., January 5, 1934; Palmer Board Minutes, April 20, 1934, Graham Papers. On board members, see Brown to Hobgood, September 27, 1933; Hobgood to Brown, September 29, 1933; Brown to Graham, October 16, 1933; Graham to Brown, October 26, 1933; Brown to Graham, November 2, 1933, Graham Papers; Samuel Eliot to Brown, October 19, 1933; W. C.

Jackson to Brown, November 8, 1933; Brown to James H. Dillard, November 20, 1933; Oscar DePriest to Brown, November 29, 1933; May B. Belcher to Brown, January 23, 1934; Brown to Hobgood, January 5, 1934; and James Weldon Johnson to Brown, March 19, 1934.

56. Brown to Frank Porter Graham, February 9, 1934, Graham Papers; "PMI Report to the President, 1934–35."

57. High School Reports, 1930–35, NE Papers.

CHAPTER EIGHT

1. AMA to Palmer, November 27, 1934, Book 745, pp. 55–60, Guilford County deeds. The amount of land was 127.63 acres. See Samuel Eliot to Brown, December 7, 1934.

2. Brown to Frank Porter Graham, November 2, 1933; "Budget for the Year September 1, 1934–August 31, 1935," S. Eliot Papers; Palmer Board Minutes, April 20, 1934, Graham Papers.

3. Samuel Eliot to Frank P. Hobgood Jr., April 25, 1934, S. Eliot Papers; Hobgood to Brown, April 30, 1934; Eliot to Brown, June 23, 1934; Elizabeth W. Mac-Mahon to Brown, July 9, 1934; Charles F. Myers to Brown, July 16, 1934; Eliot to Brown, December 7, 1934.

4. Samuel Eliot to Brown, December 7, 1934; Brown to Frank Porter Graham, November 1, 1934. The Roosevelts and the president's mother contributed to Palmer for well over twenty years. See Brown to Clyde R. Hoey, March 13, 1940, GEB Papers. Brown invited Eleanor Roosevelt to speak at a dinner in Boston before 1,000 people. Mrs. Roosevelt did not accept. See Brown to Eliot, October 30, 1933. Also included among Palmer's notable supporters was Mrs. John D. Rockefeller Jr. See Aura L. Kelly to Brown, January 11, 1936.

5. Frank Porter Graham to Brown, February 28, 1936; Brown to Graham, March 6, 1936; Jenkins, "Twig Bender, 1937–45"; *Palmer Memorial Institute Bulletin*, 1935–36.

6. *Palmer Memorial Institute Bulletin*, 1935–36, 8.

7. Ibid., 1–20.

8. Ferguson, "Some Facts about the Education of Negroes in North Carolina, 1921–1960," 4–8, NE Papers; Guilford County Board of Education Minutes, June 6, 1931; Brown to Frank Porter Graham, June 18, 1934. The state began paying one teacher's salary at Palmer in 1921 and continued until 1937.

9. Guilford County Board of Education Minutes, January 2, 1905, July 5, 1909; Batchelor, *Guilford County Schools*, 89–91, 94.

10. Batchelor, *Guilford County Schools*, 90–92.

11. J. W. Burke to State School Commission, August 5, 1935, Graham Papers.

12. Brown to Frank Porter Graham, August 6, 1935; Graham to Leroy Martin, August 7, 1935; Martin to Graham, August 8, 12, 1935; and Brown to Board, May 15, 1936, all in Graham Papers. See also Palmer Board Minutes, May 15, 1936, Graham Papers, and Brown to Board, 1938–39.

13. Brown to Frank Porter Graham, [June 1936], Graham Papers. See also Graham to Brown, July 7, 1936, and Brown to Graham, August 4, 1936, both in Graham Papers.

14. Brown to Frank Porter Graham, December 5, 1936, Graham Papers.

15. Ibid.; Brown to N. C. Newbold, December 5, 1936, Graham Papers.

16. Brown to N. C. Newbold, December 5, 1936, Graham Papers. Brown did not want any of the current black college presidents to head the proposed African American college system.

17. Ibid.; Brown to Frank Porter Graham, December 11, 1936, Graham Papers. After years of fighting against forced segregation, Brown had learned to use that unjust system to her advantage.

18. Brown to Frank Porter Graham, December 11, 1936, Graham Papers.

19. Ibid. Graham went along with Brown on almost every detail.

20. Jenkins, "Twig Bender, 1937–45," 1.

21. Ibid., 1–2. Eight to ten day students continued at Palmer because their parents were employed there. See Guilford County Board of Education Minutes, April 5, 1937, and Marteena, *Lengthening Shadow*, 68–69. Lanier taught until 1944, worked in Connecticut for a few years, and then returned to Sedalia. In the early 1950s, he became principal of the Sedalia school, where he served thirteen years. In 1966, he became a Palmer trustee; his daughter, Jeanne Lanier Rudd, worked at Palmer and later became manager of the historic site. See Rudd and Lanier, *The Family Lanier*, 11–15; Brown to Board, 1938–39, 1942–43; Jenkins, "Away from the Beaten Path"; Totton family, interviews by C. W. Wadelington, Sedalia, N.C., June 17–18, 1987; DeBerry, "Palmer Memorial Institute," 27; and Holloway, "Palmer Institute," 40.

22. Jenkins, "Twig Bender, 1937–45," 2; Marteena, *Lengthening Shadow*, 68–69. On Glover's death, see Brown to Frank Porter Graham, January 4, 1938, and Graham to Brown, January 18, 1938, both in Graham Papers; and "Nurse Ola Glover of Palmer Institute Succumbs," funeral speech, January 6, 1938. Glover passed away on January 4, 1938.

23. Jenkins, "Twig Bender, 1937–45," 3; G. C. Wilkinson to Brown, July 2, 1937; Samuel Eliot to Brown, August 12, 1937, S. Eliot Papers; Caroline F. Willis, death certificate, April 8, 1938, North Carolina Board of Health, Office of Vital Statistics, Certificates of Death, book 2020, p. 332, Raleigh, N.C. On Brown's mother's declining years, see S. Bess to Brown, April 11, 1934, and Eliot to Brown, December 7, 1934. Mrs. Willis died of complications resulting from diabetes.

24. Frances Coble, interview by C. W. Wadelington, Winston-Salem, N.C., October 29, 1986; Mildred Burris Dudley, interview by C. W. Wadelington, Philadelphia, Pa., February 23, 1987; Marie Gibbs, interview by C. W. Wadelington, Greensboro, N.C., November 8, 1984; Elsie A. Paisley, interview by C. W. Wadelington, Sedalia, N.C., August 25, 1984; Totton family interviews; Lacy, *Rise and Fall*, 45; Carol Brice, diary, February 19, 1934, Brown Collection; *Ebony*, questionnaire, 1947; "PMI Report to the President, 1934–35"; *Palmer Memorial Institute Bulletin, 1935–36*; *Palmer Memorial Institute*, brochure, [1907]; "Rules and Regulations," [1949].

25. Carol Brice, diary, 1934, Brown Collection; Coble and Totton family inter-

views; Mary Jane Brown Sitzer, interview by C. W. Wadelington, Greensboro, N.C., March 28, 1987; Holloway, "Palmer Institute," 29−30; "PMI Report to the President, 1934−35"; *Palmerite,* annual, 1946.

26. Carol Brice, diary, 1934, Brown Collection; student essays, 1936−40; Lacy, *Rise and Fall,* 47−52; Totton family interviews.

27. Jenkins, "Twig Bender, 1937−45," 3−4, 13; *Palmer Memorial Institute Bulletin,* 1937−38; scrapbook of Palmer's thirty-fifth anniversary, April 23−25, 1937.

28. Brown to Board, 1938−39; Low and Clift, *Encyclopedia,* 753. James Edward Shepard (1875−1947) in 1910 founded the National Religious Training School and Chautauqua for the education of Christian workers and teachers, and he remained its president until his death. Later operated by the state, the school became the North Carolina College for Negroes, then it was the North Carolina College at Durham, and presently it is North Carolina Central University.

29. Low and Clift, *Encyclopedia,* 172. When Jones arrived at Bennett, the school had deteriorated to the point that it had only ten students and a $100 endowment. In thirty years, he renewed the college and built up the endowment to $1.5 million. Although Jones made Bennett a "symbol of self-determination," some called it elitist. On Jones, see ibid., 477, and Chafe, *Civilities and Civil Rights,* 26−27.

30. Brown to Board, 1938−39; Brown to W. C. Jackson, February 9, 1940, and Jackson to Brown, February 16, 1940, both in Charlotte Hawkins Brown and Palmer Memorial Institute Files, W. C. Jackson Library, University of North Carolina at Greensboro, Greensboro, N.C.; Dudley and Totton family interviews.

31. Clyde R. Hoey to Brown, March 16, 1940, Hoey Papers. On Brown's proposal, see Brown to Hoey, March 6, 1940, GEB Papers, and Brown to Hoey, March 13, 1940, Hoey Papers.

32. Brown to Frank Porter Graham, March 19, 1940; Brown to M. C. S. Noble, March 19, 1940; and Graham to Brown, March 27, 1940, all in Graham Papers. Brown also asked the GEB for $30,000 to cover the two-year operating budget. See Brown to Jackson Davis, March 27, 1940, GEB Papers.

33. Brown to Frank Porter Graham, April 1, 1940, Graham Papers.

34. Brown to Board, 1940−41. See also Brown to Palmer trustees, June 18, 1940, Graham Papers; Clyde R. Hoey to Brown, April 4, August 8, 1940, and Brown to Hoey, August 5, 1940, both in Hoey Papers.

35. Brown to Clyde R. Hoey, August 7, 1940, and Hoey to Brown, August 10, 1940, both in Hoey Papers.

36. Jenkins, "Twig Bender, 1937−45," 5; Lacy, *Rise and Fall,* 48.

37. Jenkins, "Twig Bender, 1937−45," 5−6; Frank Porter Graham to Brown, November 13, 1940, Graham Papers.

38. Jenkins, "Twig Bender, 1937−45," 6−7; Brown, *The Correct Thing,* 50, 83. *The Correct Thing* was reprinted several more times.

39. Franklin and Moss, *From Slavery to Freedom,* 385−90.

40. Brown to Board, 1940−41, 1942−43; Totton family interviews. In 1943, Brown also served as a consultant to the secretary of war on recreation in military camps. See Bell, "Charlotte Hawkins Brown," 19. The gym, built about 1943, was condemned in the 1960s.

41. Brown, "Role of the Negro Woman." The four freedoms were freedom of speech, of religion, from want, and from fear. Roosevelt listed those freedoms in an address to the Seventy-seventh Congress in January 1941. See *War Volume of Compton's Pictured Encyclopedia: An Alphabetical Reference Book of the Second World War* (Chicago: F. E. Compton, 1943). Other similar speeches by Brown were "The Importance of Overcoming Discrimination" in 1943 and "Military Training for National Safety" in about 1944.

42. Jenkins, "Twig Bender, 1937–45," 7–8; *Pittsburgh Courier,* April 17, 1943.

43. Brown to Board, 1938–39, 1940–41, 1942–43; *Greensboro Daily News,* May 24, 1943; *Ebony,* questionnaire, 1947; Lacy, *Rise and Fall,* 64.

44. Jenkins, "Twig Bender, 1937–45," 7–12; *Greensboro Daily News,* June 12, 1943; Brown to Board, 1938–39, 1942–43; "Certificates, Awards, Honorary Degrees," 1939–45; Bell, "Charlotte Hawkins Brown," 18. On Brown during the years before she became known as the "First Lady of Social Graces," see Coble interview. Charlie Maye came to Palmer as a child and was practically reared by Brown. He had run the farm since 1925 and in 1942–43 produced pork, grains, vegetables, and (for the first time) $1,000 worth of tobacco. See Brown to Board, 1940–41, 1942–43; Rebecca Fuller, interview by C. W. Wadelington, Sedalia, N.C., May 22, 1986; and Lola Maye, interview by Harold Webb, Sedalia, N.C., February 12, 1987. Helped by Bethune, Brown also got federal New Deal scholarships for eleven students. See Brown to Board, 1938–39, 1940–41; *Palmerite,* annual, 1946; Ruth Totton, interview by C. W. Wadelington and Richard F. Knapp, Sedalia, N.C., April 4, 1997; Lacy, *Rise and Fall,* 50; and Brown to Palmer graduates, December 20, 1939.

45. Brown, "Annual Report of the President of Palmer Memorial Institute," 1942–43, 1–4, 8, Brown Collection; Bell, "Charlotte Hawkins Brown," 19; Brown to C. R. Wharton, September 26, 1951, in Strand Report, 1951; Strand Report, 1951; Palmer Board Minutes, April 26, November 1, 1946; Brown to Clyde R. Hoey, June 16, 1944; Thomas J. Pearsall to Brown, December 28, 1944; John Twombly to Brown, [1945]. Strand Reports cover the years 1951 to 1969. The reserve fund was used for emergencies. Among prominent new African American and white trustees and sponsors in North Carolina were governors Hoey and Broughton; life insurance company presidents Julian Price and C. C. Spaulding; state school superintendent Clyde A. Erwin; state legislator Thomas J. Pearsall; attorneys A. L. Brooks and Hugar S. King; educators James E. Shepard, Harriet Elliot, Clyde A. Milner, David D. Jones, and Ben L. Smith; newspaper editors Julian Miller and H. W. Kendall; dentists John D. Hawkins, Thomas Watkins, B. W. Barnes, and George C. Simkins; and former newspaper editor and ambassador Josephus Daniels.

46. C. Stone to Brown, April 15, November 17, 1944, March 7, 1945; *New York Times,* July 30, August 7, 1945; Stone to Brown, [1945]; Palmer Board Minutes, April 26, 1946; Brown, "Annual Report of the President of Palmer Memorial Institute," 1946–47, 4–5, Brown Collection. See also Christine Knudsen to Brown, September 10, 1945, and *Palmerite,* annuals, 1946, 1953.

47. *Dictionary of North Carolina Biography,* s.v. "Love, James Spencer"; Palmer

Board Minutes, April 25, October 17, 1947, April 30, 1948; J. Spencer Love to Brown, December 9, 1946, Davis Papers; W. G. Coltrane Jr., Certified Public Accountant, Greensboro, N.C., "Exhibit A: Assets and Liabilities," June 27, 1951; Brown, "Annual Report of the President of Palmer Memorial Institute," 1946–47, 3, Brown Collection. Davis's papers concerning Brown and Palmer were given to the Historic Sites Section by Davis in 1987. Other members of Love's family gave to Palmer. See James Lee Love to Brown, December 9, 1946, Davis Papers.

48. Palmer Board Minutes, April 26, 1946; Brown, "Annual Report of the President of the Palmer Memorial Institute," 1946–47, 2, Brown Collection; Bell, "Charlotte Hawkins Brown," 18; Holloway, "Palmer Institute," 41; Baker, "Twig-Bender," 8, 10; James Rudd, interview by C. W. Wadelington, Sedalia, N.C., September 30, 1986; Totton family interviews; Brown to Board, 1942–43.

49. Palmer Board Minutes, April 25, 1947; Brown to Board, 1938–39, 1940–41, 1942–43; Ruth Totton and Totton family interviews; Baker, "Twig-Bender," 10–11; Lacy, *Rise and Fall*, 52.

50. Griffith Davis, "Finishing School," 22–36. African American poet and writer Langston Hughes suggested the article to *Ebony* after a visit to Palmer. See Langston Hughes to John H. Johnson, March 3, 1947; Hughes to Brown, March 26, 1947; Griffith Davis to Brown, telegram, [1947]; Ben Burns to Davis, February 26, 1947; Davis to Brown, March 23, 1947; Davis to Burns, March 29, 1947; Davis to Brown, April 15, 1947; Davis to Burns, May 1, 1947; and Burns to Davis, May 5, 1947, all in Davis Papers; Brown, "Annual Report of the President of Palmer Memorial Institute," 1946–47, 9, Brown Collection; and H. M. Michaux Jr., interview by Marie Hart, Greensboro, N.C., February 26, 1981.

51. Griffith Davis, "Finishing School," 24–26; Ruth Totton, interview by C. W. Wadelington, Sedalia, N.C., June 11, 1987. Students could not smoke on campus. The article contains twenty-two excellent photos of student life and campus scenery.

52. Griffith Davis, "Finishing School," 26.

53. Palmer Board Minutes, November 1, 1946, April 25, 1947, April 30, 1948; High School Report, 1949–50, NE Papers. On Jenkins and Grant, see High School Reports, 1945–50, NE Papers, and Brown to Cecie Jenkins, telegram, October 10, 1946. As early as 1943, Brown had told the board to begin looking for a successor, a man in his thirties, to carry on Palmer's "academic, cultural, Christian training." See Brown to Board, 1942–43.

54. *Palmerite,* annual, 1946, 5; Palmer Board Minutes, April 26, 1946, April 25, 1947, April 30, 1948. D. B. Scott, former administrative assistant to Brown, also was elected a trustee. See Palmer Board Minutes, November 1, 1946.

55. Palmer Board Minutes, April 26, 1942, April 26, 1946.

56. Brown, "Annual Report of the President of Palmer Memorial Institute," 1946–47, 5, Brown Collection; Laura Phillips, National Register of Historic Places, 1988, Brown Collection. The Congregational Women's Cottage was completed in 1948 at a cost of $25,000. In 1949, $50,000 in bonds was moved to the reserve fund to finish paying for Stone Cottage and the Women's Cottage. See Palmer Board

Minutes, April 22, 1949, and Jeanne Lanier Rudd, interview by C. W. Wadelington, Sedalia, N.C., March 19, 1993. Eight or so girls lived for six weeks at a time in the Women's Cottage with a faculty adviser to learn how to run a household.

57. Palmer Board Minutes, April 26, 1946, April 22, 1949; "The Charlotte Hawkins Brown Foundation, Trust Agreement," July 2, 1949; High School Report, 1949–50, NE Papers.

58. "Wilhelmina M. Crosson," funeral program, Twelfth Baptist Church, Boston, Mass., June 1, 1991; Dannett, *Profiles*, 6.

59. Dannett, *Profiles*, 67–70; "Wilhelmina M. Crosson," funeral program, Twelfth Baptist Church, Boston, Mass., June 1, 1991; Wilhelmina Crosson, interview by Marie Hart, Boston, Mass., February 28, 1981. Alpha Kappa Alpha is a prestigious national service organization of African American women.

60. Dannett, *Profiles*, 70; Palmer Board Minutes, April 22, 1949; Crosson interview. Crosson was forty-seven years old when she began work at Palmer.

61. Four decades later, the state of North Carolina implemented a similar program requiring competency tests for graduation from public high schools.

62. For interpretation of the atmosphere in Greensboro in which white progressives and philanthropists openly supported and encouraged "safe" African Americans, see Chafe, *Civilities and Civil Rights*. Brown was well within that category of blacks and enjoyed its privileges.

63. Dannett, *Profiles*, 70; *Greensboro Daily News*, February 9, 1950.

64. *Greensboro Daily News*, February 9, 1950; Dannett, *Profiles*, 70.

65. Dannett, *Profiles*, 70; *Greensboro Daily News*, February 9, 11, 1950; Griffith Davis to Brown, February 17, 1950, Davis Papers. Insurance rates were high in Palmer's rural location.

66. Palmer Board Minutes, February 17, April 25, May 20, 1950.

67. Dannett, *Profiles*, 71; Palmer Board Minutes, June 2, 1951; Brown to C. R. Wharton, September 26, 1951, in Strand Report, 1951. Along with Brown, other longtime members of the board, such as Burke and Hobgood, were in declining health. Hobgood's health was so poor that Wharton became acting chairman in 1950. See Palmer Board Minutes, May 20, 1950.

68. Dannett, *Profiles*, 71; Fuller interview.

69. "Inaugural Exercises for Wilhelmina M. Crosson, Palmer Memorial Institute, Sunday, October 5, 1952"; *Greensboro Daily News*, October 5, 1952.

CHAPTER NINE

1. "Inaugural Exercises for Wilhelmina M. Crosson, Palmer Memorial Institute, Sunday, October 5, 1952."

2. *Greensboro Daily News*, October 5, 6, 1952; High School Report, 1952–53, NE Papers; Palmer Board Minutes, June 6, 1952.

3. Palmer Board Minutes, June 6, 1952; Strand Report, 1951–52. The reserve fund for that year was $55,500, and the endowment fund totaled $120,000. By the following year, the school's reserve fund was $60,936.79, at least $20,000 of which was earmarked for the endowment fund.

4. Palmer Board Minutes, June 6, 1952, May 22, 1953, May 14, 1954, May 14, 1955. See also Strand Reports, 1952−55.

5. Wilhelmina Crosson, interview by Marie Hart, Boston, Mass., February 28, 1981.

6. Palmer Board Minutes, May 14, 1955. Brown was the only trustee to vote against giving Crosson full control.

7. Charles W. Bundrige, interview by C. W. Wadelington, Sedalia, N.C., April 12, 1984; Richard L. Wharton, interview by C. W. Wadelington, Greensboro, N.C., May 23, 1984; Rebecca Fuller, interview by C. W. Wadelington, Sedalia, N.C., May 22, 1986; Ruth Totton, interview by C. W. Wadelington, Sedalia, N.C., June 11, 1987.

8. Palmer Board Minutes, April 19, 1956.

9. Ibid., May 22, 1958.

10. Frances Bonner to Carol Brice, June 30, 1958, Brice Papers.

11. Ibid., June 30, July 22, 1958.

12. Robert Stone to Carol Brice, August 4, 1958, and Brice to Maria Cole, August 6, 1958, both in Brice Papers; Palmer Board Minutes, June 15, 1959. For financial data on Brown's stay at the hospital, see Brown's estate records, Clerk of Court's Office, Guilford County Courthouse, Greensboro, N.C.

13. Carol Brice to C. R. Wharton, August 8, 1958, and Wharton to Brice, August 12, 1958, both in Brice Papers.

14. Robert Stone to C. R. Wharton, August 22, 1958, and Carol Brice to Hugh Thompson, September 17, 1958, both in Brice Papers.

15. Carol Brice to Hugh Thompson, September 17, 1958, Brice Papers; C. W. Wadelington, telephone conversation with Ruth Totton, March 30, 1993. See also Ruth Totton interview; Totton family, interviews by C. W. Wadelington, Sedalia, N.C., June 17−18, 1987. Crosson was against moving Brown to California.

16. Palmer Board Minutes, January 22, May 13, 1960; Crosson interview; telegrams from Crosson to Carol Brice, Lolita Brice Bluford, and others, January 11, 1961, Brice Papers. See Brown's estate records, Clerk of Court's Office, Guilford County Courthouse, Greensboro, N.C., for further details.

17. *Greensboro Daily News,* January 12, 1961; *Baltimore Afro-American,* January 21, 1961; will of Charlotte Hawkins Brown, December 4, 1953, Book 15, p. 415, Guilford County wills; James Rudd, interview by C. W. Wadelington, Sedalia, N.C., September 30, 1986; Jeanne Lanier Rudd, interviews by C. W. Wadelington, Sedalia, N.C., March 19, April 21, 1993.

18. Palmer Board Minutes, June 9, 1961. The money to buy Canary Cottage was taken from the reserve fund and was replaced later by contributions to a special fund.

19. Palmer Board Minutes, June 9, December 12, 1961.

20. Crosson, "Annual Report of the President of Palmer Memorial Institute," 1960−61, 1−10, Brown Collection.

21. Palmer Board Minutes, June 22, 1960; Crosson, "Annual Report of the President of Palmer Memorial Institute," 1960−61, 74, Brown Collection.

22. Palmer Board Minutes, May 13, 1960.

23. Ibid., October 14, 1960; Crosson, "Annual Report of the President of Palmer Memorial Institute," 1960–61, 11, Brown Collection.

24. Crosson, "Annual Report of the President of Palmer Memorial Institute," 1960–61, 12, Brown Collection; Strand Reports, 1952–62.

25. Palmer Board Minutes, May 11, 1962.

26. Crosson, "Annual Report of the President of Palmer Memorial Institute," 1960–61, 30–34, Brown Collection.

27. Ibid., 86.

28. Wilhelmina Crosson, interview by Constance H. Marteena, Greensboro, N.C., [1977], transcript, Bennett College Archives, Holgate Library, Bennett College, Greensboro, N.C., 5–6; Crosson interview by Hart; Crosson, "Annual Report of the President of Palmer Memorial Institute," 1960–61, 28, Brown Collection. The Peace Corps was a federal agency established in the early 1960s to sponsor American volunteers who helped provide education and fight poverty in Third World countries. Palmer is believed to have been the first school in North Carolina to include "Negro history" in its curriculum. Brown offered the course in the early 1940s.

29. Wilson, *For the People of North Carolina;* Trudy Holder, telephone interview by Richard F. Knapp, May 18, 1993; McCracken and Associates, "Appraisal Report of 40.057 Acre Tract," 25–26. Reynolds Hall measured 11,731 square feet on two floors, as well as a basement. The building had twenty-eight dormitory rooms, a lounge, two suites for counselors, bathrooms, and space for storage and offices. See ibid., 18–19.

30. Strand Reports, 1961–66. Use of the endowment fund was restricted, but $6,000 was removed in 1966, leaving $114,000.

31. Wharton interview; Richard L. Wharton to C. W. Wadelington, April 29, 1993.

32. Wharton interview; Richard L. Wharton to C. W. Wadelington, April 29, 1993.

33. Wharton interview.

34. Ibid.; Bundrige interview. New England preparatory schools and colleges were offering scholarships to African Americans. This new competition from public and independent schools provided a significant challenge to all historically African American schools. See Crow, Escott, and Hatley, *African Americans in North Carolina,* 157–59. Laurinburg Academy still survives today as Laurinburg Institute.

35. Wharton interview.

36. *Greensboro Daily News,* August 27, 1966; *Greensboro Daily Record,* April 29, 1968. See also Harold E. Bragg, interview by Marie Hart, Greensboro, N.C., March 5, 1981.

37. Charles W. Bundrige, interview by C. W. Wadelington, Sedalia, N.C., June 3, 1993; Bundrige interview, April 12, 1984; Rudolph D. Artis, interview by C. W. Wadelington, Greensboro, N.C., June 7, 1993; Ruth Totton interview; Elworth E. Smith, interview by C. W. Wadelington, Greensboro, N.C., July 19, 1984.

38. Strand Reports, 1967–69.

39. Wharton interview. On Bragg's spending policies, see Strand Reports, 1966–69. See also *Greensboro Daily News,* April 21, May 17, 1970, and *Greensboro Daily Record,* January 30, March 2, 1970.

40. Wharton interview; Bundrige interview, April 12, 1984. Although Wharton would not cite Bragg as the primary reason the school failed, Bundrige and several other members of Palmer's staff did not hesitate to do so.

41. Wharton interview. Board members included Ben Mayes, Willa B. Player, and Rose Butler Browne. Wharton recollected that "none of them chose to move in." Douglas was the first African American chairman. One year later, Elworth E. Smith, a Palmer graduate and successful Greensboro businessman, was elected to the position. It was under Smith's term that Palmer closed. See Smith interview and Bundrige interview, June 3, 1993.

42. *Greensboro Daily News,* May 17, June 23, 1970; Bragg interview. See also Wharton interview.

43. *Greensboro Daily News,* August 29, 1970; *Greensboro Daily Record,* August 29, 1970.

44. Bundrige interview, April 12, 1984; Ruth Totton interview; Barbara Gibson Wiley, interview by C. W. Wadelington, Sedalia, N.C., June 9, 1993; *Greensboro Daily Record,* December 4, 15, 22, 1969; *Greensboro Daily News,* December 16, 1969. A similar confrontation occurred that same year when a student tried to turn Palmer into a Black Panther guerrilla training camp. See *Greensboro Daily News,* May 17, 1970.

45. Franklin and Moss, *From Slavery to Freedom,* 444–48. On the mood of the African American community during the 1960s and early 1970s, see ibid., 448–70. On the civil rights movement in North Carolina, see Flora J. Hatley, "The Civil Rights Movement of the 1960s," in Crow, Escott, and Hatley, *African Americans in North Carolina,* 177–208.

46. *Greensboro Daily News,* October 8, 12, 1970; *Greensboro Daily Record,* October 8, 1970.

47. *Greensboro Daily News,* February 15, 1971; *Greensboro Daily Record,* February 15, 1971. The fire was classified officially as being of undetermined origin, but reliable sources indicated that a few vindictive students had set curtains ablaze.

48. *Greensboro Daily News,* February 15, 1971; Bundrige interview, April 12, 1984.

49. Wharton and Smith interviews; Bundrige interview, April 12, 1984; *Greensboro Daily News,* February 20, 21, April 11, May 30, August 27, 1971; *Greensboro Daily Record,* March 3, 1971. This series of articles provides excellent information on plans for the fund-raising campaign but gives no reasons for its failure.

EPILOGUE

1. *Durham Morning Herald,* October 14, 22, 1969; *Greensboro Daily News,* August 31, 1971; *Greensboro Daily Record,* October 15, 1971. Trustees in favor of selling the property were Smith; B. J. Battle, a savings and loan executive; Benjamin Mays, former president of Morehouse College; and Elton Price, a Howard University professor. Voting against the motion were W. H. Lanier and Douglas. Richard Wharton (the only white trustee present) abstained. If Wharton had voted, the action would have been binding since his vote would have constituted a quorum.

2. Low and Clift, *Encyclopedia,* 385; *Greensboro Daily News,* August 31, 1971.

3. *Greensboro Daily News,* September 3, 4, 1971; *Greensboro Daily Record,* Septem-

ber 3, 4, 1971. James L. Lee, MXLU's director of operations, stated that his organization's leaders were "deeply hurt" by the "division within the Sedalia community." Vina Webb said that Palmer supporters were caught completely off-guard by the trustees' willingness to sell the campus.

4. *Greensboro Daily News,* September 9, 21, October 6, 15, 23, 24, November 9, 27, 1971; *Greensboro Daily Record,* September 9, 24, October 15, 22, 23, 25, November 9, 28, 1971.

5. *Greensboro Daily News,* November 28, 1971. The property consisted of an estimated 225 acres. Trustees at the meeting were Ruth Harvey Charity, Mays, Lanier, Wharton, James Lockhart, Rosaline Epps, Bishop Wyoming Wells, Bundrige, Battle, and Smith. Executive Committee members were Smith, Battle, Bundrige, Wharton, and Lanier.

6. *Greensboro Daily News,* April 2, June 25, December 18, 1973; *Greensboro Daily Record,* June 25, 1973.

7. *New Encyclopedia Britannica,* s.v. "American Muslim Mission"; Lincoln, *Black Muslims.*

8. Tinney, "Muslims to Open N.C. College." See also *Greensboro Daily News,* August 11, 1982.

9. Tinney, "Muslims to Open N.C. College"; *Greensboro Daily News,* August 11, 1982. Bennett College sold the buildings for double the price it had paid in 1971 while retaining some 185 acres.

10. *Greensboro Daily Record,* March 17, 1981, May 10, 1983. Personnel at the University of North Carolina at Greensboro produced the videotape with funding from the North Carolina Humanities Committee and the Women of Guilford, a local nonprofit organization. After release of the video, Chauncey Smith of Whitsett led a campaign for a commemorative stamp honoring Brown. Although the endeavor failed, it brought greater public attention to Brown. See Harold Webb to Marie Hart and Gayle Wulk, February 13, 20, 1987.

11. *Greensboro Daily News,* July 28, 1983.

12. Ibid., July 13, 15, 1983. See North Carolina General Assembly, Session 1983, "An Act to Appropriate Funds to Develop a Plan to Establish the Charlotte Hawkins Brown Memorial State Historic Site," Senate Bill 561, June 1, 1983.

13. *Greensboro Daily News,* July 13, 14, 1983.

14. "Mrs. Margaret Marie Hill Gibbs," obsequies, St. Matthew's United Methodist Church, Greensboro, N.C., May 29, 1986; *Greensboro Carolina Peacemaker,* May 26, 1986; Marie Hart to Marie Gibbs, February 7, 1986; Maria Cole to Gibbs, January 31, 1986; Charlotte Hawkins Sullivan to Gibbs, January 31, 1986; William J. Kennedy III to Gibbs, February 6, 1986; and Larry Misenheimer to Gibbs, February 7, 1986, all in Brown Collection. In 1943, Marie Hill married Warmoth T. Gibbs Jr., son of North Carolina Agricultural and Technical College president Warmoth T. Gibbs Sr., a close friend of Brown's. Her activities included lifetime membership in the North Carolina Educational Association; membership on the boards of the Greensboro Association for Retarded Citizens and the Guilford County chapter of the American Cancer Society; and several terms as president of the St. Matthew's United Methodist Women. See Marie Gibbs, interview by C. W. Wadelington,

Greensboro, N.C., November 8, 1984, and interview by Marie Hart, Greensboro, N.C., March 3, 1981.

15. North Carolina Department of the Secretary of State, "Articles of Incorporation of Charlotte Hawkins Brown Historical Foundation," September 29, 1983; *Greensboro Daily News,* July 28, November 4, 1983; *Greensboro Daily Record,* November 3, 4, 1983. Publicist L. Annette Gibbs was the daughter of Marie Gibbs. Other officers included Bennett College president Isaac Miller; Marie Hart; Jeanne Lanier Rudd and Ruth Totton, former staff members at Palmer; and Cole. The remaining board members were Martin, H. M. Michaux Jr., Asa Spaulding Jr., state official Harold Webb, Greensboro school administrator Robert Saunders, educators Dorothy P. Barnett and Nan Manuel, Wharton, and Bundrige. See also *Raleigh Carolinian,* November 21, 1983; *Greensboro Carolina Peacemaker,* December 3, 1983; *Greensboro Daily News,* December 7, 1983; and *Raleigh News and Observer,* January 28, 29, 1985.

16. "Memorandum of Understanding," March 18, 1985, Book 3121, p. 344, Guilford County deeds; North Carolina General Assembly, Session 1985, "An Act to Appropriate Funds to Purchase Property and Upgrade Facilities for the Charlotte Hawkins Brown State Historic Site and Black History Center," House Bill 728, April 24, 1985; *Greensboro Daily Record,* July 25, 1985; *Greensboro Carolina Peacemaker,* July 13, 1985; *Durham Carolina Times,* August 3, 1985. See also Harold Webb to Benjamin S. Ruffin, January 28, 1987, and Webb to Marie Hart and Gayle Wulk, February 20, 1987, both in Brown Collection. H. M. Michaux Jr. (1930–) received B.S. and J.D. degrees from North Carolina Central University. He served as assistant district attorney for North Carolina's Middle District, the first black federal prosecutor in the South. See Low and Clift, *Encyclopedia,* 560–61.

17. Larry Misenheimer to Friends of Charlotte Hawkins Brown, March 13, 1987, Brown Collection; *Greensboro News and Record,* August 7, November 7, 8, 1987; *Raleigh Carolinian,* August 13, 1987; *Durham Carolina Times,* November 28, 1987.

18. *Greensboro News and Record,* November 8, 1987.

19. Charlotte Hawkins Brown Historical Foundation brochure, [1988]; *Greensboro News and Record,* February 16, 1988.

BIBLIOGRAPHY

MANUSCRIPT COLLECTIONS

American Missionary Association Papers, Amistad Research Center, Tulane University, New Orleans, La.

Mary McLeod Bethune Papers, Library of Congress, Washington, D.C.

Carol Lovette Brice Papers, Amistad Research Center, Tulane University, New Orleans, La.

Charlotte Hawkins Brown Papers, Arthur and Elizabeth Schlesinger Library on the History of Women in America, Radcliffe College, Cambridge, Mass. Microfilm, North Carolina Division of Archives and History, Raleigh, N.C.

Charlotte Hawkins Brown and Palmer Memorial Institute Files, C. W. Chesnutt Library, Fayetteville State University, Fayetteville, N.C.

Charlotte Hawkins Brown and Palmer Memorial Institute Files, Charlotte Hawkins Brown Memorial State Historic Site, Sedalia, N.C.

Charlotte Hawkins Brown and Palmer Memorial Institute Files, F. D. Bluford Library, North Carolina Agricultural and Technical State University, Greensboro, N.C.

Charlotte Hawkins Brown and Palmer Memorial Institute Files, Greensboro Public Library, Southeast Branch, Greensboro, N.C.

Charlotte Hawkins Brown and Palmer Memorial Institute Files, Bennett College Archives, Holgate Library, Bennett College, Greensboro, N.C.

Charlotte Hawkins Brown and Palmer Memorial Institute Files, W. C. Jackson Library, University of North Carolina at Greensboro, Greensboro, N.C.

Charlotte Hawkins Brown Collection, North Carolina Department of Cultural Resources, Historic Sites Section, Raleigh, N.C.

Cambridge Historical Society Papers, Cambridge, Mass.

Commission on Interracial Cooperation Papers, Trevor Arnett Library, Atlanta University, Atlanta, Ga.

Griffith Davis Papers, Charlotte Hawkins Brown Collection, North Carolina Department of Cultural Resources, Historic Sites Section, Raleigh, N.C.

W. E. B. Du Bois Papers, University of Massachusetts, Amherst, Mass.

Ebenezer Baptist Church Records, Boston, Mass.

Charles William Eliot Papers, Harvard University Library, Cambridge, Mass.

Samuel A. Eliot Papers, Harvard Theological Library, Harvard University, Cambridge, Mass.

General Education Board Papers, Rockefeller Archive Center, North Tarry-town, N.Y.

Frank Porter Graham Papers, Southern Historical Collection, Wilson Library, University of North Carolina at Chapel Hill, Chapel Hill, N.C.

Hawkins Family Papers, Southern Historical Collection, Wilson Library, University of North Carolina at Chapel Hill, Chapel Hill, N.C.

Clyde R. Hoey Papers, Governors' Papers, North Carolina Division of Archives and History, Raleigh, N.C.

W. C. Jackson Papers, University Archives, Wilson Library, University of North Carolina at Chapel Hill, Chapel Hill, N.C.

Charles Spurgeon Johnson Papers, Library of Congress, Washington, D.C.

John Price Jones Corporation Papers, Baker Library, Harvard Business School, Harvard University, Cambridge, Mass.

Charles D. McIver Papers, W. C. Jackson Library, University of North Carolina at Greensboro, Greensboro, N.C.

National Council of Negro Women Papers, National Archives of Black Women's History, Washington, D.C.

National Federation of Afro-American Women, Reports of the First Annual Convention, 1896, Boston Public Library, Boston, Mass.

North Carolina Commission on Interracial Cooperation Records, North Carolina Division of Archives and History, Raleigh, N.C.

Henry Hugh Proctor and Adeline L. Davis Papers, Library of Congress, Washington, D.C.

Franklin D. Roosevelt Papers, Franklin D. Roosevelt Library, Hyde Park, N.Y.

Julius Rosenwald Papers, Fisk University Library, Fisk University, Nashville, Tenn.

Salem State College Archives, Salem, Mass.

Mary Church Terrell Papers, Library of Congress, Washington, D.C.

Union Baptist Church Records, Cambridge, Mass.

Booker T. Washington Papers, Library of Congress, Washington, D.C.

Wellesley College Archives, Wellesley, Mass.

FEDERAL RECORDS AND PUBLICATIONS

Blose, David T., and Ambrose Caliver. *Statistics of the Education of Negroes, 1929–1930 and 1931–1932.* Washington, D.C.: Government Printing Office, 1936.

Bureau of the Census. *Historical Statistics of the United States, Colonial Times to 1957.* Washington, D.C.: Government Printing Office, 1960.

———. Index to the 1880 Population Schedule. National Archives, Washington, D.C. Microfilm, North Carolina Division of Archives and History, Raleigh, N.C.

———. *Negro Population, 1790–1915.* Washington, D.C.: Government Printing Office, 1918.

———. Ninth Census of the United States, 1870: Vance County, N.C., Population and Agricultural Schedules. National Archives, Washington, D.C. Microfilm, North Carolina Division of Archives and History, Raleigh, N.C.

————. Tenth Census of the United States, 1880: Granville County, N.C., Population and Social Statistics Schedules. National Archives, Washington, D.C. Microfilm, North Carolina Division of Archives and History, Raleigh, N.C.

————. Tenth Census of the United States, 1880: Wake County, N.C., Population and Social Statistics Schedules. National Archives, Washington, D.C. Microfilm, North Carolina Division of Archives and History, Raleigh, N.C.

————. Twelfth Census of the United States, 1900: Guilford County, N.C., Population Schedule. National Archives, Washington, D.C. Microfilm, North Carolina Division of Archives and History, Raleigh, N.C.

————. Twelfth Census of the United States, 1900: Middlesex County, Mass., Population Schedule. National Archives, Washington, D.C.

————. Thirteenth Census of the United States, 1910: Guilford County, N.C. National Archives, Washington, D.C. Microfilm, North Carolina Division of Archives and History, Raleigh, N.C.

Caliver, Ambrose. *Availability of Education to Negroes in Rural Communities.* Washington, D.C.: Government Printing Office, 1936.

Commissioner of Education in the District of Columbia. *History of Schools for the Colored Population.* Reprint. New York: Arno Press, 1971.

Department of Commerce and Bureau of the Census. *The Social and Economic Status of the Black Population in the United States: An Historical View, 1790–1978.* Washington, D.C.: Government Printing Office, 1979.

Jones, Thomas J. *Negro Education: A Study of the Private and Higher Schools for Colored People in the United States.* 2 vols. Washington, D.C.: Government Printing Office, 1917.

Senate. *Report of the Select Committee of the United States Senate to Investigate the Causes of the Removal of the Negroes from the Southern States to the Northern States.* 46th Cong., 1st and 2d sess., 1879–80. S. Rept. 693.

Smith, Charles L. *The History of Education in North Carolina.* Washington, D.C.: Government Printing Office, 1888.

STATE RECORDS AND PUBLICATIONS

Massachusetts Department of Public Health, Registry of Vital Records and Statistics. Record of marriage of Charlotte Eugenia Hawkins to Edward S. Brown, June 14, 1911, 603:402. Boston, Mass.

North Carolina Board of Health, Office of Vital Statistics. Certificates of Death. Death certificate for Caroline F. Willis, April 8, 1938, book 2020, p. 332. Death certificate for Charlotte Hawkins Brown, January 11, 1961, book 113, p. 120. Raleigh, N.C.

North Carolina Commission to Study Public Schools and Colleges for Colored People. *Report and Recommendations of the Commission to Study Public Schools and Colleges for Colored People in North Carolina.* Raleigh, N.C., [1938].

North Carolina Department of Public Instruction, Division of Negro Education Papers. North Carolina Division of Archives and History, Raleigh, N.C.

North Carolina Department of the Secretary of State. "Articles of Incorporation of Charlotte Hawkins Brown Historical Foundation," September 29, 1983. North Carolina Division of Archives and History, Raleigh, N.C.

North Carolina General Assembly, Session 1983. "An Act to Appropriate Funds to Develop a Plan to Establish the Charlotte Hawkins Brown Memorial State Historic Site," Senate Bill 561, June 1, 1983. North Carolina Division of Archives and History, Raleigh, N.C.

————, Session 1985. "An Act to Appropriate Funds to Purchase Property and Upgrade Facilities for the Charlotte Hawkins Brown State Historic Site and Black History Center," House Bill 728, April 24, 1985. North Carolina Division of Archives and History, Raleigh, N.C.

North Carolina Superintendent of Public Instruction. *Biennial Report of the Superintendent of Public Instruction* (1900–1912, 1940–42). Raleigh, N.C.: Various publishers, 1902–42.

COUNTY RECORDS

Guilford County. Deeds. Microfilm, North Carolina Division of Archives and History, Raleigh, N.C.

————. Board of Education Minutes, 1872–1965. Microfilm, North Carolina Division of Archives and History, Raleigh, N.C.

————. Estate Records. Clerk of Court's Office, Guilford County Courthouse, Greensboro, N.C.

————. "Maiden Names of Divorced Women, 1937–1969." Miscellaneous Records. Microfilm, North Carolina Division of Archives and History, Raleigh, N.C.

————. Marriage Books. Guilford County Courthouse, Greensboro, N.C.

————. School Census and Distribution of School Funds, 1876–97. School Records. North Carolina Division of Archives and History, Raleigh, N.C.

————. School Census Reports, 1895–1896. School Records. North Carolina Division of Archives and History, Raleigh, N.C.

————. Will of Charlotte Hawkins Brown, December 4, 1953. Book 15, p. 415. Wills. Microfilm, North Carolina Division of Archives and History, Raleigh, N.C.

Vance County. Deeds and Marriage Certificates. North Carolina Division of Archives and History, Raleigh, N.C.

PALMER MEMORIAL INSTITUTE PUBLICATIONS

Unless otherwise noted, the following works were published by Palmer Memorial Institute and copies can be found in the Charlotte Hawkins Brown Collection, North Carolina Department of Cultural Resources, Historic Sites Section, Raleigh, N.C.

The Alice Freeman Palmer Memorial. Brochure, [1924].

Annual Report for Palmer Memorial Institute, Sedalia, North Carolina, 1914–1915. [1915]. Copy in Charles William Eliot Papers, Harvard University Library, Cambridge, Mass.

"The Brice Trio Benefit Concert, Dedicated to Rev. John Brice, Father." Souvenir program for concert, April 10, 1965.

Conclusive Evidence: Scenes and Comments from the Work of the Alice Freeman Palmer Memorial at Sedalia, North Carolina. 1919.

Educational Rally for Palmer Memorial Institute. Brochure, July 4, 1918.

Palmerite. Annual, 1935, 1938, 1946, 1951, 1953, 1956, 1961, 1968.

Palmer Memorial Institute. Brochure, [1910].

The Palmer Memorial Institute. Brochure, November 3, 1920.

The Palmer Memorial Institute. Brochure, [1920]. Education Department Papers, Harvard University Library, Cambridge, Mass.

[Palmer Memorial Institute]. Brochure, [1941].

Palmer Memorial Institute: A Brief History. Brochure, [1919].

Palmer Memorial Institute: C. E. Hawkins, Principal. Brochure. [Greensboro, N.C., 1907].

The Palmer Memorial Institute, 1902–1953: A Pictorial Bulletin. 1953.

Palmer Memorial Institute Bulletin. 1917–18, 1931–32, 1935–38.

Palmer Memorial Institute Catalog. 1968–69.

Palmer Memorial Institute Report on Graduates: A Handbook. 1937–40.

Sentinel. Newsletter, November 25, 1936.

Slattery, Margaret. *Carolina Moon.* 1933.

Whitney, Frederic. *A Little Story of Achievement.* Framingham, Mass., 1916.

PAPERS AND SPEECHES

Unless otherwise noted, copies of the following papers and speeches are in the Charlotte Hawkins Brown Collection, North Carolina Department of Cultural Resources, Historic Sites Section, Raleigh, N.C.

"Action of the Administrative Committee of the American Missionary Association concerning Palmer Memorial Institute." 1933.

Brown, Charlotte H. "Annual Report of the President of Palmer Memorial Institute to the Board of Trustees." 1936–43, 1946–47.

———. "A Biography." [1927].

———. "Booker T. Washington's Philosophy of Education and Business." Speech presented to the Negro Businessmen's League, Birmingham, Ala., 1944.

———. "The Negro and the Social Graces." Address on *Wings over Jordan* radio program, Columbia Broadcasting System, March 10, 1940; printed and distributed by the Commission on Interracial Cooperation, Atlanta, Ga.

———. "Pronouncements of the Ideals for the New Palmer." Speech, [1930].

———. "The Quest of Culture." Speech presented to the Volkamenia Club, 1929.

———. "The Role of the Negro Woman in the Fight for Freedom." Speech, Madison Square Garden, New York, June 1943.

———. "Some Incidents in the Life of Charlotte Hawkins Brown Growing out of Racial Situations, at the Request of Ralph Bunche." [1937].

————. "Teacher's First Grade Certificate." Guilford County Superintendent of Schools. November 4, 1901.

————. "What the Negro Woman Asks of the White Women of North Carolina." Speech presented to the North Carolina Federation of White Women's Clubs, Charlotte, N.C., May 1927.

————. "What to Teach to Negro Americans." Speech presented to Kentucky Negro Education Association, Berea College, Berea, Ky., [1933].

————. "Where We Are in Race Relations." Speech, October 22, 1926.

————. "The Will and the Way: Palmer Memorial Institute, April 1927." 1927.

Crosson, Wilhelmina M. "Annual Report of the President of Palmer Memorial Institute to the Board of Trustees." 1960–61.

"Facts about the Fire at Palmer Memorial Institute Occurring Monday Evening, October 31, 1932." 1932.

Ferguson, G. H. "Some Facts about the Education of Negroes in North Carolina, 1921–1960." 1962. North Carolina Department of Public Instruction, Division of Negro Education Papers, North Carolina Division of Archives and History, Raleigh, N.C.

Jenkins, Cecie R. "Away from the Beaten Path: How One School Dares to Educate." [1940].

————. "Dr. Charlotte Hawkins Brown." [1933].

————. "Early Life." Handwritten draft of "The Twig Bender of Sedalia," [1945]. Bennett College Archives, Holgate Library, Bennett College, Greensboro, N.C.

————. "Life and Story of Charlotte Hawkins Brown." [1919].

————. "The Twig Bender of Sedalia." Typescript, [1946]. Bennett College Archives, Holgate Library, Bennett College, Greensboro, N.C.

————. "The Twig Bender of Sedalia, 1937–45." Typescript, [1946]. Bennett College Archives, Holgate Library, Bennett College, Greensboro, N.C.

McCracken, John, and Associates, Inc. "Appraisal Report of 1.98 Acres, U.S. Highway 70, Sedalia, North Carolina." Greensboro, N.C., 1984.

————. "Appraisal Report of 7.52 Acres, U.S. Highway 70, Sedalia, North Carolina." Greensboro, N.C., 1984.

————. "Appraisal Report of 40.057 Acre Tract of Land Formerly Known as the Alice Freeman Palmer Memorial Institute, U.S. Highway 70, Sedalia, North Carolina." Greensboro, N.C., 1985.

McCrea, William J. "Palmer Memorial Institute: A Southern Black Educator's Vision and Her New England Benefactors." Paper presented to the Society of Architectural Historians, Boston, Mass., 1990.

Phillips, Laura. National Register of Historic Places registration form for Palmer Memorial Institute Historic District, 1988.

"A Quarter Century of Progress." [1928].

Simons, S. B., comp. "A Volume of Letters from Friends and Admirers of the Life and Work of Dr. Charlotte H. Brown." Greensboro, N.C.: North Carolina Agricultural Teachers Association, North Carolina Agricultural and Technical State University, July 23, 1956.

Strand, Skees, Jones, and Company. "Palmer Memorial Institute, Sedalia, North Carolina, Report on Audit and Cash Receipts and Disbursements." Greensboro, N.C., 1951–69.

Wadelington, Charles. "Charlotte Hawkins Brown (1883–1901): A Biographical Sketch." 1984.

———. "The Civic Life of Dr. Charlotte Eugenia Hawkins Brown, 1895–1961." 1984.

———. "A Contemporary Analysis of Notable Events in the Life of Dr. Charlotte Hawkins Brown." 1987.

———. "Important Dates in Black Education and Famous Black North Carolinians." 1983.

———. "Important Dates in the Life of Dr. Charlotte Eugenia Hawkins Brown and the Palmer Memorial Institute." 1984.

———. "Negro Education in North Carolina: North Carolina African-American Schools." 1985.

———. "Palmer Memorial Institute Structures and Their Use." 1986.

———. "A Report on Historical Research to Restore Canary Cottage and Its Furnishings: The Private Home of Charlotte Hawkins Brown." 1987.

———. "A Report on Newspaper Articles on Charlotte H. Brown and Palmer Memorial Institute from the *Greensboro Daily News and Record*." 1984.

———. "Student Life on the Palmer Memorial Institute Campus." 1986.

Webb, Vina Wadlington. "Dr. Brown as I Knew Her." 1965. Bennett College Archives, Holgate Library, Bennett College, Greensboro, N.C.

Wilson, Francis. "A Pioneer." [1916].

INTERVIEWS

Unless otherwise noted, the following interviews are in the Charlotte Hawkins Brown Collection, North Carolina Department of Cultural Resources, Historic Sites Section, Raleigh, N.C.

Artis, Rudolph D. Interview by C. W. Wadelington, Greensboro, N.C., June 7, 1993.

Bragg, Harold E. Interview by Marie Hart, Greensboro, N.C., March 5, 1981.

Brown, Charlotte Hawkins. Interview G-56-1, Southern Oral History Program, University of North Carolina at Chapel Hill, Chapel Hill, N.C.

Bundrige, Charles W. Interview by Marie Hart, Sedalia, N.C., 1981.

———. Interviews by C. W. Wadelington, Sedalia, N.C., April 12, 1984, June 3, 1993.

Coble, Frances. Interview by C. W. Wadelington, Winston-Salem, N.C., October 29, 1986.

Cole, Maria. Interview by C. W. Wadelington, Sedalia, N.C., September 3, 1985.

Crosson, Wilhelmina. Interview by Marie Hart, Boston, Mass., February 28, 1981.

———. Interview by Constance H. Marteena, Greensboro, N.C., [1977]. Transcript, Bennett College Archives, Holgate Library, Bennett College, Greensboro, N.C.

———. Interview by C. W. Wadelington, Boston, Mass., January 15, 1984.

Dudley, Mildred Burris. Interview by C. W. Wadelington, Philadelphia, Pa., February 23, 1987.

Dyette, Levell. Interview by Marie Hart, Boston, Mass., February 28, 1981.

Edmead, Edmonia. Interview by C. W. Wadelington, Bronx, N.Y., November 17, 1989.

Felton, J. A. Interview by C. W. Wadelington, Winton, N.C., October 3, 1986.

Foust, Lottie. Interviews by C. W. Wadelington, Wadsworth, N.C., July 7–8, 25, 1986; Sedalia, N.C., July 23, 1986.

Fuller, Rebecca. Interview by C. W. Wadelington, Sedalia, N.C., May 22, 1986.

———. Interview by Harold Webb, Sedalia, N.C., February 12, 1987.

Gibbs, Marie. Interview by Marie Hart, Greensboro, N.C., March 3, 1981.

———. Interview by C. W. Wadelington, Greensboro, N.C., November 8, 1984.

Gibbs, Warmoth T. Interviews by L. Annette Gibbs and C. W. Wadelington, Greensboro, N.C., June 4–6, 1985.

———. Interview by Marie Hart, Greensboro, N.C., March 8, 1981.

———. Interview by C. W. Wadelington and Flora Hatley, Greensboro, N.C., December 6, 1983.

Green, Dannielle. Telephone interview by Richard F. Knapp, April 7, 1995.

Hardy, Lucretia. Interview by Marie Hart, Winston-Salem, N.C., February 24, 1981.

Hawkins, Charles. Interview by C. W. Wadelington, Henderson, N.C., July 11, 1984.

Hawkins, Gladys. Interviews by C. W. Wadelington, Henderson, N.C., June 25, July 11, 1984, August 21, 1990, October 24, 1991.

Hendrick, Jeremiah E. Interview by Marie Hart, Sedalia, N.C., 1981.

Holder, Trudy. Telephone interview by Richard F. Knapp, May 18, 1993.

Holmes, Mae D. Interview by C. W. Wadelington, Kinston, N.C., August 24, 1984.

Hooker, Ada. Interview by C. W. Wadelington, Burlington, N.C., June 25, 1986.

Hughes, Ruth Anita Hawkins. Interview by C. W. Wadelington, Henderson, N.C., July 27, 1984.

Ivey, Oliver. Interview by Marie Hart, Greensboro, N.C., March 6, 1981.

Johnson, Clifton. Interview by C. W. Wadelington, Durham, N.C., January 22, 1993.

Jones, Annie. Interviews by C. W. Wadelington, Wadsworth, N.C., July 7–8, 23, 1986.

Jones, Eleanor Tellers. Interview by C. W. Wadelington, Mount Airy, N.C., November 13, 1986.

Lewis, Grace D. Interview by C. W. Wadelington, Greensboro, N.C., February 13, 1985.

Maye, Lola. Interviews by Marie Hart, Sedalia, N.C., February 7–8, 1981.

———. Interview by Harold Webb, Sedalia, N.C., February 12, 1987.

Michaux, H. M., Jr. Interview by Marie Hart, Greensboro, N.C., February 26, 1981.

Miller, Blanche Foust. Interview by C. W. Wadelington, Sedalia, N.C., July 23, 1986.

Mitchell, James. Interview by C. W. Wadelington, Sedalia, N.C., September 18, 1997.

Norwood, Bernice. Interview by C. W. Wadelington, Greensboro, N.C., February 13, 1985.

Paisley, Elsie A. Interview by Marie Hart, Sedalia, N.C., 1981.

———. Interview by C. W. Wadelington, Sedalia, N.C., August 25, 1984.

Palmer Memorial Institute Atlanta alumni. Interview by C. W. Wadelington and L. Annette Gibbs, Atlanta, Ga., May 17, 1987.

Palmer Memorial Institute New York alumni. Interview by L. Annette Gibbs, New York, N.Y., December 7, 1986.

Pattishaul, Mable Cook. Interview by C. W. Wadelington, Sedalia, N.C., March 31, 1988.

———. Interview by C. W. Wadelington, Sedalia, N.C., June 12, 1991.

Puryear, James. Interview by C. W. Wadelington, Hempstead, N.Y., November 17, 1989.

Rivera, Alex M. Interview by C. W. Wadelington, Durham, N.C., March 15, 1988.

Rudd, James. Interview by C. W. Wadelington, Sedalia, N.C., September 30, 1986.

Rudd, Jeanne Lanier. Interviews by C. W. Wadelington, Sedalia, N.C., March 19, April 21, 1993.

Rudd, Myrtle. Interview by Marie Hart, Sedalia, N.C., February 7, 1981.

Rudd family. Interview by Marie Hart, Sedalia, N.C., February 7, 1981.

Shaw, Charlie. Interview by C. W. Wadelington, Burlington, N.C., July 22, 1986.

Sitzer, Mary Jane Brown. Interview by C. W. Wadelington, Greensboro, N.C., March 28, 1987.

Slade, Daisy. Interview by C. W. Wadelington, Burlington, N.C., July 22, 1986.

Smith, Elworth E. Interview by Marie Hart, Greensboro, N.C., March 3, 1981.

———. Interview by C. W. Wadelington, Greensboro, N.C., July 19, 1984.

Sullivan, Charlotte Hawkins. Interviews by C. W. Wadelington, Sedalia, N.C., August 6–7, 1987.

Totton, Ezra. Interview by C. W. Wadelington, Durham, N.C., June 24, 1987.

Totton, Ruth. Interview by Marie Hart, Sedalia, N.C., March 4, 1981.

———. Interviews by C. W. Wadelington, Sedalia, N.C., June 11, 1987, November 16, 1992, March 30, 1993.

———. Interview by C. W. Wadelington and Richard F. Knapp, Sedalia, N.C., April 4, 1997.

———. Telephone interview by C. W. Wadelington, June 11, 1997.

Totton family. Interviews by C. W. Wadelington, Sedalia, N.C., June 17–18, 1987.

Walden, Helen Brown. Interview by C. W. Wadelington, Greensboro, N.C., August 22, 1984.

Webb, Burleigh. Interview by C. W. Wadelington, Greensboro, N.C., March 15, 1984.

Webb, Haywood. Interview by Marie Hart, Sedalia, N.C., 1981.

Webb, Vina Wadlington. Interview by Marie Hart, Sedalia, N.C., 1981.

———. Interview by C. W. Wadelington, High Point, N.C., December 6, 1983.

Westerband, Henri M. Interview by Marie Hart, Greensboro, N.C., March 5, 1981.

Wharton, Richard L. Interview by C. W. Wadelington, Greensboro, N.C., May 23, 1984.

Wheeler, Eugenia Cox. Interview by Valinda Littlefield, Sedalia, N.C., June 12, 1991.

Wiley, Barbara Gibson. Interview by C. W. Wadelington, Sedalia, N.C., June 9, 1993.

Willis, Addie. Interview by Marie Hart, Boston, Mass., February 28, 1981.

NEWSPAPERS AND PERIODICALS

American Missionary, 1872–1934

Boston Chronicle, 1940

Boston Globe, 1918–91

Chicago American Muslim Journal, 1982

Durham Carolina Times, 1926–98

Greensboro Carolina Peacemaker, 1967–98

Greensboro Daily News, 1917–98

High Point Enterprise, 1985–87

New York Times, 1945

Norfolk Journal and Guide, 1929–46

Pittsburgh Courier, 1943–48

Raleigh Carolinian, 1940–98

Raleigh Times, 1984–98

Roanoke Rapids (N.C.) Progressive Herald, 1930–85

Salisbury (N.C.) Sunday Post, 1983–88

Sedalia (N.C.) Sentinel, 1936–47

Winston-Salem Journal, 1983–87

BOOKS

Adams, L. Russell. *Great Negroes Past and Present.* 3d ed. Chicago: Afro-American Publishing Company, 1969.

American Missionary Association. *Annual Report of the American Missionary Association.* New York: American Missionary Association, 1892–1933.

The American Negro: His History and Literature. New York: Arno and New York Times, 1969.

Anderson, Eric. *Race and Politics in North Carolina, 1872–1901: The Black Second.* Baton Rouge: Louisiana State University Press, 1981.

Anderson, James D. *The Education of Blacks in the South, 1860–1935.* Chapel Hill: University of North Carolina Press, 1988.

Andrews, Frank Emerson. *Philanthropic Giving.* New York: Russell Sage Foundation, 1950.

Aptheker, Betina. *Women's Legacy: Essays on Race, Sex, and Class in American History.* Amherst: University of Massachusetts Press, 1982.

Aptheker, Herbert, ed. *The Correspondence of W. E. B. Du Bois.* Amherst: University of Massachusetts Press, 1973–78.

————. *A Documentary History of the Negro People in the United States.* Vol. 2. Secaucus, N.J.: Citadel Press, 1973.

Ashe, Samuel A., Stephen B. Weeks, and Charles L. Van Noppen, eds. *Biographical History of North Carolina.* 8 vols. Greensboro, N.C.: C. L. Van Noppen, 1905–17.

Baker, Ray Stannard. *Following the Color Line.* 1908. Reprint, New York: Harper and Row, 1964.

Ballard, Allen B. *The Education of Black Folk: The Afro-American Struggle for Knowledge in White America.* New York: Harper and Row, 1973.

Bardolph, Richard. *The Negro Vanguard.* New York: Holt, Rinehart, 1959.

Barringer, Paul B. *The American Negro: His Past and Future.* Raleigh: Edwards and Broughton, 1900.

Batchelor, John. *The Guilford County Schools: A History.* Winston-Salem, N.C.: John F. Blair, 1991.

Beard, Augustus Field. *A Crusade of Brotherhood: A History of the American Missionary Association.* Boston: Pilgrim Press, 1909.

Berry, Brewton. *Almost White.* New York: Macmillan, 1963.

Billings, Dwight B. *Planters and the Making of a "New South": Class, Politics, and Development in North Carolina.* Chapel Hill: University of North Carolina Press, 1980.

Birmingham, Stephen. *Certain People: America's Black Elite.* Boston: Little, Brown, 1977.

Blackburn, George T. *The Heritage of Vance County, North Carolina.* Winston-Salem, N.C.: Hunter, 1984.

Blassingame, John W. *The Slave Community: Plantation Life in the Antebellum South.* New York: Oxford University Press, 1979.

Bond, Horace M. *The Education of the Negro in the American Social Order.* New York: Prentice-Hall, 1934.

Boulware, Marcus H. *The Oratory of Negro Leaders, 1900–1968.* Westport, Conn.: Negro Universities Press, 1969.

Bowles, Frank H. *Between Two Worlds: Negro Higher Education.* New York: McGraw-Hill, 1971.

Bratton, Theodore DuBose. *The Christian South and Negro Education.* Sewanee, Tenn.: University of the South Press, 1908.

Brawley, Benjamin. *Negro Builders and Heroes.* Chapel Hill: University of North Carolina Press, 1937.

Bremner, Robert H. *American Philanthropy.* Chicago: University of Chicago Press, 1960.

Brown, Charlotte H. *The Correct Thing to Do, to Say, to Wear.* Boston: Christopher Publishing, 1941. Reprint, Raleigh: Charlotte Hawkins Brown Historical Foundation, 1990.

————. *Mammy: An Appeal to the Heart of the South.* Boston: Pilgrim Press, 1919.

Brown, Hallie Quinn. *Homespun Heroines and Other Women Builders.* Xenia, Ohio: Aldrine, 1926.

Brown, Hugh Victor. *A History of the Education of Negroes in North Carolina.* Raleigh: Irving Swain Press, 1961.

Brownlee, Frederick Leslie. *Heritage of Freedom: A Centenary Story of Ten Schools Offering Education in Freedom.* Philadelphia: United Church Press, 1963.

————. *New Day Ascending.* Boston: Pilgrim Press, [1945].

Bullock, Henry Allen. *A History of Negro Education in the South, from 1619 to the Present.* Cambridge: Harvard University Press, 1967.

Burton, Orville B. *In My Father's House Are Many Mansions: Family and Community in Edgefield, South Carolina.* Chapel Hill: University of North Carolina Press, 1985.

Cambridge School Committee. *Annual Report of the School Committee . . . 1899.* Boston: J. A. Cummings, 1899.

————. *Rules of the School Committee and Courses of Study.* Cambridge, Mass.: Caustic and Claflin Press, 1899. Copy in Education Department Papers, Harvard University Library, Cambridge, Mass.

Chafe, William H. *Civilities and Civil Rights: Greensboro, North Carolina, and the Black Struggle for Freedom.* New York: Oxford University Press, 1980.

Chambers, Frederick. *Black Higher Education in the United States: A Selected Bibliography.* Westport, Conn.: Greenwood Press, 1978.

Cheney, John L., Jr., ed. *North Carolina Government, 1584–1974.* Raleigh: North Carolina Department of the Secretary of State, 1981.

Clifton Conference Committee. *An Era of Progress and Promise.* Clifton, Mass.: W. N. Hartshorn, 1908.

Coble, Grady W. *Coble's Home Almanac for the Year 1930 and Rural Directory of Guilford County.* Greensboro, N.C., 1929.

Commission on Interracial Cooperation. *Southern Women and Race Cooperation: A Story of the Memphis Conference, October sixth and seventh, 1920.* Atlanta: Commission on Interracial Cooperation, 1921.

Cooke, Dennis H. *The White Superintendent and Negro Schools in North Carolina.* Nashville: George Peabody College for Teachers, 1930.

Coon, Charles L. *The Beginning of Public Education in North Carolina: A Documentary History, 1790–1840.* Raleigh: Edwards and Broughton, 1908.

————. *Facts about Southern Educational Progress: A Present Day Study in Public Schools.* Raleigh: North Carolina Department of Public Instruction, 1905.

————. *The Need of a Constructive Educational Policy for North Carolina.* Wilson, N.C., 1911.

————. *Statistical Record of the Progress of Public Education in North Carolina, 1870–1906.* Raleigh: North Carolina Department of Public Instruction, 1907.

Cooper, Ann J. *The Voice from the South by a Black Woman of the South.* Xenia, Ohio: Aldrine, 1892.

Cooper, James W. *North Carolina: From Beaufort to Blowing Rock.* New York: American Missionary Association, [1903].

Cooper, Richard. *John Chavis: To Teach a Generation.* Raleigh: Creative Productions, 1985.

Cooper, William Arthur. *A Portrayal of Negro Life.* Raleigh: North Carolina Department of Public Instruction, 1936.

Cozart, Leland Stanford. *A History of the Association of Colleges and Secondary Schools, 1934–1965.* Charlotte: Heritage, 1967.

Crabtree, Beth G. *North Carolina Governors, 1585–1958: Brief Sketches.* Raleigh: North Carolina Division of Archives and History, 1958.

Crow, Jeffrey, Paul D. Escott, and Flora Hatley. *A History of African Americans in North Carolina.* Raleigh: North Carolina Department of Cultural Resources, 1992.

Crow, Jeffrey J., Paul D. Escott, and Charles L. Flynn Jr., eds. *Race, Class, and Politics in Southern History.* Baton Rouge: Louisiana State University Press, 1989.

Crow, Jeffrey, and Flora Hatley, eds. *Black Americans in North Carolina and the South.* Chapel Hill: University of North Carolina Press, 1984.

Cutlip, Scott M. *Fundraising in the United States: Its Role in America's Philanthropy.* New Brunswick, N.J.: Rutgers University Press, 1965.

Dabney, Charles W. *Universal Education in the South.* 2 vols. Chapel Hill: University of North Carolina Press, 1936.

Daniel, Sadie Iola. *Women Builders.* Rev. ed. Edited by Charles H. Wesley and Thelma D. Perry. Washington, D.C.: Associated Publishers, 1970.

Daniels, John. *In Freedom's Birthplace: A Study of the Boston Negroes.* Boston: Houghton Mifflin, 1914.

Dannett, Sylvia G. L. *Profiles of Negro Womanhood.* Negro Heritage Library. New York: M. W. Lads, 1964–66.

Davis, Lenwood G. *The Black Woman in American Society: A Selected Annotated Bibliography.* Boston: G. K. Hall, 1975.

Day, Beth. *The Little Professor of Piney Woods.* New York: Julian Messver, 1955.

Dickens, Brooks. *The History of Negro Education in North Carolina.* Jackson, Tenn.: Lane College Press, 1929.

Douglass, H. Paul. *Christian Reconstruction in the South.* Boston: Pilgrim Press, 1909.

Doyle, Bertram W. *The Etiquette of Race Relations in the South.* Chicago: University of Chicago Press, 1937.

Drago, Edmund L. *Initiative, Paternalism, and Race Relations: Charleston's Avery Normal Institute.* Athens: University of Georgia Press, 1990.

Du Bois, W. E. B. *The Autobiography of W. E. B. Du Bois: A Soliloquy on Viewing My Life from the Last Decade of Its First Century.* New York: International Publishers, 1968.

———. *Black Reconstruction in America: An Essay toward a History of the Part Which Black Folk Played in the Attempt to Reconstruct Democracy in America, 1860–1880.* New York: Atheneum Publishing, 1970.

———. *Dusk of Dawn: An Essay toward an Autobiography of a Race Concept.* New York: Harcourt, Brace, 1940.

———. *The Negro Common School.* Atlanta: Atlanta University Press, 1901.

———. *The Souls of Black Folk.* Chicago: A. C. McClurg, 1903.

———, ed. *The College Bred Negro.* Atlanta: Atlanta University Press, 1900.

Durden, Robert F. *The Dukes of Durham, 1865–1929.* Durham, N.C.: Duke University Press, 1975.

Dykeman, Wilma, and James Stokely. *Seeds of Southern Change: The Life of Will Alexander.* Chicago: University of Chicago Press, 1962.

Edmonds, Helen G. *The Negro and Fusion Politics in North Carolina, 1894–1901.* Chapel Hill: University of North Carolina Press, 1951.

Egerton, John. *Speak Now Against the Day: The Generation before the Civil Rights Movement in the South.* New York: Knopf, 1994.

Embree, Edwin R., and Julian Waxman. *Investment in People: The Story of the Julius Rosenwald Fund.* New York: Harper, 1949.

Emory, Frank, et al., eds. *Paths towards Freedom: A Biographical History of Blacks and Indians in North Carolina by Blacks and Indians.* Raleigh: North Carolina State University, 1976.

Escott, Paul D. *Many Excellent People: Power and Privilege in North Carolina, 1850–1900.* Chapel Hill: University of North Carolina Press, 1985.

Fite, Gilbert. *Cotton Fields No More: Southern Agriculture, 1865–1980.* Lexington: University Press of Kentucky, 1984.

Foster, M. Marie Booth. *Southern Black Creative Writers, 1829–1953.* New York: Greenwood Press, 1988.

Franklin, John Hope. *The Free Negro in North Carolina.* Chapel Hill: University of North Carolina Press, 1943.

Franklin, John Hope, and Alfred A. Moss Jr. *From Slavery to Freedom.* 6th ed. New York: Knopf, 1988.

Franklin, Vincent P., and James D. Anderson, eds. *New Perspectives on Black Educational History.* Boston: G. K. Hall, 1978.

Frazier, E. Franklin. *Black Bourgeoisie.* Glencoe, Ill.: Free Press, 1957.

———. *The Negro Family in the United States.* Rev. ed. New York: Dryden Press, 1948.

———. *Negro Youth at the Crossways.* Washington, D.C.: American Council on Education, 1940.

Gaines, Kevin K. *Uplifting the Race: Black Leadership, Politics, and Culture in the Twentieth Century.* Chapel Hill: University of North Carolina Press, 1996.

Gates, Henry L., Jr., ed. *African-American Women Writers, 1910–1940. "Mammy": An Appeal to the Heart of the South* and *The Correct Thing to Do — to Say — to Wear,* by Charlotte Hawkins Brown. New York: G. K. Hall, 1995.

Gatewood, Willard B. *Aristocrats of Color: The Black Elite, 1880–1920.* Bloomington: Indiana University Press, 1990.

General Education Board. *The General Education Board: An Account of Its Activities, 1902–1914.* New York: General Education Board, 1915.

Giddings, Paula. *When and Where I Enter: The Impact of Black Women on Race and Sex in America.* New York: Morrow, 1984.

Gilbert, John F. *Crossties through Carolina: The Study of North Carolina's Early Day Railroads.* Raleigh: Helios Press, 1969.

Gilman, Arthur, ed. *The Cambridge of 1896.* Cambridge, Mass.: Riverside Press, 1896.

Gilmore, Glenda Elizabeth. *Gender and Jim Crow: Women and the Politics of White Supremacy in North Carolina, 1896–1920.* Chapel Hill: University of North Carolina Press, 1996.

Glasscock, Jean, ed. *Wellesley College, 1875–1975: A Century of Women.* Wellesley, Mass.: Wellesley College, 1975.

Goldfield, David R. *Black, White, and Southern: Race Relations and Southern Culture, 1940 to the Present.* Baton Rouge: Louisiana State University Press, 1990.

Goldstein, Rhoda L. *Black Life and Culture in the United States.* New York: Thomas Y. Crowell Company, 1971.

Graham, Lawrence Otis. *Our Kind of People: Inside America's Black Upper Class.* New York: HarperCollins, 1999.

Gutman, Herbert G. *The Black Family in Slavery and Freedom, 1750–1925.* New York: Pantheon Books, 1976.

Haley, John. *Charles N. Hunter and Race Relations in North Carolina.* Chapel Hill: University of North Carolina Press, 1987.

Hall, Jacquelyn Dowd. *Revolt against Chivalry: Jessie Daniel Ames and the Women's Campaign against Lynching.* New York: Columbia University Press, 1979.

Harlan, Louis R. *Booker T. Washington: The Making of a Black Leader, 1856–1901.* New York: Oxford University Press, 1972.

———. *Booker T. Washington: The Wizard of Tuskegee, 1901–1915.* New York: Oxford University Press, 1983.

———. *Separate and Unequal: Public School Campaigns and Racism in the Southern States, 1901–1915.* Chapel Hill: University of North Carolina Press, 1958.

———, ed. *The Booker T. Washington Papers.* Urbana: University of Illinois Press, 1972–84.

Hawks, Joanne V., and Sheila L. Skemp. *Sex, Race, and the Role of Women in the South.* Jackson: University Press of Mississippi, 1983.

Hennings, Lloyd. *The American Missionary Association: A Christian Anti-Slavery Society.* Oberlin, Ohio: Oberlin College, 1933.

Henri, Florette. *Black Migration: Movement North, 1900–1920.* Garden City, N.Y.: Anchor Press, 1975.

Hine, Darlene Clark, and Kathleen Thompson. *A Shining Thread of Hope: The History of Black Women in America.* New York: Broadway Books, 1998.

Holder, Rose H. *McIver of North Carolina.* Chapel Hill: University of North Carolina Press, 1957.

Hopkins, Charles H. *The Rise of the Social Gospel in American Protestantism, 1865–1915.* New Haven: Yale University Press, 1940.

Hornsby, Alton, Jr. *The Black Almanac.* Woodbury, N.Y.: Barron's Educational Series, 1972.

Hughes, Ruth Anita Hawkins. *Contributions of Vance County People of Color.* Henderson, N.C.: Sparks Press, 1988.

Hunter, Charles N. *Review of Negro Life in North Carolina, with My Recollections.* Raleigh: Irving Press, [1925].

Johnson, Charles S. *Growing Up in the Black Belt.* Washington, D.C.: American Council on Education, 1941.

———. *The Negro College Graduates.* Chapel Hill: University of North Carolina Press, 1938.

Johnson, Clifton H., Juanita V. Williamson, and Wesley A. Hotchkiss. *Our American Missionary Association Heritage.* New York: American Missionary Association, 1966.

Johnson, Daniel, and Rex Campbell. *Black Migration in America: A Social and Demographic History.* Durham, N.C.: Duke University Press, 1981.

Jones, Jacquelyn. *Labor of Love, Labor of Sorrow: Black Women, Work, and the Family from Slavery to the Present.* New York: Basic Books, 1985.

Jones-Wilson, Faustine C., et al., eds. *Encyclopedia of African-American Education.* Westport, Conn.: Greenwood Press, 1996.

Kennedy, Albert J. *The Zone of Emergence: Observations of the Lower and Middle and Upper Working Class Communities of Boston, 1905–1914.* Cambridge: M.I.T. Press, 1962.

Kirby, John H. *Black Americans in the Roosevelt Era: Liberalism and Race.* Knoxville: University of Tennessee Press, 1979.

Knight, Edgar W. *Public School Education in North Carolina.* Boston: Houghton Mifflin, [1916].

Lacy, Leslie. *Cheer the Lonesome Traveler: Life of W. E. B. Du Bois.* New York: Dial Press, 1970.

———. *The Rise and Fall of a Proper Negro: An Autobiography.* New York: Macmillan, 1970.

Larkins, John Rodman. *Pattern of Leadership among Negroes in North Carolina.* Raleigh: Irving Swain Press, 1959.

Leavell, Ullin W. *Philanthropy in Negro Education.* Nashville: George Peabody College for Teachers, 1930.

Lefler, Hugh T., and Albert R. Newsome. *North Carolina: The History of a Southern State.* 3d ed. Chapel Hill: University of North Carolina Press, 1973.

Leloudis, James L. *Schooling the New South: Pedagogy, Self, and Society in North Carolina, 1880–1920.* Chapel Hill: University of North Carolina Press, 1996.

Lerner, Gerda. *The Majority Finds Its Past: Placing Women in History.* New York: Oxford University Press, 1979.

———, ed. *Black Women in White America: A Documentary History.* New York: Vintage Books, 1972.

Lewis, David L. *W. E. B. Du Bois: Biography of a Race, 1868–1919.* New York: Henry Holt, 1993.

Lieberson, Stanley. *A Piece of the Pie: Blacks and White Immigrants since 1880.* Berkeley: University of California Press, 1980.

Lincoln, C. Eric. *The Black Muslims in America.* Boston: Beacon Press, 1961.

Link, William A. *The Paradox of Southern Progressivism.* Chapel Hill: University of North Carolina Press, 1992.

Litwack, Leon F. *Been in the Storm So Long: The Aftermath of Slavery.* New York: Knopf, 1979.

Locke, Alain, ed. *The New Negro.* New York: Atheneum, 1975.

Logan, Frenise. *The Negro in North Carolina, 1876–1894.* Chapel Hill: University of North Carolina Press, 1964.

Logan, Rayford W. *The Negro and the Post-War World: A Primer.* Washington, D.C.: Minorities Publishers, 1945.

———, ed. *What the Negro Wants.* Chapel Hill: University of North Carolina Press, 1944.

Logan, Rayford W., and Michael R. Winston, eds. *Dictionary of American Negro Biography.* New York: Norton, 1982.

Long, Hollis Moody. *Public Secondary Education for Negroes in North Carolina.* New York: Bureau of Publications, Teachers College, Columbia University, 1932.

Low, W. Augustus, and Virgil A. Clift, eds. *Encyclopedia of Black America.* New York: McGraw-Hill, 1981.

Lowenburg, Bert, and Ruth Begin, eds. *Black Women in Nineteenth Century American Life.* University Park: Pennsylvania State University, 1976.

McKinney, Theophilus E., ed. *Higher Education among Negroes.* Charlotte: Johnson C. Smith University, 1932.

McPherson, James M., et al. *Blacks in America: Bibliographical Essays.* Garden City, N.Y.: Doubleday, 1971.

Magot, Richard, ed. *Philanthropic Giving: Studies in Varieties and Goals.* New York: Oxford University Press, 1989.

Marable, Manning. *Race, Reform, and Rebellion: The Second Reconstruction in Black America, 1945–1990.* 2d ed. Jackson: University Press of Mississippi, 1991.

Margo, Robert A. *Race and Schooling in the South, 1880–1950: An Economic History.* Chicago: University of Chicago Press, 1990.

Marks, Carole. *Farewell—We Are Good and Gone: The Great Black Migration.* Bloomington: Indiana University Press, 1989.

Marteena, Constance Hill. *The Lengthening Shadow of a Woman: A Biography of Charlotte H. Brown.* Hicksville, N.Y.: Exposition Press, 1977.

May, Henry F. *Protestant Churches and Industrial America.* 2d ed. New York: Octagon Books, 1977.

Mayo, Amory D. *Southern Women in the Recent Educational Movement in the South.* Baton Rouge: Louisiana State University Press, 1978.

Meier, August. *Negro Thought in America, 1880–1915: Racial Ideologies in the Age of Booker T. Washington.* Ann Arbor: University of Michigan Press, 1963.

Meier, August, and Elliott Rudwick. *From Plantation to Ghetto.* Rev. ed. New York: Hill and Wang, 1970.

Morris, Aldon D. *The Origins of the Civil Rights Movement: Black Communities Organizing for Change.* New York: Free Press, 1984.

Moss, Alfred. *The American Negro Academy: Voice of the Talented Tenth.* Baton Rouge: Louisiana State University Press, 1981.

Murphy, Ann M. *An Inventory of Historical Architecture: Henderson, North Carolina.* Henderson, N.C.: Vance County Historical Society, 1981.

Murray, Percy. *The History of the North Carolina Teachers Association.* Washington, D.C.: National Education Association, 1984.

Myrdal, Gunnar. *An American Dilemma.* New York: Harper, 1944.

Neverdon-Morton, Cynthia. *Afro-American Women of the South and the Advancement of the Race, 1895–1925.* Knoxville: University of Tennessee Press, 1989.

Noble, Marcus Cicero Stephens. *A History of the Public Schools of North Carolina.* Chapel Hill: University of North Carolina Press, 1930.

The North Carolina Yearbook. Raleigh: News and Observer, 1900–1931.

Norton, Mary Beth, et al. *A People and a Nation: A History of the United States.* 2d ed. Boston: Houghton Mifflin, 1986.

Orr, Oliver H., Jr. *Charles Brantley Aycock.* Chapel Hill: University of North Carolina Press, 1961.

Palmer, George Herbert. *The Life of Alice Freeman Palmer.* Boston: Houghton Mifflin, 1908.

Parkman, Mary R. *Heroines of Service.* New York: Century, 1917.

Peace, Samuel Thomas. *"Zeb's Black Baby"—Vance County, North Carolina: A Short History.* Henderson, N.C.: Seeman Printery, 1955.

Pleck, Elizabeth Hofkin. *Black Migration and Poverty: Boston, 1865–1900.* New York: Academic Press, 1979.

Powell, William S. *North Carolina through Four Centuries.* Chapel Hill: University of North Carolina Press, 1989.

Prather, H. Leon. *Resurgent Politics and Educational Progressivism in the New South: North Carolina, 1890–1913.* Rutherford, N.J.: Fairleigh Dickinson University Press, 1979.

Richardson, Joe M. *Christian Reconstruction: The American Missionary Association and Southern Blacks, 1861–1890.* Athens: University of Georgia Press, 1986.

———. *A History of Fisk University, 1865–1946.* Tuscaloosa: University of Alabama Press, 1980.

Riegel, Robert E. *American Women: A Story of Social Change.* Rutherford, N.J.: Fairleigh Dickinson University Press, 1970.

Roell, Craig H. *The Piano in America, 1890–1940.* Chapel Hill: University of North Carolina Press, 1989.

Rouse, Jacqueline A. *Lugenia Burns Hope, Black Southern Reformer.* Athens: University of Georgia Press, 1989.

Rudd, Jeanne Lanier, and Patricia Lanier. *The Family Lanier: A Continuing History.* N.p.: Privately published, 1976.

Scott, Anne Firor. *The Southern Lady: From Pedestal to Politics, 1830–1930.* Chicago: University of Chicago Press, 1970.

Sicherman, Barbara, et al., eds. *Notable American Women: The Modern Period—A Biographical Dictionary.* Cambridge: Harvard University Press, 1980.

Silcox-Jarrett, Diane. *Charlotte Hawkins Brown: One Woman's Dream.* Winston-Salem, N.C.: Bandit Books, 1995.

Sitkoff, Harvard. *A New Deal for Blacks: The Emergence of Civil Rights as a National Issue—The Depression Decade.* New York: Oxford University Press, 1978.

Smith, Dwight L. *Afro-American History: A Bibliography.* Santa Barbara: ABC-CLIO, 1974.

Smith, Jessie Carney, ed. *Notable Black American Women.* Detroit: Gale Research International Limited, 1992.

Smith, Steven T. *An Historical Account of the American Muslim Mission, with Specific Reference to North Carolina.* N.p., 1984.

Southern, Eileen. *Music of Black Americans: A History.* New York: Norton, 1970.

Spivey, Donald. *Schooling for the New Slavery: Black Industrial Education, 1868–1915*. Westport, Conn.: Greenwood Press, 1978.

Stanley, Alfred Knighton. *The Children Is Crying: Congregationalism among Black People*. New York: Pilgrim Press, 1979.

Sternsher, Bernard. *The Negro in Depression and War: Prelude to Revolution, 1930–1945*. Chicago: Quadrangle Books, 1969.

Styron, William. *Confessions of Nat Turner*. New York: Random House, 1967.

Sullivan, Charlotte Hawkins. *A Bit of This, a Bit of That*. N.p.: Privately published, n.d.

Swint, Henry Lee. *The Northern Teacher in the South, 1862–1870*. Nashville: Vanderbilt University Press, 1941.

Terborg-Penn, Rosalyn, and Sharon Harley, eds. *The Afro-American Woman: Struggles and Images*. Port Washington, N.Y.: National University Publications, 1978.

Terrell, Mary Church. *A Colored Woman in a White World*. Washington, D.C.: National Association of Colored Women's Clubs, 1968.

Thernstrom, Stephen. *The Other Bostonians: Poverty and Progress in the American Metropolis, 1880–1970*. Cambridge: Harvard University Press, 1971.

Tindall, George B. *Emergence of the New South, 1913–1945*. A History of the South, no. 10. Baton Rouge: Louisiana State University Press, 1967.

Vaughn, William Preston. *Schools for All: The Blacks and Public Education in the South, 1865–1877*. Lexington: University Press of Kentucky, 1974.

Walker, Vanessa Siddle. *Their Highest Potential: An African American School Community in the Segregated South*. Chapel Hill: University of North Carolina Press, 1996.

Walters, Raymond. *Negroes and the Depression: The Problem of Economic Recovery*. Westport, Conn.: Greenwood Press, 1970.

Washington, Booker T. *The Education of the Negro*. Albany, N.Y.: J. B. Lyons, 1904.

———. *My Larger Education, Being Chapters from My Experience*. Garden City, N.Y.: Doubleday, Page, 1911.

———. *Up from Slavery: An Autobiography*. Garden City, N.Y.: A. L. Burt, 1901.

Washington, E. Davidson, ed. *Selected Speeches of Booker T. Washington*. Garden City, N.Y.: Doubleday, Doran, 1932.

Watkins, John Bullock, Jr. *Historic Vance County and "Happy, Healthy, Hustling Henderson."* Henderson, N.C.: Henderson Daily Dispatch, 1941.

Webb, Vina Wadlington. *History of the Bethany United Church of Christ*. Sedalia, N.C.: Bethany United Church of Christ, 1985.

Wesley, Charles H. *The History of the National Association of Colored Women's Clubs: A Legacy of Service*. Washington, D.C.: National Association of Colored Women's Clubs, 1984.

Wheeler, Edward L. *Uplifting the Race: The Black Minister in the New South, 1865–1902*. Lanham, Md.: University Press of America, 1986.

Williams, Mildred M., et al. *The Jeanes Story: A Chapter in the History of American Education, 1908–1968*. Jackson, Miss.: Jackson State University Press, 1979.

Wilson, Emily H. *For the People of North Carolina*. Chapel Hill: University of North Carolina Press, 1988.

Woods, Frances Jerome. *Marginality and Identity: A Colored Creole Family through Ten Generations.* Baton Rouge: Louisiana State University Press, 1972.

Woodson, Carter G. *The Education of the Negro prior to 1861.* New York: Arno Press, 1968.

Woodward, C. Vann. *Origins of the New South, 1877–1913.* Baton Rouge: Louisiana State University Press, 1951.

———. *The Strange Career of Jim Crow.* 3d ed. New York: Oxford University Press, 1974.

ARTICLES

Arter, Edna. "Biographical Sketch of Mrs. Charlotte H. Brown." *Women's Missionary Magazine of the United Presbyterian Church* 44 (August 1930): 12–14.

[Baker, Joseph V.] "A Bit of New England in North Carolina." *Brown American* 1 (Summer 1958): 20–38.

———. "The Twig-Bender of Sedalia." *Brown American* 1 (Fall/Winter 1944–45): 8–12.

Bell, Leonard H. "Charlotte Hawkins Brown—Pride of New England." *Spotlighter* 1 [1944]: 18–19.

Blanchard, Frederick Q. "Quarter Century in the American Missionary Association." *Journal of Negro Education* 9 (April 1940): 177–82.

Bland, Sidney R. Review of *Lugenia Burns Hope,* by Jacqueline A. Rouse. *Journal of Southern History* 56 (November 1990): 769.

Brownlee, Frederick L. "Moving In and Out: The Story of the American Missionary Association." *Phylon* 9 (1948): 146–50.

"Charlotte H. Brown." *Federation Journal* 31 (Spring 1984): 1–2.

Chittenden, Elizabeth F. "As We Climb: Mary Church Terrell." *Negro History Bulletin* 38 (1975): 351–54.

Cott, Nancy F. "The South and the Nation in the History of Women's Rights." In *A New Perspective: Southern Women's Cultural History from the Civil War to Civil Rights,* edited by Priscilla C. Little and Robert C. Vaughan, 11–19. Charlottesville: Virginia Foundation for the Humanities, 1989.

Davis, Griffith. "Finishing School: Wealthiest Families Send Children to Palmer for Polishing." *Ebony* 11 (October 1947): 22–27.

Derry, Cecil Thayer. "Pages from the History of the Cambridge High and Latin School." *Proceedings of the Cambridge Historical Society* 35 (1954): 95–107.

Doddy, Hurley H. "The Progress of the Negro in Higher Education." *Journal of Negro Education* 32 (1963): 485.

Fultz, Michael. "African American Teachers in the South, 1890–1940: Powerlessness and the Ironies of Expectation and Protest." *History Education Quarterly* 35 (Winter 1995): 401–22.

Gatewood, W. B. "Eugene Clyde Brooks: Educational Journalist in North Carolina, 1906–1923." *North Carolina Historical Review* 36 (July 1959): 325.

Gibbs, Annette. "Unfailing Courage and Unfaltering Faith." *Tar Heel Junior Historian* 23 (Spring 1984): 20–21.

Hanchett, Thomas W. "The Rosenwald Schools and Black Education in North Carolina." *North Carolina Historical Review* 65 (October 1988): 387–444.

Hotchkiss, Wesley Akin. "The Congregational and Christian Churches (AMA): The Rationale Underlying Support of Negro Private Colleges." *Journal of Negro Education* 29 (Summer 1960): 289–98.

Huddle, Mark A. "To Educate a Race: The Making of the First State Colored Normal School, Fayetteville, North Carolina, 1865–1877." *North Carolina Historical Review* 74 (April 1977): 135–60.

Hunter, Tera. "The Correct Thing: Charlotte H. Brown and the Palmer Institute." *Southern Exposure* 11 (September/October 1983): 37–43.

Johnson, Guy B. "Some Factors in the Development of Negro Social Institutions in the United States." *American Journal of Sociology* 40 (November 1934): 329–37.

Johnson, Isaac J. "Pattern for Living." *Message,* June 1953.

Karif, Wali Rashash. "Black Muslims." In *Encyclopedia of African American Civil Rights: From Emancipation to the Present,* edited by Charles D. Lowery and John F. Marszalek, 52–53. New York: Greenwood Press, 1992.

King, William E. "Charles McIver Fights for the Tarheel Negro's Right to an Education." *North Carolina Historical Review* 41 (July 1964): 360–69.

Laney, Lucy Craft. "The Burden of the Educated Colored Woman." In *Hampton Negro Conference,* vol. 3, edited by Hugh Brown et al., 3:39–41. Hampton, Va.: Hampton Institute Press, 1899.

Leslie, Elmer A. "Alice Freeman Palmer." In *Women Leaders,* edited by Philip Henry Lotz, 86–95. New York: Association Press, 1940.

Lewis, William H. "With Booker T. Washington: William H. Lewis on One of the Negro Leader's Typical Trips South," *Boston Transcript,* November 12, 1910. In *The Booker T. Washington Papers,* edited by Louis R. Harlan, 10:455–68. Urbana: University of Illinois Press, 1972–84.

Logan, Rayford. "Nat Turner, Fiend or Martyr?" *Opportunity* 9 (1931).

McCluskey, Audrey T. "'We Specialize in the Wholly Impossible': Black Women School Founders and Their Mission." *Signs: Journal of Women in Culture and Society* 22 (Winter 1997): 403–26.

McCusker, John J. "How Much Is That in Real Money?: A Historical Price Index for Use as a Deflator of Money Values in the Economy of the United States." *Proceedings of the American Antiquarian Society* 101 (1992): 297–373.

Miller, Eugene. "She Built a School on Labor, Dignity." *The State: A Weekly Survey of North Carolina,* October 27, 1951.

"Miss Glover Dies at Sedalia." *North Carolina Teachers Record* 9 (January 1938): 11.

Newbold, N. C. "Common Schools for Negroes in the South." *Annals of the American Association of Political and Social Science* 140 (November 1928): 209–23.

Perkins, Linda M. "The Black Female A.M.A. Teacher in the South, 1861–1870." In *Black Americans in North Carolina and the South,* edited by Jeffrey J. Crow and Flora J. Hatley, 122–36. Chapel Hill: University of North Carolina Press, 1984.

Pleck, Elizabeth H. "The Two-Parent Household: Black Family Structure in Late Nineteenth-Century Boston." *Journal of Social History* 6 (Fall 1972): 1–31.

Prichett, Jonathan B. "The Burden of Negro Schooling: Tax Incidence and Racial

Redistribution in Postbellum North Carolina." *Journal of Economic History* 49 (December 1989): 966–73.

"Recitals: Carol Brice Contralto, Town Hall." *Musical America,* December 15, 1955, 22.

Saunders, Lucinda. "An Idea That Grew from a Shanty into a Million Dollar Project." *Abbott's Monthly* 1 (November 1930): 34–36, 88.

Scott, Neil. "Carol Brice Is Just a Typical American Girl." *Opportunity,* Spring 1947, 93–94.

["Sedalia Singers Visit White House"]. *Time,* December 18, 1933, 1.

Smith, Elaine M. "Mary McLeod Bethune." In *Notable Black American Women,* edited by Jessie Carney Smith, 86–90. Detroit: Gale Research International Limited, 1992.

Smith, Sandra N., and Earle H. West. "Charlotte Hawkins Brown." *Journal of Negro Education* 51 (Summer 1982): 191–206.

Taylor, Joseph H. "The Great Migration from North Carolina in 1879." *North Carolina Historical Review* 31 (January 1954): 18–33.

"Teachers Hold First District Meeting." *North Carolina Teachers Record* 8 (January 1937): 3–4.

Tinney, James S. "Muslims to Open N.C. College for Teachers." *National Leader,* September 2, 1982, 23.

Vick, Marsha C. "Charlotte Hawkins Brown (1883–1961): Educator, School Founder, Author, Civic Leader." In *Notable Black American Women,* edited by Jessie Carney Smith, 109–14. Detroit: Gale Research International Limited, 1992.

"Voice Like a Cello." *Time,* March 11, 1946, 74.

Wadelington, Charles. "The Development of the Palmer Memorial Institute Curriculum: Its Founding Philosophy." *Afro-American Historical and Genealogical Society Journal* 10 (Summer and Fall 1989): 104–16.

———. "What One Young African American Woman Could Do: The Story of Dr. Charlotte Hawkins Brown and the Palmer Memorial Institute." *Tar Heel Junior Historian* 35 (Fall 1995): 22–26.

Wagoner, Jennings L., Jr. "The American Compromise: Charles W. Eliot, Black Education, and the New South." In *Education and the Rise of the New South,* edited by Ronald Goodenow and Arthur White, 26–46. Boston: G. K. Hall, 1981.

Washington, Booker T. "How to Build a Good School in the South." *Tuskegee Student* 13 (September 14, 1901): 4.

———. "A Plain Talk as to Securing Negro Homes." *Tuskegee Student* 13 (August 10, 1901): 2.

"Wilhelmina M. Crosson Reports on International Education in Mexico." *Negro History Bulletin* 10 (December 1946): 55–60, 68–71.

Zipf, Karin L. "'Among These American Heathens': Congregationalist Missionaries and African American Evangelicals during Reconstruction, 1865–1878." *North Carolina Historical Review* 74 (April 1977): 111–34.

DISSERTATIONS AND THESES

Batley, M. Grant. "John Chavis: His Contributions to Education in North Carolina." Master's thesis, North Carolina College for Negroes, 1954.

Boggs, Wade H., III. "State Supported Higher Education of Blacks in North Carolina, 1877–1945." Ph.D. dissertation, Duke University, 1972.

Burns, Augustus M. "North Carolina and the Negro Dilemma, 1930–1950." Ph.D. dissertation, University of North Carolina at Chapel Hill, 1970.

Chujo, Ken. "The Black Struggle for Education in North Carolina, 1877–1900." Ph.D. dissertation, Duke University, 1988.

Clement, Rufus E. "History of Negro Education in North Carolina, 1865–1928." Ph.D. dissertation, Northwestern University, 1930.

Davis, Owena Hunter. "A History of Mary Potter School, Oxford, North Carolina." Master's thesis, North Carolina College for Negroes, 1942.

DeBerry, Charles. "A Study of the History and Development of Palmer Memorial Institute." Master's thesis, New York University, 1939.

Drake, Richard Bryant. "The American Missionary Association and the Southern Negro, 1861–1888." Master's thesis, Emory University, 1957.

Holloway, Evelyn F. "A Study of the Aims, Growth, and Functions of Palmer Institute." Master's thesis, Fisk University, 1935.

Holmes, Dwight O. W. "The Evolution of the Negro College." Ph.D. dissertation, Columbia University, 1934.

Hunter, Tera. "A Biographical Study of Charlotte Hawkins Brown: Unearthing One of the Many Brave." Senior thesis, Duke University, 1982.

Jones, Maxine Deloris. "A Glorious Work: The American Missionary Association and Black North Carolinians, 1863–1880." Ph.D. dissertation, Florida State University, 1982.

King, William E. "The Era of Progressive Reform in Southern Education: The Growth of Public Schools in North Carolina." Ph.D. dissertation, Duke University, 1969.

Kitchen, G. H. "The Status of Physical Education in Colleges for Negroes Sponsored by the American Missionary Association." Master's thesis, University of Michigan, 1940.

Patterson, Joseph Norenzo. "A Study of the History of the Contributions of the American Missionary Association to the Higher Education of the Negro." Master's thesis, Cornell University, 1956.

Welch, Eloise Turner. "The Background and Development of the American Missionary Association's Decision to Educate Freedmen in the South." Ph.D. dissertation, Bryn Mawr College, 1976.

Westin, Richard B. "The State and Segregated Schools: Negro Public Education in North Carolina, 1863–1923." Ph.D. dissertation, Duke University, 1966.

White, Frank H. "The Economic and Social Development of Negroes in North Carolina since 1900." Master's thesis, New York University, 1960.

VIDEOS

Copies of the following videos are in the Charlotte Hawkins Brown Collection, North Carolina Department of Cultural Resources, Historic Sites Section, Raleigh, N.C.

Aristo Club Dinner. Narrated by Marie Hart. Boston, March 1, 1981.

Charlotte Hawkins Brown. Raleigh: North Carolina Department of Cultural Resources, Historic Sites Section, and the Charlotte Hawkins Brown Historical Foundation, 1988.

Charlotte Hawkins Brown State Historic Site. OPEN/net, November 11, 1988. Raleigh: North Carolina Agency for Public Telecommunications, 1988.

The Journey Continues. Greensboro, N.C.: Charlotte Hawkins Brown Historical Foundation, 1988.

McLeansville Railroad Crossing. Greensboro, N.C.: Suite Five Productions, 1981.

Palmerite, yearbook, 1956, 1961, 1965, plus clippings. Narrated by Marie Hart. Sedalia, N.C., February 7–8, 1981.

Palmer Memorial Institute: The Mission and the Legacy. Narrated and directed by Marie Hart and Gayle Wulk. Greensboro, N.C.: Suite Five Productions, 1981.

Palmer Memorial Institute Grounds and Photographs. Narrated by Marie Hart. Sedalia, N.C., February 4, 1981.

"The Twig Bender." *Carolina Saturday,* WRAL-TV, Raleigh, 1988.

INDEX